## Manchester Medieval Sources Series

*series advisers* Rosemary Horrox and Janet L. Nelson

This series aims to meet a growing need among students and teachers of medieval history for translations of key sources that are directly usable in students' own work. It provides texts central to medieval studies courses and focuses upon the diverse cultural and social as well as political conditions that affected the functioning of all levels of medieval society. The basic premise of the series is that translations must be accompanied by sufficient introductory and explanatory material, and each volume, therefore, includes a comprehensive guide to the sources' interpretation, including discussion of critical linguistic problems and an assessment of the most recent research on the topics being covered.

*also available in the series*

Mark Bailey *The English Manor c. 1200–c. 1500*

Malcolm Barber and Keith Bate *The Templars*

Simon Barton and Richard Fletcher *The world of El Cid: Chronicles of the Spanish Reconquest*

Andrew Brown and Graeme Small *Court and civic society in the Burgundian Low Countries c. 1420–1520*

Samuel K. Cohn, Jr. *Popular protest in late-medieval Europe: Italy, France and Flanders*

Trevor Dean *The towns of Italy in the later Middle Ages*

P. J. P. Goldberg *Women in England, c. 1275–1525*

Rosemary Horrox *The Black Death*

Simon Maclean *History and Politics in Late Carolingian and Ottonian Empire: The Chronicle of Regino of Prüm and Adalbert of Magdeburg*

Anthony Musson and Edward Powell *Crime, law and society in the later middle ages*

I. S. Robinson *Eleventh-century Germany: The Swabian Chronicles*

I. S. Robinson *The papal reform of the eleventh century: Lives of Pope Leo IX and Pope Gregory VII*

Michael Staunton *The lives of Thomas Becket*

Craig Taylor *Joan of Arc: La Pucelle*

Elisabeth van Houts *The Normans in Europe*

David Warner *Ottonian Germany*

Diana Webb *Saints and cities in medieval Italy*

# MONASTICISM IN LATE MEDIEVAL ENGLAND, *c.* 1300–1535

Manchester University Press

# MedievalSources*online*

Complementing the printed editions of the Medieval Sources series, Manchester University Press has developed a web-based learning resource which is now available on a yearly subscription basis.

MedievalSources*online* brings quality history source material to the desktops of students and teachers and allows them open and unrestricted access throughout the entire college or university campus. Designed to be fully integrated with academic courses, this is a one-stop answer for many medieval history students, academics and researchers keeping thousands of pages of source material 'in print' over the Internet for research and teaching.

*titles available now at* MedievalSources*online include*

Trevor Dean *The towns of Italy in the later Middle Ages*

John Edwards *The Jews in Western Europe, 1400–1600*

Paul Fouracre and Richard A. Gerberding *Late Merovingian France: History and hagiography 640–720*

Chris Given-Wilson *Chronicles of the Revolution 1397–1400: The reign of Richard II*

P. J. P. Goldberg *Women in England, c. 1275–1525*

Janet Hamilton and Bernard Hamilton *Christian dualist heresies in the Byzantine world, c. 650–c. 1450*

Simon MacLean *History and politics in late Carolingian and Ottonian Europe: The Chronicle of Regino of Prüm and Adalbert of Magdeburg*

Anthony Musson with Edward Powell *Crime, law and society in the later Middle Ages*

Rosemary Horrox *The Black Death*

Graham A. Loud and Thomas Wiedemann *The history of the tyrants of Sicily by 'Hugo Falcandus', 1153–69*

Janet L. Nelson *The Annals of St-Bertin: Ninth-century histories, volume I*

Timothy Reuter *The Annals of Fulda: Ninth-century histories, volume II*

R. N. Swanson *Catholic England: Faith, religion and observance before the Reformation*

Elisabeth van Houts *The Normans in Europe*

Jennifer Ward *Women of the English nobility and gentry 1066–1500*

Visit the site at *www.medievalsources.co.uk* for further information and subscription prices.

# MONASTICISM IN LATE MEDIEVAL ENGLAND, *c.* 1300–1535

*selected sources translated and annotated with an introduction*
*by* Martin Heale

Manchester University Press
Manchester and New York

*distributed exclusively in the USA by Palgrave Macmillan*

Copyright © Martin Heale 2009

The right of Martin Heale to be identified as the author of this work has been asserted by him in accordance with the Copyright, Designs and Patents Act 1988.

*Published by* Manchester University Press
Oxford Road, Manchester M13 9NR, UK
*and* Room 400, 175 Fifth Avenue, New York, NY 10010, USA
www.manchesteruniversitypress.co.uk

*Distributed exclusively in the USA by*
Palgrave Macmillan, 175 Fifth Avenue, New York, NY 10010, USA

*Distributed exclusively in Canada by*
UBC Press, University of British Columbia, 2029 West Mall,
Vancouver, BC, Canada V6T 1Z2

*British Library Cataloguing-in-Publication Data*
A catalogue record for this book is available from the British Library

*Library of Congress Cataloging-in-Publication Data applied for*


ISBN   978 0 7190 7174 4 *hardback*
          978 0 7190 7175 1 *paperback*

First published 2009

18  17  16  15  14  13  12  11  10  09        10  9  8  7  6  5  4  3  2  1

Typeset in Monotype Bell
by Koinonia Ltd, Manchester
Printed in Great Britain
by the MPG Books Group

For my parents

# CONTENTS

# SERIES EDITOR'S FOREWORD

This volume fills a gap not only in the provision of sources for the exploration of late medieval English monasticism but in providing the context for that exploration. As Martin Heale discusses in his introduction, medieval monastic history after the glory days of the eleventh and twelfth century reforms has been neglected of late. In part this is because of the belief, emphasised in the magisterial work of Dom David Knowles, that the later centuries saw a progressive decline of the monastic ideal. It surely also owes something to the modern emphasis on 'popular' religion, by which is usually meant the study of attitudes rather than institutions, and the attitudes of the laity rather than the clergy. Monasteries have tended to miss out on both grounds. The extensive surviving sources have been mined far more thoroughly to show the monasteries in their role as landowners and, more recently, as consumers, than to try and engage with their primary, spiritual function. The present collection does not ignore those roles, but reminds us how much more can be drawn from the sources and, in the process, shows where exploration might be taken further. Thus the introduction not only offers a useful synthesis of recent work but in important areas – notably in discussion of how the monasteries' closer engagement with the world might be interpreted – offers exciting new ideas. Although the range of sources deliberately stops before the Dissolution, which would demand a whole volume to itself, the editor also has interesting points to make about which previous developments might have facilitated that process. In all of this, Dr Heale is not using the sources to force a particular reading on his audience but to open up the subject to new questions and approaches. This is an extremely rich volume that will bring late medieval monasticism back in from the cold as a fruitful topic of investigation even for those primarily interested in the attitudes of the pre-Reformation laity or in the Reformation itself.

Rosemary Horrox
Fitzwilliam College, Cambridge

# PREFACE AND ACKNOWLEDGEMENTS

Records relating to late medieval monasteries survive in enormous quantities. The thorough study of the archives of certain individual houses (such as Durham Priory or Westminster Abbey) would require a lifetime's work; and a great many late medieval monastic accounts, charters, registers, letters, inventories, leases and rentals, service books and study books have still not been investigated in detail. To produce a sourcebook on this theme, therefore, is to be spoilt for choice. This problem has been exacerbated by my early realisation that an extended introduction would be needed to set the documents in context. There is no student-friendly guide to late medieval English monasticism available, and the last extended treatment of the subject, by David Knowles, is now more than fifty years old. The decision to devote a third of the book to an overview of this topic has inevitably reduced the space available for documents, but I felt this approach would maximise the usefulness of the volume to students. In selecting documents, I have also aimed for quality rather than quantity. All fifty-five documents are, I hope, a convenient size for discussion in seminars and tutorials, and I have eschewed very long or very short documents, or decontextualised gobbets.

It has accordingly been necessary to be highly selective in my choice of documents. I have tried to include sources which illustrate all the main facets of late medieval monastic life, and which represent a cross-section of houses – male and female, large and small and over a range of religious orders. In the absence of any comparable collection, it seemed most useful to include a number of relatively well-known, but often inaccessible, sources alongside more obscure documents. I have also tried consciously to augment and complement the only two existing collections of translated sources for late medieval monasticism: the relatively short section on this subject in *English Historical Documents IV* (which focuses mainly on the great Benedictine houses); and Joyce Youings' *The Dissolution of the Monasteries* (which naturally deals principally with the suppression of religious houses, a topic that lies beyond the scope of this volume). And although I am aware that monastic records can be profitably used to shed light on many important facets of medieval life, the documents chosen are intended to illustrate the experience of monastic communities rather than the wider application of their archives. Many have been printed before in the original Latin or middle English, several (albeit not infallibly) in the earliest and greatest monastic sourcebook, Sir William Dugdale's *Monasticon Anglicanum*. A few have been previously translated, but in all but five cases I have made my own translations – indicated by the formula 'translated from' rather than 'translation taken from'. In these translations, it has been my intention to retain something of the flavour of the original text and style of each document (including, no doubt unsuccessfully, in the poetical works).

This volume has been much improved by the generous advice and assistance of several colleagues and friends. Brother Anselm J. Gribbin O.Praem., Julian Luxford and Nicholas Orme commented very helpfully on earlier versions of the introduction. Brother Anselm, Paul Botley, Paul Booth, Marios Costambeys, Brigitte Resl and David Smith have all very kindly shared their time and expertise to assist with particular translations and queries; whereas James Davis and Chris Briggs have put at my disposal their acquaintance, respectively, with bread and dung. I also profited from a conversation with Joan Greatrex about the scope of the collection, and from the comments of the book's anonymous external reviewer. To all of the above, I am extremely grateful: I alone am responsible for all the faults which remain.

I also wish to record my sincere gratitude to The National Archives (document no. 30), Sutton Publishing (45) and the University of Toronto Press (51) for their generous permission to reproduce translations to which they hold the copyright; and to the Dean and Canons of Windsor, the Chapter of Durham Cathedral, the British Library, the Bodleian Library, University of Oxford, and to The National Archives again for permission to publish the contents of manuscripts in their custody in translation for the first time. I am also very grateful to all the staff at Manchester University Press for their skill and patience, and to Rosemary Horrox for first suggesting this project to me and for her subsequent support and advice.

Special thanks must go to Mel, Jonathan and Beth for their good-humoured tolerance and unfailing support while I was excessively preoccupied with this book; and also to my parents, to whom the dedication of the volume is but a small return for all they have done for me.

## Note on money and dates

The rendering of monetary amounts can often be a source of confusion. In order to minimise this, I have rounded up totals where the original writer has not divided them neatly into pounds (£), shillings (s) and pence (d). Several documents also give sums in marks, which were equivalent to two-thirds of a pound, or 13s 4d. All dates given are in the new style.

# INTRODUCTION: MONASTICISM IN LATE MEDIEVAL ENGLAND, c. 1300–1535

We associate the middle ages with monks, and with good reason: monasticism was at the heart of medieval life and culture. In the preservation and dissemination of learning, the spread of Christianity throughout Europe, the periodic reform of the Church, the stimulation of the economy and much else, the monastic contribution to the medieval world needs no elaboration.[1] All these achievements, however, are associated with the early and high middle ages: the monastic 'golden age' was over by 1200. After centuries of expansion, the later middle ages saw few novel monastic foundations, and no major reform movement (at least in England). The perceived lack of importance of late medieval monasticism can be readily illustrated by the amount of space devoted to the period after 1300 in general works on the subject. C. H. Lawrence's popular textbook, *Medieval Monasticism*, now in its third edition, gives a total of 16 out of 294 pages to the later middle ages.[2] Similarly, a number of important works on the late medieval Church in England have very little to say about the religious orders. Robert Swanson's *Church and Society in the Late Medieval England* contains only nine pages on the religious or regular clergy (i.e. those following a monastic rule), while Eamon Duffy's influential *The Stripping of the Altars* has a single entry under 'monasteries' in its index.[3] The implication of this lack of attention is that monasteries were no longer central players in the religious and social life of the day.

This characterisation of late medieval monasticism has a long pedigree, and a number of factors have contributed to its entrenchment. It is in part a product of a long-established view of the later middle ages as a period of decline, following the glories of the 'high' medieval period.[4] In this view, the twelfth and thirteenth centuries are set up as the epitome of medieval civilisation, with the later period portrayed as a falling away from this ideal. Pure feudalism is succeeded by greedy bastard feudalism, chivalry by mercenary self-interest, social harmony

1 Zarnecki (1972); Brooke (2003).
2 Lawrence (2000).
3 Swanson (1989); Duffy (1992).
4 For a classic exposition of this argument, see Huizinga (1924).

and representative government by popular revolt and civil war, and a thriving and self-renewing Church by a corrupt and moribund one. Historians of the later middle ages have naturally sought to study this period on its own terms, but it is still common to find something not dissimilar to this portrayal of the later middle ages in general works of medieval and early modern history. Equally, the representation of late medieval monasteries as inferior versions of their high medieval predecessors remains a very popular approach today.

Another important factor in the negative depiction of late medieval monasticism is the long tradition of Protestant historiography in England. From the outset of the English Reformation, the religious orders were the object of particular disdain among evangelicals[5] (see below, pp. 70–2). To the reformers, monasteries were closely associated with a number of undesirable features of medieval religion, including 'superstitious' pilgrimage and the cult of saints, clerical celibacy, Church wealth and privilege, and prayers for the dead in Purgatory.[6] This trend was exacerbated by the fact that a significant number of early English reformers were themselves former monks or friars, reacting strongly against their former way of life [52]. Protestant hostility towards the religious orders was further enflamed by the unpopularity of the Jesuits entering Elizabethan England from the 1580s, who quickly became associated with the papacy, foreign invasion and treason. The stereotype of the scheming, vicious monk entered English folklore and was reflected in many historical (and literary) depictions of pre-Reformation monasticism. Eighteenth- and nineteenth-century histories of medieval England often single out the monk for particular criticism, although it should be noted that the hostile nature of much of this writing was in part provoked by the romantic depictions of universally kindly and saintly monastics often advanced by pro-Catholic writers.[7]

An essentially negative portrayal of late medieval monasticism remained widespread in the first half of the twentieth century, as more detailed research was carried out by scholars such as G. G. Coulton, Geoffrey Baskerville and (for the nuns) Eileen Power.[8] This negativity, in part the product of Protestant preconceptions, also proceeded from these histo-

---

5 An alternative term to 'Protestant' or 'Lutheran' favoured by many historians of the early English Reformation, since it implies a more fluid set of beliefs, influenced by a range of continental reformers.

6 E.g. Parish (2005), esp. 45–70.

7 E.g. Hume (1780); Froude (1867–83). For much more sympathetic treatments, see Cobbett (1827); Gasquet (1893).

8 Coulton (1923–50); Baskerville (1937); Power (1922).

rians' particular reliance on one genre of source material: the visitation record. Coulton, especially, delighted in reciting at length the faults uncovered by these periodic inspections of the quality of monastic life, carried out by bishops or monastic visitors. The visitation record is by far the most vivid and accessible source surviving for the internal life of late medieval monasteries [18, 19], and the appearance of several editions of such records between the late nineteenth and mid-twentieth centuries understandably influenced all historians of this period. Visitation records are, however, an inherently critical source, designed to reveal faults in observance so that they can be corrected. When this genre of evidence is contrasted with our main source of information about the monastic life of the early and high middle ages, the chronicles written by monks in order to celebrate the achievements of their houses, it is hardly surprising that the late medieval religious appear considerably less heroic or sympathetic figures.

Another reason for the chequered reputation of late medieval monasticism is the hiatus in the creation of new monastic orders between 1200 and 1540. After the ferment of the eleventh and twelfth centuries when the Cistercian and Carthusian monks and the Augustinian, Premonstratensian and Gilbertine canons were all founded, the establishment of new orders stalled. The thirteenth century saw the appearance of the friars, a new form of religious life based on preaching and charity, supported by begging (mendicancy) rather than a landed endowment; but there were no new orders of monks, canons or nuns.[9] Indeed, the only new late medieval monastic order was the relatively small Bridgettine Order of nuns, established by St Bridget of Sweden in the 1340s, and formally recognised by the Church in 1378. A single Bridgettine house was established in England, although Henry V's foundation of Syon quickly became the wealthiest and most prestigious nunnery in the kingdom. This pattern of foundation is significant, since monastic history has commonly been viewed according to a cyclical model of revival and decline. According to this model, a newly founded order shows great rigour in its early years, before its zeal and commitment gradually fall away. In its place, another zealous new order grows up before this in turn loses its early enthusiasm and succumbs to mediocrity [cf. 51]. This approach finds its classical expression in the historiography of the Cistercians, which has emphasised the monks' gradual movement away from the early ideals of the order (including

9 The friars, who represent a very different approach to the religious life, fall outside the scope of this volume.

austerity of life, the avoidance of ornate artistic and architectural styles, and the rejection of feudal sources of income such as manors and parish churches) until the late medieval Cistercians became almost indistinguishable from other orders.

If this 'boom and bust' grand narrative of monastic history is accepted, the lack of new orders in the later middle ages looks like a symptom of stagnation or even decline. This conception, however, was not widely held in late medieval Europe. The Church councils of the thirteenth century prohibited the creation of new rules and suppressed a number of more recent religious orders as an unnecessary and unhelpful diversification of the monastic ideal.[10] The proliferation of monastic orders also attracted criticism from reformers such as Pierre d'Ailly in the later middle ages, for contributing to disunity within the Church; and to some early sixteenth-century commentators the consolidation of existing orders seemed a much more valuable reforming measure than the creation of new ones.[11] It is also no coincidence that the explosion of new orders in high medieval Europe, and again during the sixteenth-century Catholic Reformation, took place at times of economic and demographic expansion: there is clearly more than just a spiritual dynamic at work in the establishment of new orders and new religious houses. It might be added that recent work on the Cistercians has questioned whether the ideals of the order's founders were ever universally recognised and applied, and therefore whether such a clear normative picture of the order's ideals can be advanced.[12]

There is no doubt, however, that there was a gradual refashioning of earlier monastic rules and practices in the later middle ages. The late medieval 'reforms' of the Benedictine Order included a relaxation of observances on diet, the common life and private property, and little of the Cistercians' primitive austerity can be found in late medieval houses of the order. These developments, which will be considered more fully below (see pp. 22–6), provided the basis for Dom David Knowles' critical interpretation of English monastic life in the later middle ages.[13] Knowles remains without question the most influential historian of medieval English monasticism. His four volumes, tracing the history of the religious orders in England from St Dunstan (d. 988) to the Dissolution, are historical classics by any standards and have not

10 Andrews (2006), 173–230.

11 E.g. Oakley (1979), 301–12; Evennett (1958); Olin (1969), 182–97.

12 Cassidy-Welch (2001), 12–16; Jamroziak (2005), 9–18.

13 Knowles (1963); Knowles (1948–59).

been superseded nearly fifty years on. Knowles combined a rare literary talent with the ability to capture broad and complex developments in a single judicious paragraph. His deep knowledge of monasticism in other countries and periods (in part drawn from his own experience as a monk) also enabled him to identify what was most remarkable and representative in each phase of medieval English monasticism. It is remarkable how much of Knowles' oeuvre still appears fresh and justified today.

Nevertheless, for all its many qualities, Knowles' work is the product of a particular standpoint on the monastic life which itself needs to be closely scrutinised. His standards were exacting, and many prominent medieval monks were deemed spiritually undeveloped by his measure, with his appraisal of individual epochs of monastic history tied closely to the number of saintly regulars he could identify.[14] Apart from signs of spiritual excellence, of which he found little trace in late medieval England, Knowles' main barometer for the health of a generation of monasteries was the fidelity with which they followed their founder's rule, 'for the religious the only safe path'.[15] For this reason, above all, the monasticism of the later middle ages, with its modifications of sixth- and twelfth-century practice, was found wanting; and this verdict has been highly influential in subsequent evaluations of the period. Furthermore, Knowles' study, as he himself acknowledged, was principally a history of the great male Benedictine monasteries of medieval England and their Cluniac and Cistercian offshoots. Much less space is devoted to the regular canons, whom Knowles considered not fully monastic, and to the nuns who, it has been calculated, receive less than fifteen pages throughout the entire four volumes.[16]

Perhaps because Knowles' work on English monasticism appeared so definitive, the next generation of historians turned their attention to other facets of late medieval religion. However, in more recent years there has been a renewal of interest in the later history of the religious orders, which has begun to rehabilitate the reputation of the nuns, canons and monks of this period. This work has been stimulated in part by the revisionist rehabilitation of the pre-Reformation Church in England, but it is also a product of the appreciation that there remains an enormous quantity of archival material relating to late medieval monasticism that has hardly been assimilated by historians. This introduction

14 E.g. Knowles (1948–59), I, ix, II, vii.

15 *Ibid.*, III, 468.

16 Greatrex (2002), 45.

– divided into two sections covering internal life and monastic relations
with the outside world – seeks to provide an overview reflecting recent
research on this subject, and to set the documents that follow in their
proper context.

## Part one: monastic life in late medieval England

The later middle ages was an era of evolution in English monastic
life. Traditional rules and practices were modified, with a general
movement away from the more austere monasticism of earlier centuries. There was a major contraction in the monastic population as
the Black Death of 1348–49 killed perhaps 40 per cent of the monks,
canons and nuns in England; and in its wake there followed a significant economic downturn which prompted many houses to adapt their
estate management and internal organisation. The monasteries of this
period also faced increasing competition from other branches of the
Church, making it difficult to attract the levels of lay patronage forth-
coming in the past (see below, pp. 44–51). Late medieval monasteries
clearly faced a range of new challenges; but whether these developments justify the traditionally downbeat assessment of the monastic
life of this period has come increasingly to be questioned. The majority
of houses rode out the economic vicissitudes of the period successfully,
and continued to recruit steadily. Standards of observance, moreover,
were arguably higher than historians, over-reliant on visitation records,
have allowed. James Clark has recently suggested that the late medieval
modifications of monastic life criticised by Knowles and others might
be better understood as a 'bold attempt at modernisation' rather than
evidence of decline – not least because many of these adaptations were
the result of deliberate policy, rather than laxity or a lack of commitment.[17] The monasticism of this period was above all outward-looking,
as the religious sought – with some success – to demonstrate that they
still had something to offer late medieval society.

### Numbers and recruitment

By 1300, around 800 monasteries had been founded in England
and Wales. A variety of different monastic orders were represented,
reflecting a diversity of approaches to the religious life. These included
the Benedictines, or black monks (as they were known after the colour

17 Clark (2002), 10–12. The phrase in the quotation was originally coined by Sir Richard
   Southern.

of their robes), following the sixth-century Rule of St Benedict [1]. The black monks counted among their number several wealthy Anglo-Saxon and Anglo-Norman foundations, as well as more than 150 smaller daughter houses of English and French monasteries. Also following the Benedictine Rule were the orders based on the French abbeys of Cluny and Fontevrault, and the Cistercians (or white monks, named from their plainer undyed garments) – an order which had set out, in the years around 1100, to lead a life of greater austerity and stricter observance of the Rule than the Benedictines. There were also a small but growing number of Carthusian monasteries (often known as charterhouses), whose monks lived largely in solitude in individual cells around a large cloister. Almost as numerous as the monks were houses of regular canons. Many of these communities were in origin groups of priests who had adopted a monastic way of life (generally following the Rule of St Augustine, based on the writings of this Church Father), and as a result the regular canons often maintained some association with the parish. Over 200 houses of Augustinian canons were established in England and Wales between 1100 and 1300, making them the single most popular order in the kingdom. They were joined by the Premonstratensian canons (who adopted a white habit and stricter observances in imitation of the Cistercians) and the Gilbertines, the only order indigenous to medieval England. The Gilbertines were in fact a double order of canons and nuns, and most of the aforementioned religious orders also had female branches. Nevertheless, numbers of nunneries never approximated those of monks and canons in medieval England and Wales, and only about 150 female houses were established.

Not only were there hundreds of monasteries in early fourteenth-century England, but in the years around 1300 these houses were probably more populous than at any other time in their history. The only sustained research into the size of the medieval monastic population, carried out in the 1950s and 1960s, suggested that there were somewhere around 13,000 religious at this time (out of a total English population of perhaps five million), with the largest houses, such as St Albans and Shaftesbury, containing more than 100 monks and nuns respectively.[18] But the upward trend in the monastic population that had persisted up to c. 1300 was soon to be reversed. Numbers fell over the first half of the fourteenth century, in line with wider population trends, and the Black Death brought about a major (and permanent) contraction of the monastic life in England. By the end of the fourteenth

18 Knowles and Hadcock (1971), 488–95.

century, there may have been fewer than 7,000 nuns, canons and monks in English monasteries. After 1349 it was rare for even a major house to hold more than fifty inmates, although Canterbury Cathedral Priory, the largest monastery of the realm, maintained about seventy monks [cf. **2**]; and Syon Abbey, the biggest nunnery in late medieval England, was founded for sixty nuns (supported by thirteen priests, four deacons and eight lay brothers). Many smaller houses, meanwhile, saw their numbers fall to single figures, with a minority of priories, mainly daughter houses, never holding more than two or three religious for the remainder of their existence.[19]

Nevertheless, there was no recruitment crisis among late medieval English monasteries [cf. **52**]. Most houses sought to maintain an ideal size of community proportionate to their financial resources, with larger monasteries receiving groups of four to six novices every few years in order to keep step with mortality in the community.[20] The numerical stability experienced by many houses over the course of the fifteenth century indicates that the desired number of recruits were generally available, at least to the wealthier monasteries. More significantly, numbers of religious apparently rose steadily over the fifteenth century to around 9,000 by 1500: a rather better rate of recovery than for the population more generally. In the first decades of the sixteenth century there are further signs of accelerating recruitment, in line with the beginnings of economic and demographic recovery in the country at large. Under the energetic leadership of Abbot Marmaduke Huby, numbers at Fountains Abbey rose from twenty-two monks in 1495 to fifty-two in *c.* 1520, and the community at Missenden expanded from five canons to fourteen between 1518 and 1530.

There is, therefore, no indication that vocations for the monastic life were failing in the years leading up to the Dissolution, and the appeal of entering a religious house may even have been growing at this time. The motivation and suitability of monastic recruits is, of course, rather more difficult to judge. Late medieval novices were required to meet certain social and intellectual expectations and to demonstrate their commitment to their new way of life through a year of proba-tion [**2, 3, 28**]. Yet the noviciate of this period, it has been remarked, 'contained little of the specific training in spiritual life and rigorous testing of vocation' found, for example, among the Franciscan friars or

19 Dobson (1995); Heale (2004a), 297–300.
20 E.g. Harvey (1993), 73–7.

(in a later period) the Jesuits.[21] Certainly not all recruits appear to have been entirely suitable [**19**], and some reformers echoed the sixteenth-century humanist Thomas Starkey in calling for 'fewer religious men in number but better in life'.[22] The majority of recruits seem to have hailed from the house's locality, often from its estates, and (with the exception of the Carthusians and the brethren of Syon, who were often mature entrants) were professed in their late teens or early twenties.[23] Most canons and monks, moreover, came from the middling sections of urban and rural society; and aristocratic recruits, not uncommon in the high middle ages, were unusual figures in late medieval male monasteries. This development, which does not seem to denote a lack of aristocratic interest in the monastic life (see below, pp. 46–51), can perhaps be attributed to the elites' well-founded assurance that they could maintain a satisfactory level of control over monastic resources and affairs as patrons and stewards, without needing family members presiding over these houses.

It used to be thought that recruits to late medieval nunneries came from a much more elevated social background than those to male houses, but recent research has qualified this conclusion. The wealthiest nunneries continued to attract women from the highest echelons of society, such as Edward I's niece Isabella of Lancaster, who was placed in the nunnery of Amesbury when still a girl and became prioress in 1343. But aristocratic recruits did not dominate the larger nunneries, with the most common entrants coming from gentry or wealthy urban families. Smaller female monasteries, always the large majority, seem to have been populated with nuns from the parish gentry or well-off townsmen;[24] although it should be noted that this was still a higher social background than many recruits to male houses. Another difference between recruitment into male and female monasteries in England was the much more limited number of places available for women. Nunneries comprised fewer than 20 per cent of English houses, and of the 9,000 or so inhabitants of these monasteries in *c.*1500, only about 2,100 were nuns. These female houses, moreover, were not at all evenly distributed geographically, with very little provision in the north-west and south-west of England (or indeed in Wales). It may be a sign of the high demand for available places that small female houses contained

---

21 Harvey (2002), 51–2.
22 Mayer (1989), 104.
23 E.g. Dobson (1973), 56–61.
24 Oliva (1998), 52–61; Cross (2002).

many more inmates than male monasteries of comparable resources, with even the very poorest convents often housing ten or more nuns throughout the period.[25]

## The monastic economy

If recruitment to religious houses held up in the face of difficult circumstances, the same might be said of the monastic economy in late medieval England. Even at times of economic hardship, the wealth held collectively by English monasteries was very substantial. The well-known 1535 tax assessment, the *Valor Ecclesiasticus*, records an aggregate income for the monastic order in England of £165,500 per year. Since this assessment undervalues certain elements of monastic income, in particular land cultivated directly by the religious, it is likely that a figure of £200,000 per year is closer to the mark: a sum nearly twice the Crown's ordinary income at this time.[26] Moreover, as all the evidence points to falling monastic incomes over much of the later middle ages, it is probable that these sums had been higher in the fourteenth century. It is not surprising, then, that it was their wealth which most impressed foreign visitors to the major English monasteries in this period [**15**].

Nevertheless, these revenues were not at all evenly distributed among religious houses. The wealthiest abbeys in 1535 were Glastonbury and Westminster with gross incomes approaching £4,000 a year. Twenty-six other houses (mostly of Benedictine monks, but including three houses of Augustinian canons, one each of Cistercian and Cluniac monks, and the nunneries of Syon and Shaftesbury) possessed annual revenues of over £1,000. In all, 20 per cent of English monasteries enjoyed incomes of more than £300 per year, putting them on a par with the higher aristocracy of the realm. This level of wealth, however, was far from the experience of many houses. According to the *Valor*, nearly half had at their disposal an income of less than £100 per year in 1535, and 9 per cent of monasteries had less than £50. Nunneries as a group were particularly poorly endowed, with nearly two-thirds of female houses having an annual income of under £100, although a small number of (mostly) Anglo-Saxon female foundations were much richer. Generalisations about wealthy monasteries therefore require considerable qualification.

Monastic revenues came from a variety of sources. 'Temporal' income, comprising about three-quarters of the total, consisted of the proceeds

25 Gilchrist (1994), 43.
26 Savine (1909); Knowles (1948–59), III, 241–59.

from manors, granges, urban property, trade or the profits of justice; and 'spiritual' income came largely from parish churches, principally tithes and offerings. All these sources of revenue tended to fall in the period following the Black Death. From the last quarter of the fourteenth century the price of grain and other staples fell significantly, and remained at low levels throughout the 1400s. This rendered unsustainable the large-scale direct cultivation of estates ('high farming') undertaken by many monasteries in the decades around 1300, particularly when combined with steadily rising agricultural wages from *c.* 1360, which greatly added to labour and transport costs. As a result, religious houses, together with the great secular landlords, were forced to lease out the majority of their estates, with many monasteries making the switch in the years between 1380 and 1420 [**4, 5**]. Since the rents charged needed to leave some margin for the lessee's profit, this inevitably brought about a fall in monastic revenues. Livestock farming was scarcely more profitable than arable in the later fourteenth century, with falling prices and the decline of the overseas wool trade badly hitting those abbeys that had previously specialised in large-scale sheep farming. Nor did the switch to a rentier economy necessarily simplify matters. Numerous monastic account rolls from the fifteenth century show large deficits of rents as lessees and tenants were either unable or unwilling to pay the full amount they owed. Many landlords were therefore forced to lower their expectations or risk losing tenants.[27]

The temporal income of many monasteries therefore fell significantly from the late fourteenth century; but it may be that the decline in spiritual income was even more severe [**6, 7**]. Revenues from parish churches were always a major component of monastic income, particularly when those churches had been appropriated. Appropriation entitled the monastery to receive the tithes and offerings made by parishioners (for example, for burial or to miraculous images and relics) normally reserved to the parish priest. These spiritual revenues, however, were closely linked to broader economic and demographic trends, since any decline in the population or wealth of a parish would translate directly into falling tithe payments and offerings. It has been calculated that Durham Priory's tithe receipts fell by up to 53 per cent in the century following the Black Death;[28] and the priories of Lynn and Yarmouth, situated in towns suffering from a decline in both population and wealth over the later middle ages, saw their spiritual income drop from nearly

27 Dyer (2005), 194–210.
28 Dodds (2004).

£200 per year in the later fourteenth century to around £50 per year in the 1460s [**7**]. The high sensitivity to economic trends of this form of income was a particular problem for those monasteries which depended heavily on spiritual income, mainly lesser houses lacking large tracts of land. Houses of regular canons, which had commonly been granted parish churches owing to their historical associations with pastoral work, also depended heavily on spiritual income: the Augustinians as a whole drew 37 per cent of their revenues from this source. With the pronounced decline in spiritual income over the later middle ages, it may well have been monasteries of this kind that suffered most severely.[29]

Nevertheless all religious houses felt the strain in the later fourteenth and fifteenth centuries as their fixed incomes declined, and it is common to find complaints of financial hardship made by some of the wealthiest institutions in medieval England. The 'depression' of the mid-fifteenth century, when prices of almost all commodities fell, was a time of particular difficulty for many houses;[30] and it is noticeable that the number of financially collapsed small houses – though always small – was at its peak between 1440 and 1470 (see below, pp. 42–3). Northern houses were also badly affected by Scottish raids across the border, particularly in the early years of the fourteenth century. The resulting damage necessitated the reassessment of these houses' income for taxation purposes, and the inhabitants of Bolton Priory and the small nunneries of Moxby and Rosedale (all in Yorkshire) were even forced to abandon their houses for a short time in 1320 to avoid attack.[31]

The religious were not helpless in the face of these wider economic trends, however, and they developed a number of strategies to cope with the prevailing conditions. Houses might seek to acquire additional revenues, either through donations, or payments for their spiritual services, or by appropriating additional parish churches (see below, pp. 46–51, 62). Monasteries seem to have been able to find creditors when necessary, and in general to have managed their debts competently: even a small house like Wallingford Priory could, with careful management, pay off debts of more than £70 (nearly half its annual income) in a single year [cf. **54**].[32] Poor nunneries, in particular, could also rely on gifts and loans from well-wishing neighbours, often local gentlewomen, to help them overcome short-term financial difficulties

29 Heale (2004a), 237–49; Robinson (1980), 128.
30 Hatcher (1996).
31 Kershaw (1973), 14–17; Tillotson (1989), 38n.
32 Heale (2004a), 268n.

[**6**]. Alternatively, the religious raised money by taking lay boarders into their cloister, either by selling corrodies – board and lodging in the monastery in return for a gift of property or lump sum in cash – or by accepting short-term paying guests. This latter practice again seems to have been particularly common among nunneries at times of hardship, with the East Anglian communities of Carrow, Redlingfield and St Radegund's Cambridge all drawing more than 10 per cent of their income from lay boarders in the mid-fifteenth century [**6, 18**].[33] Some houses developed their industrial activity, while others sought to increase revenues from lands by exploiting them more intensively. The medium-sized Warwickshire houses of Merevale and Maxstoke, for example, specialised in cattle farming in the forest of Arden in the fifteenth century, and by such means were able to weather the economic storms of the period.[34]

This kind of enterprise was increasingly common in the generation before the Dissolution when economic conditions were becoming more favourable, at least for pastoral farming. The dairy of Sibton Abbey was producing significant quantities of cheese and butter for the market in the early sixteenth century, and several monasteries situated near the centres of the cloth trade in the Cotswolds and East Anglia began to take part in large-scale wool production. The nuns of Carrow expanded their sheep flocks from 152 animals in 1485 to more than 800 in 1520, and Norwich Cathedral Priory enlarged its flocks to ten times that number over the same period. The majority of monastic estates remained leased out, but the improved economic outlook permitted some religious houses to raise rents, or to demand higher entry fines from new tenants [cf. **52**].[35] If the number of major building projects undertaken by monasteries of all sizes is any guide (see below, pp. 18–22), many houses were experiencing a rise in prosperity in the early sixteenth century after decades of stagnation.

The difficult and shifting economic conditions of the later middle ages inevitably affected the character of monastic life itself. Declining income created anxiety and must have made attracting lay patronage appear more necessary than ever. The move to widespread leasing of monastic estates also had far-reaching ramifications for many houses, most notably the Cistercians and their imitators, the Premonstratensians and the Gilbertines. A major element in the Cistercian Order's

33 E.g. Tillotson (1989); Oliva (1998), 111–38.
34 Watkins (1994); Watkins (1996).
35 Harper-Bill and Rawcliffe (2004), 96; Youings (1990).

attempts to isolate themselves from worldly distractions in the twelfth century was their employment of lay brothers to work their lands, which were organised into compact estates or granges. However, from the early fourteenth century, many houses of these orders began to find it more profitable to lease out some of their granges, a process greatly accelerated after the collapse in grain prices in the 1370s. With the decline of their grange economy, Cistercian, Premonstratensian and Gilbertine houses had little need for lay brothers, who were in any case much harder to recruit in an age of labour shortages and high wages. The Cistercian abbey of Meaux had held ninety lay brothers in the mid-thirteenth century, but there were only seven remaining on the eve of the Black Death and none at all by 1396 [4]. Indeed, by 1400 it was rare to find more than a handful of lay brothers in any house in England, and a major element in the distinctiveness of these orders had evaporated.

## Monastic administration and heads of houses

A further effect of this shift to a rentier economy may have been a lightening of the administrative burden faced by some monasteries, as the need to supervise closely the management of individual estates was reduced. But the contrast between time-consuming direct management and a more relaxed policy of leasing can easily be overdrawn. Monasteries still needed to ensure that lessees did not dilapidate their properties, and even after the leasing of an estate the religious often retained responsibility for the upkeep of its buildings [5]. The finding of suitable tenants could also be a laborious task in fifteenth-century England, and vigilance was necessary to preserve the powers and income of the manorial court.[36] As a result, their status as major landholders still weighed heavily on the inmates of late medieval monasteries. Religious houses divided the management of their property among the more senior members of the community, who were assigned various offices (or 'obediences'). Monastic lands were usually apportioned between these obedientiaries, who were charged with the responsibility of supervising estates, maintaining buildings, holding courts, hiring labour, purchasing provisions or materials and providing an account of their administration at the yearly audit [6, 8, 10]. It was normal in larger houses for at least half the community to hold an obedience, many with their own lands to manage; and smaller monasteries might need to call on an even higher proportion of their convent to contribute to the priory's administration [19]. The same practice obtained in nunneries, and despite traditional

36 Dyer (2005), 102–3.

claims that 'the nuns were never very good business women', there is little evidence that female religious were any less competent managers of their property than the monks and canons [10].[37] In male and female houses alike, promotion to important obediences was dictated by the experience and ability of the inmates, and surviving financial records from nunneries cannot be distinguished in their form or professionalism from those of male monasteries of a comparable size.

The financial wellbeing of a monastery was also dictated by the competence of its superior.[38] A large proportion of many houses' revenue – often between a quarter and a half – was devoted solely to the upkeep of the head of house and their guests. Monasteries could become seriously indebted through their head's profligacy or mismanagement, as at Huntingdon Priory in 1439 where the prior and his mother allegedly 'squandered and wasted' large sums of money without the community's consent.[39] The Benedictine Rule accorded a great deal of power to the abbot in the management of the monastery. The head, to whom complete obedience was owed by all members of the community, was encouraged to consult senior brethren in important decisions but ultimately the decisions to be taken were his [11]. Nevertheless, in practice, certain checks and balances tempered the power of the superior. Both lay patrons and the ecclesiastical authorities monitored monastic administration closely to ensure the performance of spiritual services or the long-term financial viability of houses were not jeopardised, with abbesses and prioresses coming under particularly close episcopal supervision.[40] Attempts to impose constitutional limitations on the superior's authority also ensued from within monastic communities, with some heads of houses required to swear on their appointment that they would observe the monastery's customs, rule consensually and not interfere with the revenues assigned to the conventual obedientiaries [28]. These 'constitutional movements' were particularly strong in the late twelfth and thirteenth centuries, with the heads of several large Benedictine abbeys forced to accept formal limits on their powers beyond those specified in the Rule;[41] and even in the early fourteenth century, new agreements of this kind were promulgated at Burton, Gloucester and Ramsey.

37 Power (1922), 228; Oliva (1998), 75–110.
38 The best discussion of the late medieval abbot currently available can be found in Knowles (1948–59), I, 270–9, II, 248–54.
39 Thompson (1914–29), II, 148–55.
40 Spear (2005), 41–58.
41 E.g. Gransden (1975).

Although many of these customs remained in force, this was the high water mark of the monastic constitutional movement in medieval England. Over the later middle ages, the internal authority of the superior gradually strengthened. By the later fifteenth century, it was not uncommon to find heads managing several monastic obediences themselves (the prior of Rochester held six in 1511), or taking the most important conventual office into their own hands. Such centralisation often made economic sense, but it brought the house's management firmly under the control of its head. A growing emphasis on the status of the abbatial office can also be discerned in the later middle ages. A wide range of houses acquired the rank of mitred abbeys, permitting their superiors to adopt the regalia and some of the ceremonial powers of a bishop [53]. Abbots and priors also increasingly sought their own coats of arms, with even the heads of some smaller houses such as the Cornish priories of Bodmin and Tywardreath obtaining this privilege in the early sixteenth century. The growing dominance of superiors in the internal life of their monasteries was also expressed through their households, which grew considerably in size over the later middle ages, in common with trends in secular and episcopal households. In 1505/6, Robert Kirton, abbot of Peterborough, maintained 116 attendants, dwarfing the 43 men retained by Abbot Wenlock of (the wealthier) Westminster in 1300. The lavish residences built to domicile these households also underline the rising status of the late medieval superior (see below, pp. 20–2).

The same trend can be seen in the growing public role of abbots and priors in the later middle ages [53]. Heads of houses had always served on government commissions in their localities, for example as tax collectors or supervising public works, and occasionally taking on more important roles such as diplomacy. But from the last years of the fifteenth century, monastic involvement in public affairs increased significantly. Between 1494 and 1509, there were sixteen appointments of monks and canons to the episcopal bench, proportionately a very large increase on the previous 100 years.[42] This included the promotion of Henry Deane, prior of Llanthony Secunda, to the archbishopric of Canterbury in 1501: the first monk appointed to this office since Simon Langham (abbot of Westminster) 135 years earlier. This pattern continued into the reign of Henry VIII, with seven further promotions of monastic superiors to the rank of bishop in the 1530s. Accompanying

---

42 One appointment every year, as opposed to approximately one every six years: Dobson (1999b); Haines (2003).

this sudden increase in the promotion of monks and canons to bishoprics was a comparable rise in the number of religious appointed as suffragan (or deputy) bishops. The superiors employed in this way were not from the greatest houses, and included priors from apparently insignificant monasteries such as Alvecote and Bicknacre. The status that attended appointment as a suffragan has been questioned, but the fine residences built for themselves by some of the heads favoured in this way, such as Thomas Chard of Forde and Thomas Vivian of Bodmin, suggests that they regarded their appointments as a mark of dignity.[43] Whether female superiors enjoyed a similar rise in status is less clear-cut; and it may be significant that in double houses of the Gilbertine order the male canons – initially subservient to the nuns – had achieved dominance over administrative affairs by the later middle ages.[44]

## Standards of living and monastic building

It was not only monastic superiors who saw their material position improve over the later middle ages: all inhabitants of monasteries benefited to some degree from the general increases in living standards in late medieval England. From the twelfth century, a barrage of satirical writings had mocked the luxurious fare enjoyed by communities vowed to poverty, and recent archaeological research on monastic skeletons has suggested that the stereotype of the corpulent monk had consider-able basis in fact.[45] By the early fourteenth century, attempts to enforce the vegetarianism of the Benedictine Rule had been defeated, and in 1336 Pope Benedict XII permitted meat-eating among the black monks on four days of the week, providing it did not take place in the monastic refectory. Studies of monastic diet at Westminster Abbey and Durham Cathedral Priory have confirmed that the inmates of major houses dined in a manner similar to the greater gentry, consuming large quantities of meat, fish and alcohol: indeed the ordinary allowance of ale or beer for a monk was a gallon (or eight pints) a day.[46] On greater festivals, when most of the day would be spent in choir, the community was rewarded with particularly lavish fare, as well as a generous allocation of wine on top of their usual alcoholic provision [10]. The inmates of smaller monasteries, though, cannot have enjoyed the luxuries accorded to the monks of Westminster and Durham. Numerous complaints about rotten

43  Emery (1996–2006), III, 560–5, 624–6.

44  Golding (1995), 133–7.

45  Gilchrist and Sloane (2005), 212–13.

46  Harvey (1993), 34–71; Threlfall-Holmes (2005), 34–74.

meat and poor quality bread and ale can be found in late medieval visitation records, although even these sources indicate that the occupants of religious houses expected to be well fed for their labours.[47]

Nevertheless, living standards in houses of all sizes seem to have risen over the later middle ages. By the mid-fourteenth century, monks, canons and nuns were regularly granted pocket money, often amounting in the larger houses to several pounds a year [8]. These allowances (alongside gifts to individuals from lay testators and payments for saying masses for benefactors) allowed supposedly possessionless inmates to build up sizeable book collections, purchase devotional aids or even hire personal servants [9].[48] Pocket money might also be spent on individuals' wardrobes, sometimes with fashionable intent: Henry V's proposed reforms of 1421 included complaints about the 'great excesses in monks' frocks, so that the sleeves of them in many places stretch right to the ground' [cf. 19].[49] Inmates were also permitted periodic holidays, either to manors set aside for the purpose or to visit friends and relatives [8]. The increasingly comfortable standard of living enjoyed in many religious houses is also apparent from the study of their built environment. The sophistication of the domestic buildings within the greater monasteries can perhaps be seen most vividly in their water management and sanitation which, with its vaulted drains, flushed latrines and clean running water, often exceeded anything found in elite secular residences of the period.[50] Moreover, despite a significant reduction in the number of major rebuilding projects involving monastic churches undertaken between c. 1380 and 1500,[51] a product presumably of the economic difficulties of this period, the renovation of domestic buildings proceeded largely unabated during the later middle ages.

The considerable expenditure on claustral buildings within late medieval monasteries was driven primarily by two developments. Firstly, convents were forced to adapt to the demographic and economic imperatives of the post-Black Death era. Buildings constructed for much larger communities were now uncomfortable, difficult to maintain and in some cases obsolete. As a result, in several houses, communal buildings such as the dormitory (Durham, Fountains and Valle Crucis) or the refectory (Cleeve and Holy Island) were converted into part of the superior's

47 Harper-Bill (1985).
48 Doyle (1988); Knowles (1948–59), II, 240–7.
49 Myers (1969), 788.
50 Bond (2001).
51 Morris (1979), 177–236.

residence. Cistercian and Premonstratensian houses, designed with a significant population of lay brothers in mind, were in particularly urgent need of remodelling, with many buildings, particularly in the west range of the cloister, now redundant. At the Cistercian Sawley Abbey, the abbot converted the vacated west range into a commodious house, and much of the church's nave was demolished.[52] Secondly, the later middle ages was a period of considerable improvement in domestic amenities outside the cloister. It is the nature of domestic buildings that they continually require renovation, and it was perhaps inevitable that monasteries should be influenced by developments in modern living conditions, just as twenty-first-century religious communities might wish to have access to television or the internet. In any case, institutions which viewed hospitality as one of their principal functions (as well as one of the most effective ways to attract influential lay support) could scarcely afford to present honoured guests with outdated accommodation [13, 40].

This combination of expediency and the desire to keep step with advances in general living conditions stimulated building work in monasteries of all descriptions [12–14]. The largest and wealthiest houses spent considerable sums on domestic buildings, such as the refashioning of the Durham dormitory in the early fifteenth century, at an estimated cost of £400.[53] Lavish new cloisters (with glazing to keep out cold winds) were constructed at numerous houses – including surviving examples at Gloucester, Lacock, Norwich and Durham again – in order to provide a more comfortable environment for monastic study, education and ceremony. Monasteries were also influenced by the move towards privacy in the domestic architecture of the period, a trend immediately perceptible in the design of late medieval residences and almshouses.[54] Monastic inventories of the later middle ages indicate the influence of secular houses on domestic arrangements, listing the contents of rooms such as the hall, chambers, buttery and pantry instead of the more traditional refectory, dormitory, warming room and so on [cf. 12]. At the same time, a wide range of monasteries, from Durham Priory to the small nunnery at Littlemore, can be found partitioning

---

52 Emery (1996–2006); Coppack (2002).

53 Dobson (2003); although more than half of this sum was apparently donated by Bishop Walter Skirlaw of Durham.

54 E.g. Grenville (1997), 89–120; Dyer (2005), 51–8. Private quarters were not new in elite residences, but this period witnessed the extension of notions of privacy further down the social spectrum, as shown by the multiplication of chambers in secular houses.

their dormitories into individual cells, or rooms [8]; and it became increasingly common in larger houses for the senior obedientiaries and university students to be given their own private quarters within the infirmary or elsewhere in the precinct. This practice was also prevalent in the wealthier nunneries, where communities often lived and ate in two or three separate households rather than in common.[55]

The other characteristic building enterprises carried out by late medieval monasteries involved the gatehouse and the living quarters of the superior. Numerous imposing gatehouses were constructed by monasteries in the fourteenth and fifteenth centuries, for example at Bury St Edmunds, Butley and Thornton. These buildings were provided in part to preserve the monastery's security and enclosure in an age of some civil unrest (see below, pp. 61–2), but they also served as an eloquent symbol of power and lordship. Superiors' houses also received considerable attention in the later middle ages. In major Benedictine monasteries, such as Westminster and Battle, already large living quarters were greatly extended and beautified over the later middle ages. Lavish building programmes, however, were also carried out at the medium-sized Cluniac priories of Castle Acre and Wenlock, where modest priors' lodgings were converted in the mid-fifteenth century into stately buildings with galleries, bay windows and commodious living quarters. Standards of decoration were also high, as can be seen from surviving buildings such as the beautifully roofed abbots' halls of Cleeve (Cistercian) and Milton (Benedictine), and the state-of-the-art houses built by the heads of Forde, Thame (both Cistercian) and Notley (Augustinian) in the fifteenth and early sixteenth centuries. This spending, moreover, was matched on the country residences of heads, which might number several in the case of the wealthiest abbots and priors [14].[56] With the particularly lavish fare reserved for the superior's table and his guests, there is no doubt that many late medieval heads lived like aristocrats.

The early years of the sixteenth century saw an 'Indian summer' of building activity within the monastic precinct.[57] Not only did domestic buildings continue to be adorned and updated, but ambitious alterations to the monastic church were now again widely countenanced, following the fifteenth-century lull. At Glastonbury, Abbot Richard Bere (in office 1494–1525) constructed three new chapels, dedicated to

55 Platt (1984), 136–72; Harvey (1993), 77; Power (1922), 317–22.

56 Emery (1996–2006); Thompson (2001), 95–101.

57 Platt (1984), 209–18.

Our Lady of Loreto, the Holy Sepulchre and King Edgar, in or annexed to the conventual church [14]; and at Bath Cathedral Priory an entirely new church was begun in the early sixteenth century, although the work had not been completed by the time of the house's suppression in 1539. Other alterations were more cosmetic, including the impressive new towers at Bolton (Augustinian), Shap (Premonstratensian) and Fountains (Cistercian). This new flowering of building activity, undertaken by houses of all sizes and orders and continuing into the 1530s, shows the confidence of the monastic order on the eve of the Dissolution. The purpose of much of this activity was display, to the glory of God and the house's patron saints, but also to convey to outsiders the efficacy of monastic prayers and the continuing vitality of the monastic way of life. This message must have got across, but it may have inadvertently contributed to the new wave of criticism directed at monastic wealth in early Tudor England (see below, pp. 68–72).

It seems clear, then, that the inmates of late medieval monasteries enjoyed a more comfortable existence than their forebears. Nevertheless, this improved standard of living did not guarantee longevity of life. Studies of the mortality rates of the monks of Christ Church Canterbury and Westminster have indicated that their life expectancy at the age of twenty (i.e. how many more years on average they would live beyond this age) dropped significantly during the second half of the fifteenth century, from about thirty years to less than twenty.[58] It should also be remembered that a significant minority of communities subsisted on inadequate incomes over the later middle ages. Recent work on female monasteries, in particular, has drawn attention to the modest living standards found in many poorly endowed nunneries. The diet experienced in these houses contained few luxuries, with the nuns of Marrick Priory spending only 15d on spices in 1415/16, compared to the £7 spent on behalf of the monks of Selby Abbey the following year.[59] Roberta Gilchrist has even suggested that modest buildings and primitive sanitation were deliberately maintained by many nunneries as acts of austerity appropriate to their monastic vocation. The emphasis on poverty and privation in contemporary female spirituality makes this a plausible theory, although it should be noted that our knowledge of water management in nunneries remains limited, and that undeveloped buildings and basic levels of sanitation can also be found in small male

58 Harvey (1993), 112–45; Hatcher (1986).
59 Tillotson (1989), 16–17.

houses.[60] On economic grounds alone, a much simpler lifestyle must have obtained in many nunneries. It would seem, however, that only a small number of monastic communities were living in serious hardship in early Tudor England. When the Henrician commissioners for the suppression of the smaller monasteries in 1536–37 reported back on the condition of these houses, they regularly commented not only on the good quality of many of the buildings, but also on their recent construction – as at the small, Augustinian Buckenham Priory, described as 'newly built and in marvellous good reparation' [cf. **12**].[61]

## Monastic observance

Despite these caveats about smaller (particularly female) monasteries and falling life expectancy, there remains a certain incongruity about religious communities vowed to poverty enjoying such a comfortable standard of living. Several historians have highlighted the extent to which late medieval observance differed from the simplicity of the Benedictine Rule [**1**] or the austere practices adopted by the reformed monasticism of the twelfth century. The most searching critique of the way of life followed within late medieval monasteries remains that of Dom David Knowles (see above, pp. 4–5). In Knowles' judgement, the modifications of observance now adopted – generally with the authorisation of the general chapters of each order – contravened the essence of the monastic way of life. The Benedictine Rule's conception of the monastery as a family was damaged, he argued, by the late medieval retreat from the common life, as refectories and dormitories were abandoned, superiors withdrew to their own houses and monks and canons were sent to university. Similarly, the disregard for the Rule's prohibition of private property and meat-eating was interpreted as a symptom and cause of laxity among the religious of this period.[62]

It has not only been historians, like Knowles, who have felt that the religious life practised in many late medieval monasteries was not characterised by particular austerity or zeal: similar charges were also made by the monks' medieval contemporaries. This criticism is commonly found in late medieval literature (see below, pp. 64–6), but it was also manifested in two serious attempts to enforce a return to stricter forms of observance by Henry V and Cardinal Wolsey. Henry V's interest in the reformed monastic life is indicated by his foundation

---

60 Gilchrist (1994), 92–127; Bond (2001).
61 Knowles (1948–59), III, 314–15.
62 *Ibid.*, II, esp. 240–7, 354–64.

of the Carthusian Sheen and the Bridgettine Syon in 1414–15, and also by his abortive plans to introduce into England the rigorous Celestine Order, which sought to observe the Benedictine Rule to the letter. Allegedly at the prompting of the Carthusian prior of Mount Grace, Nicholas Love,[63] the king called an extraordinary meeting of the Benedictine general chapter at Westminster to discuss reform in May 1421. His proposals were relatively modest, including criticisms of meat-eating, private property and the retreat from the common life. However, Henry V's death in France a few months later allowed the black monks to deflect his reforming programme without absorbing any of the proposed changes. Here the matter rested until Cardinal Wolsey sought to introduce a similarly modest return to more traditional practices for all the major monastic orders in 1519–20 [17, 20]. Wolsey's proposals to the black monks were met with a frank, but arresting response: 'in this our age (with the world now drawing to its end), those who seek austerity of life and regular observance are very few and very rare'. If adopted, the monks' response continued, these reforms would prompt widespread defection and the drying up of new recruits [17]. Once again, there is no sign that this attempted reform had any serious influence on monastic observance.

It is also significant that the fifteenth-century Observant movement to restore strict and primitive practice, so prominent among the friars in continental Europe but also influencing monks and canons (most notably, with the groups of Benedictine monasteries that affiliated themselves to the 'reformed' abbeys of Bursfeld in Germany and Monte Cassino in Italy), made very little headway in late medieval England.[64] The Observant Franciscan friars were eventually introduced into England in 1482 (though on a rather smaller scale than in contemporary Scotland and Ireland), but no reformed houses of monks, canons or nuns were ever established. This reluctance to embrace the more rigorous practices found in some branches of contemporary European monasticism again conveys something of the character of English houses, which might be described as more relaxed or more moderate depending on one's perspective.

The only orders which routinely adopted a more austere form of monasticism were the Carthusians and the Bridgettines of Syon. Practices such as the wearing of hair shirts, total abstinence from meat-eating (even for the sick), regular fasting on bread and water and a long night

63 Smith (2006).
64 Knowles (1969), 135–41.

office were widely observed within late medieval charterhouses [9]. The Bridgettine rule, and the English additions to it, also required strict observance from the nuns and brethren of the order, for example in the regulations concerning private property and fasting. Nevertheless, even the Carthusian Order saw some significant modifications of its primitive observance in the later middle ages. Twelfth-century Carthusians had fasted on bread and water four days a week, whereas this practice was adopted only once a week in late medieval houses and then only for the young and healthy; and some level of private ownership of property was permitted by the early sixteenth century [9]. Ornamentation was also introduced into Carthusian churches, with archaeological finds from the Coventry Charterhouse showing elaborately decorated screenwork, floor tiles and glass. Excavation of Mount Grace Priory has similarly revealed that a high standard of accommodation was provided for the monks, with spacious and comfortable cells accessorised with pleasant gardens and sophisticated sanitary arrangements.[65] These developments were connected with the late medieval Carthusians' retreat from isolationism (see below, p. 34), and represented a significant departure from their original statutes.

The gradual movement away from traditional observances can therefore be traced in every corner of monastic England. Indeed, the lament of the Benedictine chapter that few contemporaries sought a life of austerity and regular observance appears on closer examination to be more than special pleading. Simplicity of life could still be found within the cloister, and gradations of austerity continued to exist between houses and orders. But asceticism comparable to that widely practised in the high middle ages was rare in late medieval England. This shift can also be viewed in other departments of medieval religion. Late medieval hermits were more likely to perform practical services, such as the maintenance of bridges, than adopt the savagely ascetic practices of Godric of Finchale and other twelfth-century solitaries. Patterns of official canonisation also suggest changing ideals in late medieval Europe, as theologians and bishops were considered more fitting emblems of sanctity than the ascetic saints of the preceding period; and the later middle ages saw a more relaxed attitude to penance on a popular level, through an emphasis on the remittance of sins after death in Purgatory rather than through penitential activity in this life.[66] These broader cultural and theological changes, of which monastic practices were

---

65 Thompson (1930), 103–30; Coppack and Aston (2003), 76–97.

66 Clay (1914); Vauchez (1997), 387–412; Burgess (1988).

only one component, should caution us against judging the religious of the later middle ages by the standards of the twelfth century. But if we were to do so, even the Carthusians of fifteenth-century England would suffer by comparison with the severe life followed by St Hugh of Witham (*c.* 1140–1200) and his contemporaries.

If deviation from monastic rules or from earlier practice is not necessarily a sign of laxity or lack of commitment to the religious life, this does not in itself invalidate Knowles' assessment of declining standards of observance among late medieval monasteries. As we have seen, the most informative source for assessing the quality and vitality of the religious life in late medieval England is the visitation record [**18, 19**]. Despite the inherently negative character of these inspection reports, it remains the case that they reveal a significant minority of communities where even the fundamentals of the monastic life are barely present. At Dorchester in 1441 the canons frequented taverns, engaged in hunting and hawking and regularly admitted women into the cloister. Several canons were accused of sexual incontinence, including the abbot who was said to have had five mistresses, including one Joan Baroun 'with whom he was taken in a suspect manner in the steward's chamber'. Matters there had improved little by 1530, when the canons' enclosure was still little observed, and their attendance at divine service was poor: one canon, indeed, had apparently appeared in choir only three times during the previous year.[67] Examples of such flagrant neglect of monastic vows and vocation are relatively rare, and it should be noted that they come from larger houses as often as smaller ones. It has been calculated that only about 5 per cent of the Premonstratensian canons subjected to visitation between 1478 and 1503 by Richard Redman, the commissary-general of the order in England, were accused of sexual incontinence. But if we should not exaggerate the levels of vice found in late medieval monasteries, it must also be acknowledged that complaints about inmates staying up to drink after the last service of the day, Compline (causing them to miss the night office), leaving the precinct to socialise with layfolk, or engaging in unsuitable secular pursuits are all commonplace in late medieval visitation records.[68]

Coulton, Knowles and others found in such reports a spiritual tepidity, an easy-going atmosphere of mediocrity that seems to tally with the retreat from traditional observances found in this period. The recurring problems highlighted in visitation records cannot simply be ignored, as

67 Thompson (1914–29), I, 68–78; Thompson (1940–47), II, 115–23.
68 Knowles (1948–59), II, 204–18, III, 62–86; Gribbin (2001), 40–100.

some recent revisionist treatments of the late medieval religious orders have come close to doing. They display many genuine faults, which make it difficult for the historian to declare that all was entirely well with English monasticism in the later middle ages. At the same time, it is unlikely that evidence of this nature would reveal deep spirituality where it existed; and it is also significant that a comparison between thirteenth- and fifteenth-century visitation reports does not indicate any significant decline in standards. It is therefore necessary to set other kinds of evidence against that of the visitation record in order to assess the spirituality and vitality of the monasteries of this period. This is not an entirely straightforward task owing to the nature of the surviving evidence, which tends to shed more light on the administrative than the devotional activities of communities. However, sufficient material survives to illuminate three topics – spirituality, the liturgy and learning – that present a different facet of monastic life in late medieval England.

## Monastic spirituality

Monastic spirituality can rarely be accessed through visitation evidence or administrative records, and although an impression of the devotional climate within individual houses is occasionally provided by monastic chronicles [**22, 23**], this genre of source becomes increasingly rare after *c.* 1350. Something of the devotional character of a house can also be learned from its books [**9**]. Numerous book lists and catalogues survive from late medieval houses, together with about 5,000 surviving volumes, often annotated by their monastic readers. The libraries of the larger houses were extensive and wide-ranging, and included many works of biblical commentary and the writings of the Church Fathers, the traditional staple of monastic devotional reading. In trying to take the spiritual temperature of late medieval houses, however, historians have tended to pay considerably more attention to evidence of monastic engagement with contemporary devotional trends, and in particular the literary productions of the English mystics[69] and the *Devotio Moderna*.[70] There is little evidence of sustained interest in these works in the many surviving books and book lists of the black monks; although the mystical (or contemplative) writings of a monk of Durham dwelling on Farne Island in the later fourteenth century indicate that the great Benedic-

---

69 Late medieval writers, such as Richard Rolle, Walter Hilton and Julian of Norwich, who wrote of their experiences of union with God through contemplation.

70 A north European devotional movement of the later middle ages, which stressed the inner life and meditative piety over ritual.

tine houses of late medieval England were not entirely insulated from this branch of devotion. It may be that some houses of the Augustinian canons were more receptive to this contemplative spirituality [cf. **24**]. Not only did this order produce one of the most important English mystics, Walter Hilton, a canon of Thurgarton, but surviving late medieval book catalogues from Southwark and Thurgarton Priories also reveal good collections of up-to-date contemplative and devotional literature.[71] It should also be remembered that the last medieval Englishman to be canonised, in 1401, was an Augustinian canon, John Thweng, prior of Bridlington (d. 1379).

The largest collections of late medieval devotional and contemplative works were owned by houses of the stricter orders: the Carthusians and the Bridgettines of Syon [**9**]. The Carthusians, who spent their days in solitude, were naturally interested in works of contemplative spirituality, and played a major part in the dissemination of this kind of literature to a lay audience. Similarly, the library of the Syon brethren contained large numbers of devotional and mystical titles in the early sixteenth century, many of them recently printed works from the continent. The Syon brothers were rather less involved in the publication of mystical works than they have sometimes been given credit for, but they did produce some of the most popular manuals of lay devotion in early Tudor England, with the practical religious writings of Thomas Betson and, in particular, Richard Whitford. Carthusian monks, too, wrote devotional works for a wider audience, most notably *The Mirror of the Blessed Life of Jesus Christ* – a translation of a well-known Latin life of Christ, wrongly attributed to St Bonaventure – by the prior of Mount Grace, Nicholas Love, in the 1410s.[72]

Although the abbey's surviving library catalogue relates only to the collection of the Syon brethren, it is clear that the Bridgettine sisters also took a strong interest in the literature of late medieval spirituality. Several of the nuns' books survive, with contemplative works strongly represented. The Carthusians of Sheen are known to have provided texts of this kind for the Syon sisters, and a number of late medieval devotional works, including the *Dialogues* of St Catherine of Siena (under the title *The Orchard of Syon*), were translated into English for their benefit by the Syon brothers.[73] This interest in vernacular

---

71 Pantin (1944); Webber (1997). Very few book lists survive from Augustinian houses, so it is impossible to know the extent of this phenomenon.

72 Sargent (1976); Gillespie (1999); Ellis (1997).

73 Rhodes (1993).

contemplative literature can also be found in other nunneries in late medieval England. Barking Abbey acquired a copy of Nicholas Love's *Mirror* soon after its publication, and the nuns of Dartford and the London Minories owned works by Walter Hilton. A good deal of late medieval contemplative literature was written with a female audience in mind, and it would appear that nunneries were more receptive to contemporary spirituality than many male houses. About half of the surviving books which can be connected with an English nunnery are of works dating from the fifteenth and early sixteenth centuries, in stark contrast to the extant books associated with male houses, 87 per cent of which are of older works.[74] There is also good reason to believe that nunneries were closely integrated with lay female spirituality in this period. Not only were nuns an obvious source of imitation by pious laywomen, such as Cecily Neville, duchess of York, who were attracted to the 'mixed life' (a combination of the active life of the world with the contemplative pursuits of the cloister), but female monasteries also shared a vernacular reading culture with pious women outside the cloister. Nuns can be found exchanging devotional literature with laywomen, and owned exactly the same kinds of books as female readers outside the cloister [**24**].[75]

## The liturgy

Nevertheless, a community's openness to the writings of late medieval mystics should not be the sole measure of their spirituality. Monastic devotion was expressed and developed not only through meditative private reading (the *lectio divina*), but also through ritual. Indeed, when late medieval monastic observers such as the chronicler Henry Knighton or the Premonstratensian commissary-general Richard Redman took pride in the spiritual reputation of their houses or orders, they were usually referring to high standards of monastic observance and the dignified performance of divine service (or liturgy). Despite the complaints in some visitation records about poor attendance in choir [**19**], it is clear – not least from the remarkably large sums spent by religious houses on elaborate vestments and plate [**13, 15**] – that many communities took their liturgical commitments seriously. Moreover, the late middle ages was a time when certain aspects of the monastic liturgy were greatly elaborated through the introduction of polyphonic music, in imitation of the choirs of secular colleges and the royal

---

74 Bell (1995), 33–56; Bell (1999).

75 E.g. Erler (2002), 127–47.

household. This highly technical chanting was generally performed by professional singers and specially trained choirboys in the Lady Chapel or nave, rather than by the religious themselves in choir – for whom (in the words of Wolsey's 1519 statutes for the Augustinian canons) the 'wanton melodies' of the new style of music were not always considered an appropriate replacement for 'plain chant and the modest dignity of psalm-singing' [20]. Nevertheless, several monasteries can be found in the fifteenth and early sixteenth centuries investing considerable sums in the provision of high-quality and up-to-date polyphonic music to augment their ordinary services.[76]

This commitment to the liturgy is perhaps unsurprising, since a good deal of the monastic day was consumed with divine service. Aside from the eight daily offices, which principally consisted of the communal recitation of the psalms and other biblical texts, the convent also attended the communal Morrow Mass and High Mass. On feast-days and in the week leading up to Easter, more elaborate services were performed consuming the greater part of the day. The monastic liturgy, which differed according to order, did not remain static throughout the medieval period. During the later middle ages, most houses adopted additional 'votive' offices on certain days of the week, dedicated to a particular saint, in place of the ordinary Hours (or services) of the day. The Little Office of the Virgin was widely celebrated on Saturdays by the early fourteenth century [28], and communities often took up other votive offices in honour of saints with close devotional associations to their house or order. Therefore, by the early fifteenth century, Peterborough Abbey was celebrating weekly offices in commemoration of the Virgin, St Peter, St Benedict, St Oswald (whose severed arm was the centrepiece of the abbey's relic collection) and the Office of Relics. These offices impinged on the traditional recitation of the psalms by the community (already cut down by the Benedictine general chapter in 1277–78), mirroring lay prayer books (or books of Hours) which increasingly preferred more personalised devotions to particular saints to psalms as the later middle ages progressed.[77]

Monastic practice demonstrated its receptiveness to broader devotional influences in other ways. New cults, such as the Holy Name of Jesus, were swiftly adopted in late medieval houses [21]. The English charterhouses, moreover, were rebuked by the general chapter of their order on more than one occasion for observing the votive Office of the Virgin on

---

76 Bowers (1994).
77 Roper (1993); Catto (1985).

Saturdays, in common with standard English practice but at variance with the Carthusian rite. Similarly, some late medieval Premonstratensian abbeys adopted practices associated with secular rites, such as the 'Office of the Passion', and kneeling instead of bowing at the elevation of the Host during Mass.[78] The overriding impression from the study of the monastic liturgy in late medieval England, therefore, is of an elaborate and evolving form of worship, which was highly responsive to contemporary developments outside the cloister. It should also be noted that a significant proportion of this liturgical activity was performed publicly. Processions which led outside the precinct (often including sermons and masses), in order to display the house's relics or to pray for God's mercy to the wider community at times of crisis, were an increasingly common element of monastic ritual in the later middle ages.[79] It would also appear that the laity regularly had access to monastic services and masses for their devotional edification [16, 18, 21].

Notwithstanding this public dimension, these extensive liturgical commitments must have been the principal channels of monastic devotion to God, the Virgin and the saints. Monastic churches were adorned with wall paintings, stained-glass windows, carved and sculpted images, screenwork, altarpieces and tapestries, all of which underscored and elaborated the meaning of the liturgy and the Mass to the community [15, 21]. The later middle ages saw great expenditure on all these embellishments [13], most of which have subsequently been lost. But occasionally their devotional impact can be sampled in surviving monastic buildings, such as the series of more than 1,000 carved roof bosses preserved in the church, cloister, chapter house and refectory at Norwich Cathedral, depicting episodes from Scripture and the lives of the saints.[80] Together with the devotional images owned by many late medieval monks and nuns, this religious artwork stimulated and channelled monastic piety, while bolstering *esprit de corps* by drawing attention to the history of the community and to the virtues and powers of the saints with which their house and order were associated.

## Monastic learning

Another indication of the potential vitality within late medieval precincts is the intellectual life of the community. Pre-Reformation monasteries have not traditionally been associated with high standards

78 Thompson (1930), 264–6; Gribbin (2001), 101–31.

79 Clark (2000b).

80 Gilchrist (2005), 86–90.

of learning. The achievement of a small number of monk-scholars, such as the theologian John Uthred of Boldon (a monk of Durham), the poet John Lydgate (Bury St Edmunds) and the chroniclers Ranulf Higden (Chester) and Thomas Walsingham (St Albans) has long been recognised. However, in contrast to the preceding period, few major works of scholarship came out of the late medieval English cloister, and few monastic chronicles continued into the fifteenth century. Nevertheless, in recent years the reputation of late medieval monastic scholarship has begun to be rehabilitated, most notably by James Clark.[81] The intellectual contribution of the black monks to the Church's response to John Wyclif and the Lollard heresy he inspired (see below, pp. 67–8) has been highlighted. At the same time, renewed attention has been given to the flourishing of writing about the origins and history of monasticism in late medieval England. Inspired by attacks from the friars and by Wycliffite writings, numerous apologetic treatises of this kind were produced seeking to defend the monastic way of life as both meritorious and biblical. The antiquity of the Benedictines in particular was stressed, and this intellectual programme widely communicated through art and architecture. Monasteries were also receptive to humanist learning, as the sixteenth-century correspondence of the Evesham monk Robert Joseph shows; and they were enthusiastic purchasers of printed books in the early sixteenth century, with some houses even maintaining their own printing presses.[82]

It seems clear, therefore, that late medieval monasteries were as fully integrated with the main intellectual currents of their age as they were with devotional and liturgical trends. This intellectual integration was closely connected with monastic engagement with the universities. Until the late thirteenth century (in stark contrast to the friars, who adopted university studies from the outset) monks and canons had had little contact with the Schools. Amid concerns that they were thereby losing influence, formal accommodation was provided for Benedictines and Cistercians wishing to study at Oxford in the 1280s, with the first monk-graduates soon receiving degrees. This involvement was further stimulated by Pope Benedict XII's 1335–39 constitutions for the Cistercians, Benedictines and Augustinians which required that all larger houses should send one in twenty inmates to university. This edict was followed unevenly, and university learning was not embraced uniformly across the monastic order [**25**]. The Augustinians and

81 E.g. Clark (2004).
82 Clark (2002).

Cistercians sent a steady stream of inmates to Oxford, although desig-
nated colleges were not provided for their students of these orders until
the mid-fifteenth century.[83] A small Gilbertine college was also established in Cambridge in 1291, but no house of studies was ever furnished
for the Premonstratensian canons, although members of that order did
study at the universities.

The Benedictines, however, took up university learning with considerable
enthusiasm. Most of the larger houses sent a regular stream of monks to
Gloucester College in Oxford (founded in 1283) or Buckingham College
in Cambridge (1428), the order's general houses of studies; and some
greatly exceeded the ratio of one in twenty required by Benedict XII's
constitutions [**25**]. The cathedral priories of Durham and Canterbury
even founded their own eponymous Oxford colleges, to which they sent
up to a third of their communities. As a result, the greater Benedictine
monasteries were almost entirely managed by a university-educated
elite in the later middle ages. Monastic involvement in the universities, moreover, was intensifying in the early sixteenth century for every
order. More than a third of all Cistercian monks and Augustinian canons
known to have studied at Oxford are recorded between 1500 and 1540;
and by this time the black monks comprised the single largest grouping
in the university, with more Benedictines obtaining degrees than friars
of all four orders together in these years. A further impression of the
importance of the Benedictines in early Tudor Oxford can be gleaned
from the fact that the humanist Brasenose and Corpus Christi colleges
were both initially conceived as monastic foundations.[84]

What Knowles disapprovingly termed 'the drift of monks to the universities' affected the character of monastic life and leadership in the decades
leading up to the Dissolution in a number of ways.[85] The monastic
training undertaken in major Benedictine houses was transformed in
the later middle ages in order to align it with the university curriculum,
leading to a considerably extended noviciate which might last several
years [**26**].[86] Not only was the character of monastic studies altered,
but a university education also provided links with the outside world for
individual religious. This could be a source of concern, with signs that
some monk-students found it difficult to reintegrate themselves back

83 Rewley Abbey, founded in 1282 for Cistercian monks studying in Oxford, seems to
    have lost its original function by the late fourteenth century.
84 Greatrex (1994); Dobson (1992); Dobson (1999a); Clark (2002).
85 Knowles (1948–59), II, 359.
86 Harvey (2002); Clark (2004), 42–78.

into the life of the community. Rather more fruitfully, a rising number of monks and canons were promoted to senior positions in the Church in the late fifteenth and early sixteenth centuries (see above, pp. 16–17), and the beneficiaries were almost without exception university-trained [cf. 7].

## Late medieval monastic life and the wider world

In a number of ways, therefore, monastic culture was becoming more closely aligned with that of the world outside the cloister in the later middle ages. For the nunneries, this was predominantly a devotional development, with nuns and pious laywomen comprising a 'textual community' based on vernacular religious literature. For the male houses, this integration was more obvious in an intellectual, artistic and liturgical context, as can also be seen in the hiring of professional lay scribes, artists and musicians, so widespread among religious houses in this period.[87] It is noteworthy that all these areas of apparent vitality stemmed from the receptiveness of late medieval monasteries to contemporary trends outside the cloister. In fact, it is arguably its creative responsiveness to contemporary trends outside the cloister – in religious and secular matters alike – that is the most salient character- istic of late medieval English monasticism. This should not be viewed as worldliness or laxity; rather it reflects a more outward-looking interpretation of the monastic ideal.

There is inherent within the religious life a fundamental tension between withdrawal from and engagement with the world. In broad terms, different emphases have prevailed at different periods of monastic history. In the twelfth century, the isolationist strain of monasticism was strong, as is indicated by the popularity and influence of the Cister- cian Order. But in the later middle ages, greater value was placed on a less introspective form of monasticism. This is perhaps most evident in the dramatic spread of the friars throughout Europe in the thirteenth century, with their ministry of preaching and charity, but the same trend can be seen among the enclosed religious. The only new monastic order authorised in late medieval Europe, the Bridgettines, while demanding strict enclosure from its nuns, required from its male brethren a preaching, educational ministry. That such activity was indeed carried out extensively at Syon can be seen not only from the great quantity of sermon literature found in the brethren's library, but also from the literary productions emanating from the abbey, principally 'handbooks

87 E.g. Doyle (1990); Harrison (1963), 2.

of moral improvement' aimed at a lay audience. Syon also attracted many layfolk to its precinct by its reputation as a source of spiritual direction and by its possession of the *Vincula* pardon, an indulgence granting 300 days' remission from time spent in Purgatory to those attending the brethren's sermons.[88] It is also indicative that most of the new religious orders established in sixteenth-century Europe emphatically set out to engage with the world rather than withdraw from it. The Jesuits combined personal spirituality with missionary and educational zeal, while other new orders, such as the Barnabites or the Ursulines, were devoted to preaching, teaching or the care of the sick.[89]

The importance attached to this outward-looking version of the monastic ideal in the later middle ages is also evident in the way that existing orders adapted their practice. The late medieval Cistercians have often been condemned for moving away from the ideals of the order's founders, but they were not alone in allowing (and indeed encouraging) greater contact with their secular neighbours in the later middle ages [16]. A similar process can be observed taking place among the late medieval Carthusians, that most eremitic of orders. The establishment of the London Charterhouse in 1371 (preceded by a similar foundation in Paris) epitomises the order's retreat from the desert [29]. The urban charterhouses of late medieval England were unable (and perhaps unwilling) to insulate themselves entirely from their lay neighbours, who sought and obtained access to the monks' churches to attend services and for the burial of their bodies. Thomas More was not the only layman to lodge within a Carthusian house in the early sixteenth century, and visitors of both sexes seem to have been common: Lady Margaret Beaufort, for example, acquired a papal bull in 1504 allowing her access to the priory of Sheen with six maidservants; and Coventry and Sheen Charterhouses even ran schools within their precincts.[90] Carthusian communities also encouraged contact with the outside world through their spiritual mentoring of pious layfolk, forging close relationships highlighted by the numerous bequests to individual monks in late medieval wills [9, 23]. Devout men and women in late medieval England sought spiritual leadership, not isolation, from their religious houses and the Carthusian Order was happy to oblige.

The sole, and striking, exception to this trend can be seen in ecclesiastical attitudes towards female enclosure in this period, embodied

---

88 Gillespie (2000); Gillespie (2002); Rhodes (1993).

89 Evennett (1958).

90 Gillespie (1989); Coppack and Aston (2003), 93–7.

by the papal bull *Periculoso* in 1298. This required that nuns should cut themselves off as far as possible from the outside world, with no seculars permitted to enter their cloisters without episcopal licence. Only the head of the house was to be allowed to leave the monastic precinct to carry out the business of the monastery, and then only when absolutely necessary and with the permission of the bishop.[91] This legislation was grounded not on the positive advocacy of a secluded and contemplative female monasticism, but on the belief that women were inherently sinful and unable to preserve their own chastity [cf. 18, 55]. The concept of the nun as the 'bride of Christ' also encouraged a strict policing of female chastity, by greatly intensifying the gravity of any lapse [3]; and contemporary concerns about groups of beguines, laywomen living quasi-religious lives in urbanised parts of northern Europe, contributed to the draconian nature of these measures.

In practice, however, *Periculoso* proved impossible to enforce. The nuns protested that strict enclosure of this kind would prevent the efficient management of their estates and the attraction of the lay patronage on which their solvency depended [cf. 6]. Moreover, it is clear that the nuns' secular neighbours did not support measures of this kind. Late medieval nunneries not only played an important role in the stimulation of female piety, but there was also considerable demand among layfolk for boarding and schooling within these houses (see below, pp. 54–5). In fact, in the face of this opposition, there is little sign that *Periculoso* had any significant impact on female monasticism in late medieval England. The fifteenth-century canon lawyer William Lyndwood bemoaned the general failure of the bishops to enforce the bull in England, and the nunneries themselves put up considerable resistance. After they had been presented with their copy of the bull by their bishop in 1300, the nuns of Markyate 'hurled the said statute at his back and over his head' as he departed, 'declaring unanimously that they were not content in any way to observe such a statute'.[92] The failure of *Periculoso* is yet another indication of the strongly outward-looking character of monasticism in the later middle ages.

It is also worth noting that late medieval English monasteries were in some respects more receptive to the influence of the secular Church than that of the wider culture of European monasticism. Not only did continental monastic reform movements make little headway in England, but contacts between English houses and the continent became

91 Makowski (1999).
92 *Ibid.*, 101–21; Power (1922), 351–2.

progressively weaker over the later middle ages. In the fourteenth century, there were still a large number of French priors and monks serving Cluniac and alien priories in England. However, this internationalism suffered a major setback as a result of the Hundred Years War, with the suppression of the majority of the alien priories (see below, pp. 41–2) and the expulsion of foreign religious [**30**]. The later middle ages also saw the weakening of ties between Cluniac, Premonstratensian and Cistercian monasteries and their French mother houses. Owing to the war, the general chapters of Cluny, Prémontré and, to a lesser extent, Cîteaux had to relinquish hands-on control over their English provinces. These orders were particularly badly hit by the Great Schism of 1378–1409, when English houses officially recognised a different pope from their general chapters. As a result, English abbots or priors were appointed as commissary- or vicar-generals, in effect exercising the power of the general chapter of the order over the houses of their province. The Cluniac and Premonstratensian houses of fifteenth-century England enjoyed a large measure of independence thereafter, although the latter continued to seek guidance from their general chapter until a dispute with Prémontré led to the English province's acquisition of a papal bull granting full autonomy in 1512.[93] The Bridgettines of Syon, meanwhile, obtained constitutional independence from their Swedish mother house, Vadstena, as early as 1425. The English Cistercians retained greater contact with their general chapter throughout the later middle ages, but it was only the Carthusians which remained fully integrated with their order in this period, regularly submitting questions for guidance to their general chapter and at times receiving rebukes for departing from the order's statutes. Some exchange of personnel with continental charterhouses also continued throughout the later middle ages. Nor did the majority of late medieval English monasteries preserve very close contact with the papacy, which was principally a source of legal resort and dispensation from Church law and monastic rules [**15**]. This growing (although far from complete) insularity was another important characteristic of the late medieval monastic order in England, setting it apart from the monasticism of the high middle ages.

There are many reasons, therefore, why the later middle ages should be seen as a distinct era in monastic history, to be studied on its own terms and not merely in comparison with the 'golden age' of the twelfth century or any other period. Although monastic traditions continued

93 Graham (1929), 46–90; Gribbin (2001), 1–19.

to be strongly emphasised (for example in late medieval writings about monastic origins and history), the monasticism of this period drew a good deal of its strength and inspiration from other sources. If this desire to engage with the world outside the cloister made the religious more susceptible to trends – such as greater privacy and higher living standards – arguably at odds with the monastic ideal, it also provided an opportunity to demonstrate their continued relevance to their lay neighbours. The precise nature of these contacts with the outside world, and the extent to which canons, nuns and monks succeeded in this endeavour is the subject of the second part of this introduction. But if late medieval modifications to the monastic life were readily explicable and not in themselves deleterious, there remains the question of whether the monastic order was strengthened or weakened by such adaptation. Knowles' case that these changes represented an impoverishment of the monastic ideal may still contain some truth. As Benjamin Thompson has put it, 'perhaps, paradoxically, in integrating more closely into the locality, monasticism narrowed the original breadth of its spiritual vision'.[94] Despite their continued vitality, there is certainly little sign that monasteries (the Carthusians and perhaps Syon aside) provided sustained religious leadership in late medieval England. This is not an easy question for the historian to resolve: ultimately we are faced with another embodiment of the ageless debate over strict fidelity to an original ideal against adaptation to meet the challenges of the day. The monks, canons and nuns of the later middle ages for the most part chose the latter path. They were truly creatures of their time, and this was both their greatest strength and their greatest weakness.

## Part two: monasteries and the world

In comparison to earlier centuries, the later middle ages witnessed few new monastic foundations and few major grants of property to existing religious houses. This state of affairs raises fundamental questions about the continued vitality and relevance of monasticism in this period. Were monasteries outdated institutions, relics from a previous age which had little to offer late medieval society? This is indeed the impression given by some accounts of the pre-Reformation Church, which scarcely mention the religious orders. However, as we have seen, the monasteries of this period were outward-looking institutions, concerned to engage with the social, intellectual and devotional trends of their day.

94 Thompson (1999), 29.

In addition, they provided a range of valuable services to late medieval society, including prayers and masses for the souls of benefactors, pilgrimage shrines, hospitality, education and charity. Nevertheless, lay attitudes towards the religious cannot simply be adduced from an evaluation of monastic utility. The position of many monasteries as major landowners added another layer of complexity to the relations between religious houses and their neighbours. This included the potential for conflict with tenants or rivals, and the criticism of monastic wealth that recurs in late medieval literature cannot be ignored. The apparent ambivalence of lay attitudes towards monks, nuns and canons is also suggested by the willingness of the English people to purchase or loot the property of newly suppressed monasteries in the 1530s and 1540s, while showing no trace of hostility to the religious themselves and even a little guilt.[95] Relations between monasteries and society, moreover, were shifting over the later middle ages in the face of the broader social, economic, intellectual and political developments of the period. The religious orders were in no sense isolated from the world, and nor were they insulated from the turbulence of early Tudor religion and politics.

## New religious foundations

The relevance of monasteries to late medieval society and religion might be assessed in a variety of ways. One of the most popular measures used by historians is the number of new religious foundations made in this period. In fact, of the 800 or more houses of monks, canons and nuns founded in medieval England, only 23 were established in the fourteenth and fifteenth centuries [28, 29]. This statistic alone explains why the later middle ages has often been viewed as a time of monastic stagnation; but it is not in itself an indication that monasteries were no longer valued. Arguably, monastic England had already reached saturation point, and new foundations were no longer required. It is notable that late medieval founders showed a clear preference for novel kinds of monasteries which might complement existing provision rather than duplicate what already existed. Two new orders of nuns were introduced into England with the foundation of the Dominican priory at Dartford by Edward III in 1356, and the Bridgettine abbey of Syon by Henry V in 1415. Similarly, the austere Carthusians, previously confined to two modest houses in Somerset, flourished with the planting of seven major new foundations between 1343 and 1414; and a small number of

95 Shagan (2003), 162–96.

university colleges were also established in Oxford and Cambridge to meet a specific new monastic need (see above, pp. 31–3).

Another explanation for the paucity of new monastic foundations in the later middle ages is the great – and growing – expense involved. The establishment of a monastery was always a major financial commitment; but the economic conditions of the later middle ages, in contrast to those of the twelfth and thirteenth centuries, were certainly not conducive to the endowment of large religious houses. Not only did the elites find it difficult to profit from their lands in an age of low prices and high wages (see above, pp. 10–14), but the foundation of religious houses was complicated by the Statute of Mortmain (1279), which required potentially expensive licences to be obtained from the Crown for making endowments to the Church.[96] It is no surprise that the majority of those founding late medieval monasteries were extremely wealthy, comprising mainly kings, prominent noblemen and aristocratic widows. Moreover, a number of these foundations (including Syon and several Carthusian priories) were largely financed by recycled monastic wealth, in the form of property confiscated from the alien priories during the Hundred Years War (see below, pp. 41–2). The success of the Carthusian Order in attracting lay patronage was also in part a product of the potential for collective endowment of their priories. Rather than one benefactor financing the entire foundation, individual patrons could pay for the construction of a single cell in return for the hypothecated prayers of its occupant. The charterhouses of London and Coventry were largely endowed in this piecemeal fashion, which combined personalisation with affordability in a highly attractive manner [**29**].

But if the prohibitive expense of establishing a traditional monastery contributed to the paucity of new monastic foundations after 1300, this downturn was also the product of increased competition as newer kinds of intercessory institutions grew in popularity. Above all, what late medieval founders sought from religious houses was intercession in the form of prayers and masses, in order to guide their souls safely through Purgatory into heaven [**28, 29**]. These 'suffrages' could be performed by monks, canons and nuns, or by the friars, who seem to have been very popular intercessors judging from their regular appearance as beneficiaries in wills. But they might also be carried out by secular (i.e. non-monastic) priests; and the majority of late medieval foundations were of this kind. The simplest intercessory institution was the chantry, consisting of one or two priests employed to pray and

96 Raban (1982).

sing masses for the founder's soul. Chantries were established in their thousands across late medieval England. Some were based within monasteries, staffed by the religious themselves or by hired chaplains [33], but the large majority were placed in parish churches.[97] Benefactors might also choose to establish larger foundations consisting of several priests, who adopted a communal existence which included the dignified performance of divine service; and over 100 of these chantry (or secular) colleges were established in late medieval England. A large number of schools and almshouses were also set up, combining educational or charitable work with intercession for the founder's soul.

Why did layfolk prefer to make these kinds of secular foundation instead of establishing new monasteries in this period? This shift might be attributed in part to monastic failings, but it also stemmed from broader developments in the theological and devotional landscape of late medieval Christendom, beyond the control of the religious. In particular, the later middle ages saw greater emphasis placed on the performance of masses as the means for expediting souls through Purgatory. Since, according to the Church's teaching, the efficacy of the Mass could not be affected by the character of the celebrant, the identity of the intercessor and their way of life became of secondary importance. This development should not be overemphasised: benefactors still valued holiness of life (as can be seen from the popularity of the Carthusians), and sought the prayers of favoured groups of clergy. But it did help to tip the balance in favour of those institutions which could offer the best value for money. An endowment of £5 per year was sufficient to support a perpetual chantry (although in practice the acquisition of the land and the requisite mortmain licence ensured that it would cost several times this amount to make a foundation); and many endowed schools and almshouses were also relatively small establishments, within the reach of less wealthy benefactors. Even a secular college was generally cheaper to endow than a monastery, not least because many founders insisted on a relatively frugal lifestyle for the community, with limited expenditure on hospitality and the head's household. These founders might still have chosen to endow existing monasteries, of course, as a means of economising; but it is not surprising that they preferred to establish their own customised secular foundation, whose primary function was to pray for them and their friends.

The popularity of chantries, colleges, almshouses and schools, not to mention the friars, inevitably drew patronage away from monasteries.

97 Rosenthal (1972), 31–52.

Indeed, several of the monasteries founded in the fourteenth and fifteenth centuries were initially conceived as secular colleges, and a number (such as Maxstoke and Edington) were given statutes similar to those provided for collegiate foundations [28]. The growing influence and appeal of these alternative forms of religious institution leave no doubt that the age of monastic dominance had passed by 1350, if not before. Nuns, canons and monks now had to compete with other branches of the Church in order to demonstrate their continuing relevance to late medieval society, a relevance that could no longer be taken for granted.

## The suppression of monasteries in late medieval England

Nevertheless, the superseding of monasteries in the economy of new religious foundations in late medieval England does not in itself signify the obsolescence of the monastic ideal. The large number of pre-existing monasteries which continued to operate throughout the later middle ages must also be brought into the equation. Indeed, it is striking how few monasteries were closed down during the fourteenth and fifteenth centuries, particularly given the number of very small and poorly endowed houses in medieval England.[98] The sole exception to this trend was the suppression in the fifteenth century of about eighty 'alien priories'. The alien priories were daughter houses of French monasteries established in England in the decades following the Norman Conquest by an invading elite who wished to reward and to preserve ties with favoured religious houses on the continent. Although some of these 'priories' were conventual, in the sense that they housed a sizeable community of monks, the majority served mainly as depots (staffed by one or two inmates) for the collection and despatching of English revenues to their French mother houses. This function was initially uncontroversial, but became unacceptable after the outbreak of war between England and France in 1294 and again following the commencement of more sustained (though still intermittent) hostilities from 1337. During times of conflict, alien houses were forbidden to maintain contact with their mother houses or to send any money overseas, although they were generally permitted to retain their properties, paying in return a large 'farm' (or subsidy) to the Crown. The lay elites were keen to enjoy a share of these spoils, and eventually succeeded in petitioning the king in Parliament to adopt sterner measures. In 1378, French monks and canons were exiled for

98 Heale (2004b).

the duration of the war, with laymen permitted to enjoy the priories' revenues in their absence. This was only a temporary solution, and in 1414 the House of Commons pressed successfully for the permanent suppression of all the non-conventual alien priories [**30**]. In practice it took several decades to complete the process of suppression and to determine which houses should be permitted to survive, but by the final quarter of the fifteenth century all previous connections with French monasteries had been severed.[99] Lay enjoyment of alien priory property continued for some decades after 1414, but in due course, and under pressure from the papacy, the Crown ensured that all former monastic property was reallocated to ecclesiastical institutions (mainly secular colleges and Carthusian priories).

Historians have been divided in their assessment of the significance of these events. The suppression of so many houses cannot be considered a minor development, but it remains true that many of the alien priories were not monasteries in any meaningful sense, but merely estate offices served by one or two monks. The principle that genuine religious houses should be permitted to continue was regularly articulated and generally adhered to, although a number of priories that were arguably conventual were suppressed collaterally. In this sense, the closure of the alien priories was no precedent for the general suppression of the 1530s, and it is significant that the confiscated property ultimately remained in the hands of the Church (and a good deal of it within the monastic order). However, this episode has also been seen as an indication of increasing lay control over ecclesiastical property.[100] Layfolk profited from the lands of the alien priories for a considerable period of time, and freely redistributed monastic property to more fashionable institutions, refocusing traditional suffrages on themselves in the process [cf. **31**]. The lay elites' ability to interfere with monastic endowments in order to satisfy their own religious needs and tastes arguably points to the vulnerability of institutions struggling to maintain former levels of influence.

Nevertheless, the dissolution of the alien priories was not accompanied by any significant number of suppressions among English houses. During the fourteenth and early fifteenth centuries, the closure of such monasteries was almost unknown. A trickle of suppressions took place in the middle decades of the fifteenth century, a period of economic depression. However, it was more common in these years for impov-

99 Knowles (1948–59), II, 157–66; Matthew (1962), 73–142.
100 Thompson (1994a).

erished and collapsed priories to be converted into daughter houses of larger monasteries, in order to preserve monastic service at their site. Equally, several intended suppressions in the later middle ages did not take place. For example, the attempts of William Waynflete, bishop of Winchester, between the 1450s and 1480s to dissolve the priories of Dodnash, Luffield, Sele and Selborne in order to endow his foundation of Magdalen College, Oxford were strongly resisted by the monks, and succeeded only in the last two instances.[101] The closure of even small and struggling monasteries was not taken lightly in fifteenth-century England.

In the last years of the 1400s, however, this pattern began slowly to change. Eleven small English priories were dissolved between 1475 and 1525, mainly by bishops seeking property to endow their new educational foundations at Oxford or Cambridge [**31**]. This trend reached a climax in the second half of the 1520s, with the suppression of twenty-nine houses by Cardinal Wolsey, in order to provide a princely endowment for his twin educational establishments of Ipswich College and Cardinal College, Oxford. Wolsey was less fastidious than his predecessors in this process, selecting houses for suppression according to their location and the suitability of their endowment rather than for any financial or spiritual decay. His targets included relatively wealthy and flourishing houses, such as St Frideswide's Oxford and Tonbridge, and unsurprisingly provoked considerable opposition. Patrons were antagonised at the loss of their houses, and both the religious and their lay neighbours resisted suppression. At Bayham a crowd of around 100, led by the canons, took to the streets for eight days in an (unsuccessful) attempt to force the priory's restoration; and, when a group of Tonbridge townsmen were offered a school for forty children in place of the priory, it was reported that 'all the said inhabitants except only one answered that they were minded and desirous to have the canons restored again'.[102] Wolsey's suppressions nevertheless went ahead, providing a blueprint for the closure of religious houses in the face of local opposition. Wolsey, moreover, countenanced the closure of monasteries on a much larger scale than ever considered before, acquiring papal bulls in 1528–29 (shortly before his fall) authorising the union of all monasteries with fewer than twelve inmates with larger houses, a measure not dissimilar to that carried out by Henry VIII in 1536–37 [**55**].

---

101 Heale (2004b); Davis (1993), 125–51.
102 National Archives, SP1/35, fos 48–48v.

## Monastic patronage

Looking beyond the statistics of foundation and dissolution alone, levels of support for the monastic ideal in late medieval England might also be assessed from the evidence of lay patronage of existing houses. Of particular importance was the interest shown in monasteries by their patron, the legal (though not always lineal) descendant of the house's founder. One of the main rationales of any monastery was to pray for their founder and his or her descendants, and in return the patron would be expected to provide assistance at times of legal or physical threat [*32*]. Benjamin Thompson, however, has suggested that aristocratic interest in the religious houses in their patronage was waning seriously in the later middle ages.[103] This was partly because many founding dynasties had died out by the second half of the fourteenth century, with new patronal families not always showing a strong interest in the foundations they had inherited. But Thompson has also demonstrated that there was a clear upward mobility of monastic advowsons[104] over this period, with a much greater proportion coming into the hands of the Crown and the nobility than had previously been the case. As a result, the greatest nobles each held the patronage of several religious houses, and it is unlikely that they would have maintained close relations with all of them. The duke of Norfolk, for example, was patron of at least nineteen monasteries in the 1530s,[105] but it was only his family mausoleum of Thetford for which he showed serious concern during the Dissolution process of that decade.

By the early sixteenth century, more than half of all English monasteries may have been in the patronage of either the Crown or one of the two dozen wealthiest aristocratic families.[106] Yet it remains difficult to estimate what proportion of monasteries might have lost meaningful contact with their patrons. The houses most likely to maintain patronal interest were those situated close to baronial residences or which were used as burial places for their families. The tombs, chantries and insignia of the dynasty on display in a monastery all served to advertise the power and status of the patronal family, while associations with an ancient religious house underlined the pedigree of any lineage. Similarly, new families inheriting a lordship would have strong reasons for establishing close ties with a monastery at the centre of their estates,

103 Thompson (1994b).
104 The legal title to the patronage of a monastery.
105 Stöber (2007), 34–5.
106 *Ibid.*, 25–64.

in order to make a statement about continuity and their legitimacy. It is clear that a significant minority of religious houses were used in this way by their patrons, including St Augustine's Bristol (by the lords of Berkeley), Boxgrove (the de la Warrs) and Tewkesbury (the Despensers) [**33**]. The geographical location and historical connections of a monastery seem often to have been as important as its size, with lesser houses such as Bourne (the Hollands) and Ulverscroft (the Ferrers) favoured by aristocratic families with nearby residences. Such monasteries maintained close relations with their patrons and served them in numerous ways, including the safekeeping of family archives or valuables. The role of the monastery as signifier of the patronal pedigree was spelt out even more vividly by the compilation by a number of religious houses, including Kingswood (the Berkeleys again), Tewkesbury (the Despensers) and Whalley (the Lacys), of genealogical accounts of their patron's family [**33**].

Many religious houses in late medieval England were not so favourably situated at the heart of a barony, and nor did the majority serve as a major patronal mausoleum. Indeed, given the importance attached to the burial place of members of one's lineage, the preference of many late medieval aristocrats (especially of gentry rank) for interment within a parish church was a serious blow to monastic prestige. Nevertheless, burial in a monastery remained popular among the upper echelons of the aristocracy, the peerage, throughout the later middle ages, with 48 per cent choosing burial in a house of monks, canons or nuns in the fourteenth century and 39 per cent in the fifteenth.[107] Religious houses, moreover, were not solely dependent on their legal patrons for support, and in practice a patronal void might be filled by other local landholders. Every monastery appointed a lay steward to oversee management of their estates, who could often fulfil the function of an absent patron very effectively. In other cases, a local family might take on the surrogate patronage of a house and receive the reciprocal patronal benefits of hospitality, burial and prayers in return for defending the monastery's interests – as, for example, at late medieval Norton Priory where the Dutton family took the place of the uninterested barons of Halton [cf. **34**].[108] The loss of regular contact with their legal patrons was evidently a problem faced by many lesser monasteries in the later middle ages, and intensified further the need to demonstrate their relevance to their lay neighbours. But it is likely that monasteries of any size, with

107 Rosenthal (1972), 81–101.
108 Greene (1989), 9–15.

the practical as well as spiritual services they could offer, would have
had the wherewithal to attract the attention of local landholders.

## Spiritual services

A more concrete indication of monastic appeal may be found in the
specific benefactions made to the religious, for which considerable
evidence survives. Gifts of land to male and female monasteries continued
throughout the later middle ages, some of them substantial. The endowment of Westminster Abbey was augmented by about £1,300 per year
in the fifteenth and early sixteenth centuries by the establishment of a
number of royal chantries in the monastery (to be served by the monks),
most notably that of Henry VII.[109] A few houses, such as Bourne and
Hulton, were provided with former alien priory lands through the influence of their patrons; and other monasteries received landed donations
in order to assist with specific building activity [35]. Major benefactions of this kind were rare, however, partly because of the competition
of other intercessory institutions, but also because of the large endowments already enjoyed by many monasteries. As the fourteenth-century
poet William Langland put it, those giving property to already wealthy
religious houses were like 'one who filled a tun full from a fresh river
/ and went forth with that water to moisten the Thames' [cf. 48].[110]
Consequently, the most promising avenue for a monastery to augment
significantly its endowment in this period (since it did not require a lay
donor to give up land) was to secure episcopal and royal assent for the
appropriation of a parish church [45]; an approach which bore fruit for
numerous houses both large and small (see below, p. 62).

But if large-scale acquisitions of property were rare, the religious were
also able to attract a multitude of smaller gifts from benefactors in return
for specific spiritual services. The most accessible evidence we have
for this purchase of monastic prayers and masses is contained in wills,
which survive in their thousands from late medieval England [36].
Numerous studies charting patterns of bequests to the religious orders
have been made, and a fairly uniform picture has emerged, indicating
that around 15–20 per cent of will-makers left money to monasteries
between c. 1350 and 1535.[111] This suggests a steady but not spectacular

109 Harvey (1977), 26–36. This took the abbey's total income to around £4,000 per
   year, although the monks were required to spend much of this extra revenue on
   charitable doles for the benefit of the benefactors' souls.
110 Schmidt (1978), 187.
111 E.g. Thomson (1965); Rosenthal (1972), 31–52; Cross (1988); Brown (1995), 26–48;
   Oliva (1998), 161–83.

level of support for the monastic order, with the proportion of bequests to monks, canons and nuns comparing unfavourably with that received by friars, cathedrals and parish churches in this period. However, the totalling of numbers of wills making bequests to particular institutions is a blunt instrument of analysis, and the statistical evidence of wills needs to be broken down if its significance is to be properly assessed.

This might be done in a number of ways. Firstly, it might be asked whether certain kinds of monastery were more popular than others. It is often asserted that the more austere Carthusian priories received considerably greater support than the mainstream monastic orders from testators; but this conclusion needs some qualification. The charterhouses of London and Sheen were particularly popular among will-makers from the capital, attracting about three-quarters of all wealthy Londoners' bequests to monasteries between the 1480s and the Dissolution. However, the wills of the citizens of Hull were rather less supportive of their local charterhouse, and the older Carthusian priories of Witham and Hinton were the beneficiaries of relatively few late medieval bequests. A study of the wills of early sixteenth-century Yorkshire, moreover, has found that the larger Benedictine, Augustinian and Cistercian monasteries were the houses most commonly remembered by testators.[112] No clear patterns emerge about the relative popularity of particular orders from this evidence; and the same might be said about patterns of bequest over time. A few studies have found falling proportions of bequests to monasteries over the later middle ages.[113] But this may be in part attributable to the changing profile of testators rather than changing attitudes towards religious houses, since many more wills of the middling ranks of society survive from the early sixteenth century than the preceding period.

A second, more promising approach is to break down bequests according to the testators' social status. Only the wealthier members of society made wills in the later middle ages, but it is still possible to differentiate between nobility, greater and lesser gentry, yeoman farmers, merchants and artisans. Studies of the wills of these different social groups have tended to produce the finding that bequests to monasteries become less common as one proceeds down the social spectrum. The upper ranks of the aristocracy continued to support traditional monasticism in their wills, a trend connected with their use of religious houses as places of burial throughout the later middle ages. A study of the Kent gentry

112 Thomson (1965); Heath (1984); Cross (1988).
113 E.g. Fleming (1984).

between 1422 and 1529, meanwhile, found that 33 per cent of knights, 24 per cent of (the less socially elevated) esquires and only 8 per cent of gentlemen made bequests to monasteries in their wills. Similarly, Marilyn Oliva's analysis of bequests to religious houses in the diocese of Norwich revealed that 14 per cent of the parish (or lesser) gentry supported male houses between 1350 and 1540, compared to only 4 per cent of yeoman farmers. This falling off of patronage according to social rank, however, was much less marked for the female houses of the diocese, which attracted bequests from 21 per cent of parish gentry and 15 per cent of yeoman farmers.[114] These figures, which appear even more remarkable when it is appreciated that there were more than five times as many male monasteries as female houses in the diocese of Norwich, also indicate a significant gendered element in lay bequests to religious houses. Oliva attributed the relative popularity of nunneries among these middling social groups to the nuns' greater attentiveness to local society and high standard of observance, and it may also have been connected to the relative poverty of female monasteries (see above, pp. 10–13).

Another potentially significant divide in lay attitudes towards monastic services was between town and country [36]. Relations between urban monasteries and townsmen were not always cordial (see below, pp. 61–2), and the proportion of merchants and artisans making bequests to monasteries was never high, with wealthier urban testators much more likely to support the friars and charitable institutions such as hospitals and almshouses. Wealthier Londoners made relatively few monastic bequests other than to the Carthusians; and it is striking how few testators from York, St Albans and Bristol left money to the great houses of monks and canons on their doorsteps.[115] Moreover, those townsmen who did make bequests to urban houses tended to dwell in the immediate environs of a religious house, and often within the liberty of the monastery. This would suggest that topographical and tenurial considerations determined the shape of patronage as much as matters of religious taste. A strong preponderance of local bequests has also been identified in studies of nunneries; and more than 50 per cent of parishioners who shared their church with a monastic community in the diocese of York made bequests to that house (see below, pp. 63–4).[116] This suggests that there was considerable support for the monastic

114 Fleming (1984); Oliva (1998), 161–83.
115 Thomson (1965); Kermode (1998), 116–55; Clark (2004), 39; Fleming (2000).
116 Oliva (1998), 161–83; Lee (2001), 67–83; Heale (2006).

life among those who observed its functioning at close quarters: a conclusion with ramifications for our judgements about the quality of monastic observance in the later middle ages.

Whether the sizeable proportion of the population of late medieval England who did not seek monastic prayers in their wills (let alone the still larger group who apparently did not make wills at all) remained apathetic towards the monastic order cannot easily be judged. Failure to mention a religious house in one's will (generally made on the deathbed) does not of course preclude the possibility of warm relations with that house during life. There may also be some significance in the particular choice of religious institutions favoured on the approach of death. The provision for the friars and the poor found in so many urban wills may have been a clearly targeted strategy for salvation, since charitable support for the poor was believed (in accordance with Christ's parable of the sheep and the goats) to be of critical importance on the Day of Judgement.[117] There are obvious dangers, therefore, in regarding bequests as plebiscites on the value of particular kinds of ecclesiastical institutions. The secular college, in many ways the most characteristic religious foundation of the late medieval period, appears seldom in wills, but this can hardly signify a lack of lay interest in collegiate foundations.

Nevertheless, it cannot be claimed that the picture provided by wills, however hazy, provides an especially positive indication of lay support for monastic prayers. Some sections of society appear to have been more interested in providing for the prayers of nuns, canons and monks than others, but this evidence does not suggest widespread admiration for the monastic life in late medieval England. Wills, however, are not the only kind of evidence to shed light on the level of popular demand for the spiritual services of religious houses: there also survive numerous records of monastic confraternity. Confraternities have not been subject to the same levels of scrutiny given to wills, but they have in recent years begun to attract the attention of historians.[118] Alongside the thousands of secular guilds or fraternities in late medieval England – associations of pious layfolk set up to provide intercessory masses, fitting funerals and social insurance for their members, and to serve as a focus for devotion to a particular saint – numerous clerical *con*fraternities also existed. These offered a share in the spiritual merit accrued by a particular religious house and a similar level of post-mortem prayer

117 Cf. Duffy (1992), 357–62.
118 In particular, Rollason (1999); Swanson (2002); Swanson (2004).

for members as would be granted to deceased monks, canons or nuns. Centralised orders like the Carthusians and Cistercians, moreover, were able to offer a share in the benefits and prayers of the monks across their entire order [37].

Monasteries appear to have offered more than one level of confraternity to their neighbours. In return for a major benefaction or important service to the community, a religious house would issue formal letters of confraternity (often elaborately decorated), specifying in detail the particular spiritual services to be provided. The benefactor was then received publicly into the monastery's confraternity in a ceremony designed to consolidate the bonds between the two parties [40]. Membership of a confraternity might also be used as a means of strengthening ties with the powerful, or as part of a negotiated settlement with one who had been in conflict with the monastery. However, not every member was, or could have been, accorded this deluxe level of service – in terms both of ceremonial and the intercessory commitment undertaken by the monastery. Accordingly, many religious houses also offered a more prosaic form of confraternity. In return for a smaller benefaction it was possible to acquire membership, conferring a share in the spiritual benefits of a monastery and some level of commemoration by the community after death.

The fuller form of confraternity is the better documented. Letters of confraternity survive from numerous monasteries, either in the form sent to the beneficiary or copied into monastic registers [37]. The majority of these formal grants were to men and women of status, and the confraternities of great Benedictine abbeys like St Albans and Bury St Edmunds numbered the leading magnates of the realm among their membership [38, 40]. Indeed, great men and women might join several of these societies, with Henry VII's mother Lady Margaret Beaufort (1443–1509), for example, known to have become a member of the confraternities of Crowland, Durham, Missenden, Thorney and the Carthusian Order as a whole.[119] Information about the less formal kind of confraternity is harder to find, but can be obtained from the occasional surviving list of entrants [38]. The late medieval lists of names in the famous Durham Priory *Liber Vitae* (or 'Book of Life') – which do not include most of the 250 people known to have received formal grants of confraternity – have been convincingly interpreted as a register of those purchasing spiritual services

---

119 Jones and Underwood (1992), 138, 147, 195; British Library, Sloane MS 747, fo. 55r.

from the community rather than a complete list of benefactors to be prayed for by the monks.[120] This book contains nearly 1,700 names (not including Durham monks), with particularly large numbers recorded between *c.* 1450 and the 1530s. Similar lists of names, again apparently denoting confraternity membership, can be found in the Hyde Abbey *Liber Vitae* and the St Albans *Liber Benefactorum* ('Book of Benefactors'). In all three cases, the members listed come from a wide social range, with a large number of local entrants. Confraternities of this kind can also be found at smaller monasteries, with sizeable lists of members surviving in the records of the humble Benedictine priories of Belvoir and Tywardreath. Confraternities are also recorded at lesser priories of Gilbertine and Premonstratensian canons and some nunneries, and must have been very widespread in late medieval England.[121]

This kind of spiritual association with monks, canons and nuns seems to have been popular, therefore, and the large numbers of entrants found at houses such as Durham, St Albans and even Belvoir must be placed alongside the evidence from wills before any rounded assessment of the value attached to monastic intercession can be made. Indeed, one explanation for the apparently limited level of support for monastic suffrages found in deathbed testaments may be that some testators had already made provision for monastic intercession for their souls during their lifetimes by joining a confraternity.[122] Confraternities also suggest an interest in the wider activities of the religious. Post-mortem masses must have been a major part of their attraction, but letters of confraternity also commonly identify the new member with the daily services, fasting and meditation continually performed within the monastery [**32, 37**]. Despite the great attention paid by benefactors to the prayers and masses for their souls carried out by monasteries and other intercessory institutions in late medieval England, it should not be forgotten that this work comprised only part of the total intercessory activity performed within a religious house.

## Other religious services

The main occupation of the nun, canon or monk was the *opus dei* (the work of God), also known as divine service (see above, pp. 28–30). This took the form of seven daily offices chanted by the community in choir

120 Rollason (1999).

121 Heale (2004a), 207–8; Golding (1995), 326–33; Colvin (1951), 258–64; Lee (2001), 73, 101–2; Orme (2008).

122 Cf. Burgess (1990).

and the night office of Matins [1]. This structured and continuous round of prayer was designed to offer up worship to God on behalf of the wider community. Lay statements about the role of monasteries suggest that they regarded the *opus dei* as just as important as the more specific intercession performed by the religious for individual benefactors. When exhorting the Benedictine Order to reform in 1421, Henry V urged that the black monks should return to the pristine observance for which they were founded, to 'pray unceasingly for him, and the state of his kingdom and the Church', in which prayers he specially trusted.[123] Indeed, concern for the 'increase of divine service' attained a particular significance in late medieval England owing to the perceived efficacy of liturgical prayer in winning God's favour for the war with France. The importance of liturgical prayer to the laity can also be seen in the foundation of numerous secular colleges in later medieval England and the provision for greater musical elaboration in parish churches in this period.[124] The monastic performance of the divine service was therefore an important component of the nation's offering of prayer to the Almighty for the realm's wellbeing.

Another important religious service carried out within late medieval monasteries was their role as centres of pilgrimage.[125] Several of the greatest pilgrimage sites in late medieval England, including the shrine of Thomas Becket at Canterbury, the cult of the Virgin Mary at Walsingham and the Holy Blood of Hailes, were housed in monasteries [15, 37]. It was not only large monasteries which attracted pilgrims to worship at their images and shrines, however. Many smaller houses sponsored cults of regional or local interest, such as that of St Leonard at the priory of that dedication outside Norwich, or the cult of the mystical writer Richard Rolle promoted by the nuns of Hampole. Moreover, a good number of the pilgrimage sites housed in parish churches and wayside chapels were managed by monks, canons or nuns [39]. The chapel of Caversham, with its popular late medieval image of the Virgin, was manned by the canons of Notley; and the cult of St Winifred in Holywell was in the hands of the Cistercian monks of nearby Basingwerk, who financed a major rebuilding of the well-chapel there in the early sixteenth century. Monastic involvement in the promotion of pilgrimage sites was therefore widespread, and was undertaken by houses of all sizes and orders, both male and female.

123 Riley (1863–64), II, 337–8.
124 Burgess (2005).
125 Heale (2007).

Many of the cults associated with monasteries were those of older saints, such as St Etheldreda (Ely), St Cuthbert (Durham) or St Edmund (Bury) [**40**]. Benedictine houses spent considerable time and money promoting the cults of these traditional saints in the later middle ages. New tombs were provided, such as that of St Edward the Martyr by the nuns of Shaftesbury and St Guthlac at Crowland, and new saints' lives were commissioned, including the English lives of St Edmund and St Alban composed by the monk-poet John Lydgate in the mid-fifteenth century.[126] But it would be wrong to portray religious houses as out of touch with more up-to-date trends in the cult of saints. Several monasteries sponsored popular shrines in honour of Christ and Mary in late medieval England, and new cults such as those of King Henry VI and John Schorne were embraced by lesser monasteries such as Yarmouth and Binham in the late fifteenth and early sixteenth centuries [**7**]. Indeed, religious houses could be highly sensitive to trends in popular devotion, and willing to take up the direction of an incipient cult by the construction of new chapels and by arranging liturgical provision at the site [**39**]. The impressive chapel of the Red Mount in Lynn was built by the Benedictine monks of that town in the 1480s, apparently in response to popular interest in a miraculous Marian image on the site. This investment stimulated an important local cult in the town which lasted for a generation. It is impossible to know what proportion of pilgrimage sites were connected with monasteries, and large numbers were also based in parish churches, wayside chapels, friaries and secular cathedrals. But there is every reason to believe that the monastic contribution to this important facet of late medieval lay religion was considerable.

## Social services

Not only was the monastic contribution to the religious life of late medieval England far from negligible, but the canons, nuns and monks also served society through their role as hosts, educators and providers of charity. Estimations of the monastic contribution to social services of this kind have oscillated fiercely over the past 200 years, but a new consensus is now forming which stresses the value of monastic provision as one of several important contributions to the welfare of late medieval society. Other institutions, such as hospitals, almshouses, colleges, endowed schools and parishes, also did much in this regard, but it is clear that the social services of the monasteries were significant and much missed after the Dissolution.[127]

126 Luxford (2005), 134–6; Clark (2000b).
127 E.g. Rushton (2001), 34; Heal (1990), 231–4.

The extent of monastic poor relief has often been questioned, with historians citing the 3 per cent of monastic income recorded as spent on almsgiving in the *Valor Ecclesiasticus* of 1535 as an indication that the record of religious houses in this regard was unimpressive. However, this tax assessment provides only a partial picture of monastic charity.[128] The *Valor* records only that portion of charitable giving that was exempt from taxation: that is, alms distributed by religious houses on behalf of lay benefactors in the manner of a modern charity (and with considerable overheads for the monastery concerned) [10]; and even this kind of almsgiving is not detailed in full. As well as distributing alms on behalf of others, monasteries administered numerous hospitals and almshouses, providing residential care [43]; and some Gilbertine houses such as St Katherine's, Lincoln themselves served as priory-hospitals. Monasteries also gave a proportion of their own revenues to the poor [7, 22] although only small cash sums appear in monastic accounts, often tailing off at times of financial difficulty. Indeed the Whalley Abbey bursar's gifts to minstrels between 1485 and the 1530s consistently outstripped his doles to the poor. The religious were also required to donate the leftovers from their table to the poor, and this must have comprised a significant quantity of almsgiving in the larger houses. Thomas More claimed that the crowds outside Westminster Abbey were so great that 'myself, for the press of them, have preferred to ride another way'; although the royal chantries established here, with their provision for large-scale doles to the poor, render Westminster exceptional.[129] Monastic almsgiving must therefore have been a cumulatively important source of support for the poor, although it was still possible for critics to argue that more income could have been devoted to charity and less to maintaining the high living standards of the religious [50, 52].

A similar assessment can be made of the monastic contribution to education. Most schooling in late medieval England was carried out in fee-paying or endowed free grammar schools, several of which were attached to secular colleges like Winchester or Eton. Nevertheless, the role played by the religious orders in running schools for children (other than their own novices) or supervising endowed schools comprised an important part of the overall educational provision in late medieval England. At least thirty houses (mainly Benedictine and Augustinian) ran free almonry schools for poor children, generally

128 Rushton (2001).
129 Harvey (1993), 7–33.

numbering ten to twenty pupils, although there is evidence that they also took in fee-paying pupils according to demand [42]. Some of these almonry boys later became monks or joined the house's service staff, but others became parish priests or took up secular employment. By the late fifteenth century a number of larger houses were also providing an education in song in order to train boys for their Lady Chapel choirs (see above, pp. 28–30), and a few monasteries even provided free town grammar schools, as at Burton-on-Trent, Evesham and Reading. The aristocracy might also send their children to monasteries to be educated, with nunneries a particularly popular destination for elite girls and for boys up to the age of about twelve. The wealthy nunnery of St Mary's Winchester was educating as many as twenty-six such girls in the mid-1530s [41]; and sixteen of the twenty-five Yorkshire nunneries (none of which were at all wealthy) are known to have boarded children in the early sixteenth century.[130] Indeed, it is likely that nunneries were the most important providers of female education in late medieval England.

Of all the social services provided by religious houses, monastic hospitality was perhaps the most extensive. The reception of guests was strongly encouraged in the Rule of St Benedict and late medieval communities took this duty very seriously [22, 40].[131] Its conscientious discharge, however, could pose serious financial problems. Even a short visit from the king or a nobleman with their retinue would be extremely expensive, and in 1275 it was considered necessary for Parliament to legislate about the excessive demands on monasteries from lay visitors other than their patrons. As a result, some houses understandably sought to economise, including the medium-sized abbey of St Benet Hulme, whose hospitality incurred the scorn of the antiquarian William Worcester in 1477: 'linen – rubbish; saltless cabbage; bed and stable – execrable; mattress – dingy; welcome – stingy'.[132] But although monastic hospitality was costly and disruptive, it also provided an opportunity for superiors to build close relations with influential lay neighbours. Very large sums of money were spent on providing the most up-to-date and comfortable guest quarters for important visitors, such as the lavish royal suites constructed at late medieval Glastonbury, St Albans and Selby [13, 40]. Abbots such as William Clown of Leicester (in office 1345–78), moreover, who were able to befriend kings and leading noblemen through their hospitality,

---

130 Orme (2006), 255–87; Bowers (1999); Cross (2002).

131 Heal (1990), 223–56.

132 Quotation from Orme (2006), 159–60.

brought great benefit to their communities through the acts of patronage these services attracted. From comments made at the Dissolution, it would seem as though it was this aspect of the monasteries' work above all that was missed by the elites of sixteenth-century England; and when we consider the free entertainment provided throughout the medieval period, this is hardly surprising.

The extent to which other sections of society had access to monastic hospitality is harder to gauge. The most important guests would stay with the abbot, with lesser guests received by the obedientiary usually known as the hostiller. However, religious houses could not accommodate every visitor, particularly if they housed a shrine or image which attracted large numbers of pilgrims. As a result, several monasteries, including Glastonbury and Christ Church, Canterbury, built inns in the later middle ages for ordinary (paying) travellers. Monastic almsgiving and education also became more discriminating over the later middle ages. In line with wider trends in charitable giving, monastic provision was increasingly targeted at the respectable poor of the neighbourhood, or diverted to institutionalised recipients, rather than to paupers gathering at the monastery gate [43]. Similarly, the places in hospitals administered by the religious were often reserved for the inmates' families and for retired servants. Candidates for monastic schooling, too, were carefully selected. It was usual for the community to take turns to nominate boys, and inevitably family members or sons of influential neighbours benefited most from this patronage [34]. In return, the boys were required to serve the monks celebrating Mass and, towards the end of the period, to act as choirboys. Monasteries therefore benefited directly from the educational work they carried out, and this perhaps explains why several houses were keen to divert income from general almsgiving to new almonry schools in the later middle ages.[133] The total amount of monastic spending on almsgiving, education and hospitality was considerable, and probably larger than has generally been appreciated; but the benefits of this work were not enjoyed equally by all sections of society, a complaint found not uncommonly in literary works of the later middle ages [cf. 52].

## Monastic distinctiveness

All this points to the conclusion that the religious and social services provided by monks, canons and nuns in late medieval England were substantial and valued. Any suggestion that monasticism was becoming

133 E.g. Harvey (1993), 31–2.

irrelevant to the religious life of the country, or that late medieval religious houses were somehow outdated, would seem therefore to be wide of the mark. But it is also clear that the significance of the services provided by monasteries cannot be fully understood unless they are placed in the broader context of late medieval provision. Monasteries were only one among several kinds of religious foundation, all offering a similar range of religious and social services. Indeed, Benjamin Thompson has argued that (with the exception of the austere communities of the Carthusians and Bridgettines) there was nothing distinctive about late medieval monasteries, since all their services were duplicated by other ecclesiastical institutions. As a result, the monks, nuns and canons were interchangeable with other similar clerical groups, and ultimately dispensable.[134]

There is clearly some substance to this hypothesis. The differences between monasteries and other intercessory institutions became considerably flattened over the later middle ages, as new kinds of foundations proliferated and as the religious themselves borrowed extensively from the secular Church (see above, pp. 26–37). This trend was further exacerbated by the tendency for elements of the monastic life previously confined to the cloister to become adopted more widely in the later middle ages. This is most obvious in the spread of the concept of the 'mixed life', which encouraged devout layfolk to adopt a quasi-monastic regime of prayer and contemplation in the world (a movement encouraged by the religious themselves, through writers such as Walter Hilton) [cf. 43]. But does this mean that monasticism no longer had anything distinctive to offer late medieval society? Such a conclusion cannot be readily applied to the nuns, since no comparable communities of spiritual women existed in medieval England; and this singularity may help to account for the continuing popularity of female monasteries highlighted in recent historiography.[135] But even the canons and monks were doing more than simply duplicating the work of others. Only the larger colleges and secular cathedrals could match the elaborate ritual carried out in monasteries; and no other kind of religious house was as widely or heavily involved in the sponsoring of saint cults. We have also seen that the specific character of monastic observance was an important part of the spiritual benefits conferred through confraternities and the performance of the liturgy. Moreover, the concern exhibited in fourteenth- and fifteenth-century England to

134 Thompson (1999); Thompson (2002).
135 E.g. Gilchrist (1994); Oliva (1998).

preserve collapsed religious houses, and to ensure wherever possible that traditionally monastic sites retained this character, again implies that late medieval monasteries retained some distinctiveness in the eyes of contemporaries (see above, pp. 42–3).

Indeed it may have been in their heritage above all that houses of monks, canons and nuns had something distinctive to offer late medieval society. Monasteries continually emphasised their ancient pedigrees, making a pointed contrast with more 'modern' competitors. In particular, they drew attention to their associations with the kings and nobles of the past (not all strictly historical), with whom current patrons may have wished to identify themselves. This was done partly through literary productions (see above, p. 31), but even more vividly through art and architecture. Many late medieval religious houses, such as Gloucester and Glastonbury Abbeys, constructed new images and tombs of kings and saints connected with their communities [14], and displayed boards (or *tabulae*) in public areas of their churches providing vernacular accounts of the glorious history of the house for a lay audience. Other monasteries deliberately preserved older buildings, or built in a traditional style (as with the retention of the western porch, or narthex, and aisleless presbytery in several late medieval Cistercian remodellings), in order to make the same visual point. In an age where antiquity was often equated with authority, this reminder of monastic pedigree could be very effective, as is suggested by the great expenditure on their heritage by late medieval houses. Drawing attention to their antiquity could also reassure benefactors that the spiritual benefits provided by monasteries were truly perpetual.[136]

Although their basic functions were similar, therefore, the services offered by different kinds of religious foundations were not identical. Even secular colleges, which resembled monasteries as centres of liturgical prayer and burial sites, appealed to patrons in subtly different ways.[137] The most plausible explanation for the multiplication and continued patronage of a variety of religious institutions in late medieval England is that they complemented one another's work rather than blindly duplicating it. But if monasteries did retain a distinctive appeal and relevance up to the Dissolution, the place of monasticism within the broader Church nevertheless shifted significantly over the middle ages. Canons, monks and nuns were now forced to compete for lay support with other equally popular institutions. Although they succeeded in retaining their

---

136 Luxford (2005), 119–50; Clark (2000b); Coldstream (1986).
137 Heale (2008b).

fair share of patronage, this constant struggle to assert their relevance to the wider world must have contributed to their willingness to modify their observance in the later middle ages (see above, pp. 22–6). The loss of monastic dominance had one further troubling implication. The tremendous investment of resources in the monastic life by the elites of Anglo-Saxon and Anglo-Norman England had been made at a time when it was a truism that this was the most praiseworthy life attainable. As that belief became increasingly questionable, the allocation of so much wealth to one valuable but unexceptional department of the English Church became much harder to justify.

## Relations with lay neighbours

Despite their obvious importance, the services performed by monasteries were only one facet of their interaction with lay society. Monks, nuns and canons were also major landowners, who exercised lordship over their tenants, servants and (in the case of some of the larger houses which enjoyed secular jurisdiction over liberties or towns) their neighbours. Any rounded assessment of the relations between monasteries and society in late medieval England must take into account the power wielded by the religious. As perpetual institutions with fixed incomes and clearly defined intercessory commitments to preserve, monasteries could not afford to be careless of their rights. Accordingly, the religious can regularly be found asserting or defending these rights against their neighbours in the courts, and monastic chronicles teem with accounts of providential victories over opponents at law [45, 47, 54]. It would be facile to assume that monastic power and wealth were inevitably the cause of lay resentment; but it is equally misleading to depict late medieval monasteries as passive entities, wholly dependent on lay support for their wellbeing.

Religious houses were therefore experienced by their neighbours in a variety of guises, bringing an ambivalence to the relations between monasteries and society, where the potential for conflict co-existed with the many avenues for creative engagement. Yet such conflict was far from endemic, either in an urban or in a rural context. Whether the religious were more generous landlords than their lay equivalents was a topic much discussed in the generation after the Dissolution and subsequently by historians. Some monasteries sought to keep wages down and to prevent the breakdown of serfdom on their estates in the years following the Black Death; and this can perhaps explain the attacks on a number of houses (mostly but not entirely male) during the Peasants'

Revolt of 1381.[138] There is, however, little sign of serious conflict with tenants after the widespread leasing of monastic estates was commenced in the late fourteenth century, a process often accompanied sooner or later by the manumission of the monastery's serfs. Indeed, as monastic land came increasingly under the management of lessees, the distinction between secular and religious landlords must have become blurred; and this trend was further enhanced by the widespread use of lay stewards by monasteries to hold their courts and administer their properties. Disputes still arose with some regularity in the fifteenth century, as legal records indicate, but general dissatisfaction with monastic landlords is difficult to discern. Recent research on Durham Cathedral Priory has suggested that the monks enjoyed good relations with their tenants in the fifteenth century, with the majority of the priory's grain acquired from this source as rent payments in kind rather than from the market, and neither party seeking to take advantage of short-term movements in prices.[139] It is also significant that monasteries' recruitment and almsgiving were frequently focused on their own estates [**43**].

A large monastery like Durham must also have had a considerable impact on the local economy as a consumer and an employer. The priory was a major purchaser of meat and luxury products from the merchants of Newcastle-upon-Tyne and other local suppliers. Durham and other religious houses also held their own fairs and markets, facilitating local exchange of goods. Monasteries, moreover, required a large number of servants to man the superior's household, carry out domestic tasks and to work on the monastery's buildings and estates on a semi-permanent or more casual basis. It is likely that most religious houses employed at least twice as many servants as they held inmates, and the general growth in the size of abbots' households over this period must have added considerably to overall numbers [**44**].[140] Evidence from Durham again, however, suggests that it is possible to exaggerate the impact of a large monastery on a town's economy. Even a major ecclesiastical corporation of this kind was still only one employer among many in the region, and few craftsmen and artisans seem to have been wholly dependent on the monks' commissions.[141] Similarly, the farmers leasing monastic estates hired their own workers, further reducing the proportion of the workforce directly employed by the religious.

138 Harvey (1977), 244–67; Knowles (1948–59), I, 263–9.
139 Threlfall-Holmes (2005), 136–61.
140 Harvey (1993), 146–78.
141 Newman (2000).

There appears to have been little friction between the monks and townsmen of Durham,[142] but relations were not always cordial in other urban centres. The majority of towns in late medieval England were royal boroughs, which were granted considerable powers of self-government by the Crown. But a small number of towns, including Bury St Edmunds, Reading and St Albans, which had grown up around monasteries, remained subject to monastic jurisdiction. Discord was most prominent in these 'monastic boroughs', and again the stormiest scenes took place in the fourteenth century. Several abbeys were attacked in 1327 (at a moment of general lawlessness following the deposition of Edward II), with particularly violent assaults made on the monks of Abingdon, Bury St Edmunds and St Albans. Similar troubles erupted during the Peasants' Revolt in 1381, as townsmen took advantage of the general disorder to advance their claims to self-government. A small number of urban monasteries were sacked, and two monks of Bury beheaded. Disputes of this vehemence did not recur, however, and the monks and townsmen seem to have co-existed relatively peacefully in the majority of monastic boroughs thereafter, although intermittent conflict still arose [**46**].[143]

Friction between town and monastery was not restricted to these boroughs, however, and many self-governing towns also witnessed clashes over the rights and liberties enjoyed by religious houses therein. These disputes too were occasionally violent, as at Norwich where full-scale assaults on the monastery took place in 1272 and 1443 (with several monastic buildings burned to the ground during the former altercation). But more common were controlled attempts by the townsmen to extend their legal and economic jurisdiction over the local monastery, as for example at Bristol in 1496.[144] In general, there seems to have been greater potential for conflict between monasteries and their neighbours in an urban setting than a rural one, owing to the development of municipal corporations with strong identities and ambitions in the later middle ages, and perhaps also to the economic difficulties faced by many towns in the fifteenth century. Nevertheless, recorded disputes seem to represent occasional flashpoints rather than a constantly simmering hostility to local monasteries. Numerous St Albans townsmen joined the abbey's confraternity and after the Dissolution there was some support within

---

142 Bonney (1990).

143 Knowles (1948–59), I, 263–9.

144 Tanner (1984), 141–66; Fleming (2000).

the town for the restoration of the monks [cf. **40**].[145] On the other hand (as we have seen) urban monasteries were rarely remembered in local wills, unless by the house's own tenants who often themselves benefited from the monks' immunity from the town corporation's jurisdiction and economic controls. And even where relations were more amicable, the benefits to be gained from the removal of their monastic neighbours or lords must have been glaringly obvious to urban elites in the 1530s.[146]

Monastic privileges also impacted on the affairs of parishioners. By the end of the middle ages, more than one-third of all English parish churches had been appropriated, in many cases to monastic rectors who drew the greater part of the revenues of the parish to themselves, and appointed a vicar to serve the parishioners on a modest stipend. Again it is very difficult to know how this affected lay perceptions of religious houses [cf. **48**]. Monastic appropriation was the subject of considerable criticism by churchmen such as Thomas Gascoigne (1404–58), chancellor of Oxford University, but examples of parochial hostility are harder to find. Much no doubt depended on how conscientious the monastic rector was in keeping the chancel of the parish church in good repair and contributing to the welfare of the parishioners. Visitation records occasionally report the failure of religious houses to fulfil these commitments, with the abbot of Langdon warned in the early sixteenth century for his neglect of the churches of Walmer and West Langdon. Architectural evidence, however, sometimes reveals a different picture: inscriptions and coats of arms indicate, for example, that Prior John Cantlow of Bath (in office 1483–99) was responsible for the renovation of at least three chancels of churches and chapels in his house's patronage.[147] Even where the monastic appropriator was diligent, the parish might still suffer from an underfunded vicarage unable to attract high-quality priests or to finance poor relief in the parish. The widespread leasing of tithes to laymen, with little interest in the functioning of the parish [**5**], might also have created tensions. On the other hand, several late medieval parish guilds included monks and canons in their membership, and abbots and priors can even be found in positions of leadership, as at Bagshot (co-founded by the prior of Sheen) or the Annunciation Guild of Walsingham, closely connected with the priory of that town.[148]

145 Clark (2000a).
146 E.g. Martin (1998).
147 Thomson (1993), 214–25; Luxford (2005), 85–7.
148 Lovatt (1992); Farnhill (2006).

As well as the many monastic rectories in late medieval England, a smaller number of parishes were served in person by a monk- or canon-priest. The Augustinian and Premonstratensian canons were particularly active in this work, reflecting these orders' traditional association with parochial service [**19**]. It is not clear how many of their many appropriated parish churches they served in person, but it does seem that this proportion was rising over the later middle ages. This development may have been partly precipitated by a shortage of secular priests following the Black Death, but also seems to have been an expedient adopted by smaller communities seeking to save money during the economic difficulties of the fifteenth century. Canons of Bolton Priory were serving five of their six parish churches in the mid-fifteenth century, and almost a quarter of Lancashire parishes were in the hands of religious, both canons and monks, on the eve of the Dissolution.[149] The impact of this activity on the relations between monasteries and their neighbours is again uncertain. Parochial visitations contain complaints about monk-priests who were not available to perform the last rites at night, suggesting that these appointments could be problematic. But there is little sign that the religious were careless of the spiritual needs of parishioners. The most popular collection of model sermons in late medieval England, the *Festial*, was written by John Mirk, the prior of the Augustinian Lilleshall Abbey, quite possibly in response to needs identified in his own house's appropriated churches. It is also likely that another popular late medieval sermon collection, the *Northern Homily Cycle*, emanated from a house of Augustinian canons. To these pastoral endeavours should be added the Gilbertine canon Robert Mannyng's *Handling Sin*, a guide for priests as confessors, and Mirk's *Instructions for Parish Priests*, both widely used clerical handbooks in the later middle ages.[150]

In more than 250 parishes (about 2.5 per cent of the total in late medieval England and Wales), the religious were even more closely connected with parochial life, with the church building divided between parishioners and monastery.[151] This arrangement, which affected houses of monks, canons and nuns in similar proportions, once again had the potential to cause conflict as two groups with very different religious and liturgical needs were confined to a single building. In a good number of cases, the inconvenience of this arrangement led to the

149 Dickinson (1950), 224–41; Kershaw (1973), 180; Haigh (1975), 122.
150 Hanna (2000).
151 Heale (2006).

construction of a new church for either parish or religious; but many churches remained shared right down to the Dissolution. Conflicting demands for space and the monastery's refusal to allow the use of bells or other amenities to the parishioners created tension in some churches, with occasional outbursts of violence. At Wymondham in 1409–10 the monks were besieged in the priory and their servants assaulted in a clash over bells [**47**]; and during a dispute at Sherborne in 1436, a parishioner fired a flaming arrow into the roof of the church, burning it to the ground. Nevertheless, as with the monastic boroughs, it would be wrong to emphasise only the evidence for conflict. It is striking that more than 50 per cent of parishioners in the late medieval diocese of York whose church was shared with a monastic community made bequests to that house in their wills. This proportion far exceeds the overall percentage of testators remembering monasteries in their wills (see above, pp. 46–9) and suggests that for the most part parishioners valued the presence of a religious house on their doorstep.

## Fourteenth- and fifteenth-century criticism of monasticism

Conflict between monasteries and their neighbours, the product of inevitable clashes of interests, was not therefore an unusual occurrence in late medieval England; but there is little sign of a deeper, more general hostility to the religious [cf. **49**]. Nevertheless, we must also confront the fact that a good deal of contemporary comment about late medieval monasticism was critical in nature. This is particularly true of references to monks and nuns in works of literature, although the connection between literary productions and lay perceptions is notoriously difficult to judge. Authors such as Chaucer wrote within strong literary conventions, and it is well known that the characters of *The Canterbury Tales* were based on traditional estates satire and played on themes that had been commonplace in European literature for generations. Nevertheless, something of the intention and impact of these works can be discerned by analysing how individual authors moulded old conventions for their own purposes and for a contemporary audience.[152] Chaucer combined traditional criticisms of wealthy and worldly monks and nuns with acute references to contemporary questions of controversy within late fourteenth-century monasticism, such as the debate over the literal observance of rules and the tension between inward- and outward-looking forms of monasticism. But if the mischievously knowing character of Chaucer's critiques serves to

152 Mann (1973), 17–37, 128–37; Pearsall (2001); Scase (1989), e.g. ix–xii.

temper their asperity, the commentary on the monastic life found in
William Langland's *Piers Plowman* (written in several drafts between
the 1360s and 1380s) contains a sharper rebuke [48]. Although the
life of the cloister was in theory the most praiseworthy of any ('For
if heaven is on this earth, and peace to any soul, it is in the cloister or
schools'), contemporary monks were not living up to their ideal.[153] At
the heart of Langland's critique was excessive monastic wealth, which,
he believed, corrupted the lives of the religious and encouraged them to
abandon their rules in favour of relaxed living. Langland's commentary
culminated with his famous warning that, unless the monks reformed
themselves, a king would come to confiscate their wealth: a prescient
remark that helped to make *Piers Plowman* a popular work in Reformation England.

An unfavourable depiction of the monk can be found in another genre
of late medieval literature: the 'rymes' of Robin Hood. These highly
popular ballads, which survive in manuscripts dating from the fifteenth
and sixteenth centuries but may represent earlier traditions, feature
monks on more than one occasion, always cast as villains.[154] In *Robin
Hood and the Monk*, the latter is an establishment figure who informs
the authorities of the outlaw's whereabouts, leading to Robin's arrest.
The monk is then intercepted by Little John and beheaded for his act
of treachery. Monasteries feature even more prominently in *A Gest of
Robyn Hood*, with the abbot of the rich abbey of St Mary's York depicted
throughout as a greedy and exploitative accumulator of property, at the
expense of an impoverished knight assisted by Robin. A similar critique
of monastic wealth and disregard for the poor can be found in the early
fifteenth-century poems *Dives and Pauper* and *Mum and the Soothsegger*,
although neither work devotes much space to the religious. Nor did
nuns feature heavily in late medieval English literature. Chaucer's
worldly and aristocratic prioress is to some extent counterbalanced by
her companion, whose demure and pious behaviour and tale might be
seen as reflecting contemporary perceptions of the ideal nun.[155] Less
positive is the unflattering depiction of a late medieval nunnery found
in the early fifteenth-century poem *Why Can't I Be a Nun*, which relates
in rather conventional terms how virtues of all kinds have fled from the
house. The role of the prioress of Kirklees in the Robin Hood ballads,
moreover, is well known.

153 Schmidt (1978), 111.
154 Field (2002).
155 Dutton (1999).

How should we interpret this literature, with its largely negative assessment of late medieval monasticism? Some historians have labelled works of this kind 'anticlerical', arguing that they represent a wider hostility to the Church.[156] The concept of anticlericalism, however, has come in for a sustained attack by revisionist historians arguing for the vitality of late medieval religion.[157] In attempting to reconcile these positions, Sean Field has drawn attention to the contrast between the piety of the Robin Hood of the fifteenth-century ballads – consisting in particular of a strong devotion to the Mass and the Virgin Mary – and the antagonism he displays towards monasteries.[158] It is argued that we should draw a distinction between lay attachment to the practices and devotions of late medieval religion on the one hand, and more negative perceptions of the institutional Church, particularly religious houses, on the other. This argument for the wholesale unpopularity of monasteries is unconvincing in the light of the evidence for the relations between the religious and their neighbours surveyed above. But it is at least conceivable that the recurrent criticisms of monastic wealth found in these and other literary productions of the period reflect, and perhaps contributed to, some level of popular disapproval towards this particular aspect of monasticism. Nor should we discount the possibility that disapproval of this kind might have co-existed with a positive appraisal of the religious and social services performed by monks, nuns and canons.

Censure of monastic wealth in late medieval England was not confined to works of literature. The years 1370–1420 witnessed considerable agitation against the rich endowments of the Church more generally from a number of quarters. This development was partly stimulated by internal ecclesiastical controversies, notably the dispute between the friars and monastic 'possessioners' (a pejorative term coined by the theoretically possession-less mendicants, which – revealingly – passed swiftly into wider currency) over which was the best form of the religious life. It was the mendicants who first brought this debate into the public arena in the early 1370s, when two Augustinian friars argued in Parliament that the wealth of the Church might be used to relieve the heavy burden of wartime taxation on the laity. This appealing argument met with a receptive audience, and the partial disendowment of the Church was discussed seriously on several occasions in Parliament in the late fourteenth and early fifteenth centuries.[159]

156 E.g. Dickens (1987); Scase (1989).
157 Most vigorously, Haigh (1987).
158 Field (2002).
159 Aston (1984).

These debates on the wealth of the Church were further stirred up and complicated by the writings of John Wyclif and his early followers. Indeed, the initial appeal of Wyclifism seems to have had much to do with its fusion with pre-existing hostility towards ecclesiastical wealth and privileges. Wyclif's critique of contemporary religion was wide-ranging, but it included a fierce attack on the monasteries. Not only should their extensive properties be confiscated by the lay authorities, Wyclif argued, but the monastic life itself was flawed. Monastic orders were sects, engaged in 'private religion', grounded on their own rules rather than the Bible; they did not even follow these rules closely; they lived luxuriously, to the detriment of the poor; and their liturgical prayer was of no value. Early Lollard writings picked up these themes, and preachers like Nicholas Hereford in his Ascension Day sermon in Oxford in 1382 vociferously argued for the confiscation of ecclesiastical revenues and their redistribution to the laity and the poor. The highlight of this campaign was the presentation of a Lollard bill for the disendowment of the Church to the 1410 Parliament, which provided a carefully costed plan for the reuse of this revenue for the good of the Crown, the country and the poor [**50**].[160]

The Church's condemnation of the writings of Wyclif and his supporters as heretical, and their association with sedition following Oldcastle's Lollard revolt in 1414, however, combined to discredit this disendowment campaign. The parliamentary criticism of monastic wealth thereafter lost much of its potency and largely disappeared for the remainder of the fifteenth century. It is noticeable that literary attacks on monastic wealth also died down after about 1420. This development was probably due in part to the association of such criticisms with heresy, but it may also have been a product of the economic conditions of this period, which favoured the lower orders at the expense of secular and ecclesiastical landlords. This was certainly the view of Abbot William Curteys of Bury, who commented about his house's finances in 1434 that 'whereas we used to be a reproach to men and despised of the people, after the common people rose up and visited their wrath upon us, we have now in some measure been brought down to the level of our neighbours'.[161] In any case, criticism of the monasteries was muted in these years, with even constructive proposals for monastic reform rarely advanced after Henry V's abortive plans for the Benedictines. Attacks on monasteries were now mainly advanced by clerical opponents, with the exemption

---

160 Hudson (1988), 334–50; Renna (1987); Aston (1984).
161 British Library, Add. MS 14848, fo. 35.

of certain monasteries from episcopal jurisdiction and appropriations targeted by secular churchmen at the general councils of Basle and Florence in the 1430s.[162] Otherwise, the religious feature little in the writing of this period.

## Humanism and evangelicalism

Suspicions that this dearth of comment was the product of the marginality of monasticism to late medieval society, however, appear groundless in the light of the return to topicality of the religious orders and their reform in the years around 1500. This was prompted above all by the influence of Christian humanism. Humanism was an intellectual technique rather than a uniform movement or set of ideas, and its impact on the English scene was accordingly diverse and variegated. As with many subjects, humanists disagreed over monasticism, but their discussions did much to bring the reform of the religious orders back onto the public agenda in early Tudor England. A number of humanist writers advocated a return to stricter monastic observance. John Longland, later bishop of Lincoln, advanced such a programme in a (subsequently published) sermon to the monks of Westminster, and John Colet, dean of St Paul's, strongly criticised the standards found in many contemporary monasteries in his famous sermon to Convocation in 1511.[163] Not all humanist responses to monasticism were critical, and Thomas More defended the monastic life of his day as rigorous and challenging, despite understandable modifications of observance. Nevertheless, humanist calls for monastic reform were not without influence. They may have informed Cardinal Wolsey's attempts to reform the Benedictine and Augustinian Orders, and the increase in the numbers of monasteries suppressed for the endowment of Oxford and Cambridge colleges in the late fifteenth and early sixteenth centuries (see above, pp. 42–3) tallies closely with the humanist prioritisation of education.

The monastic reforms proposed by English humanists were largely traditional. But a much more radical and far-reaching programme of Church reform was outlined in the early sixteenth century by the celebrated Dutch humanist Desiderius Erasmus. Erasmus developed a strong critique of many elements of contemporary religion, advocating a practical, personal piety based on the New Testament. His own experiences as a young man in the Dutch monastery of Steyn left him with a

---

162 Schofield (1966).
163 Bowker (1981), 17–18; Harper-Bill (1988).

lifelong distaste for several aspects of monasticism, and this hostility can be traced in many of his writings [**51**].[164] Erasmus' critique focused on four main facets of the religious life. Firstly, monastic emphasis on ritual prayer was ridiculed in works such as his famous *The Praise of Folly*: 'when like donkeys in church they bray out their psalms (memorised indeed, but not understood) they imagine they are ravishing the ears of the saints with infinite delight'.[165] Erasmus here contrasted ceremonialism and the monastic dependence on rules and regulations with the religion of the heart and the Gospels, dismissing the strictest branches of the monastic order as proponents of petty legalism. Secondly, the wealth enjoyed by many monasteries was judged entirely excessive for the contribution they were making to early sixteenth-century society; and Erasmus, like some of his fellow humanists, was keen to offer alternative good causes for this income – in particular, education. Thirdly, monasteries were castigated (most notably in the colloquy, *A Pilgrimage for Religion's Sake*) for encouraging superstition through their widespread involvement in the promotion of pilgrimage. And fourthly, monastic university learning, with its reliance on traditional scholastic authorities, was dismissed as foolish and ignorant (although it was the mendicants who were the principal targets of Erasmus' sarcasm on this score).

This attack on the religious life represented the most searching critique of monasticism from within the Church for many generations. Earlier orthodox critics of monasteries, including Chaucer and Langland and the older literary tradition they represent, essentially attacked the religious for not living up to their own ideals, and highlighted eradicable abuses such as excessive wealth or relaxed observance. But Erasmus' critique was much more dangerous, because it focused on precisely those elements of late medieval monasticism that arguably comprised its greatest strengths: the dignified performance of the liturgy, the stricter, 'observant' branch of monasticism, the monks' growing engagement with university learning, the popularity of monastic pilgrimage sites and the success of the religious in maintaining their solvency. All of these activities, which were at the very heart of the late medieval variety of monasticism, Erasmus condemned as unnecessary or nefarious. He never laid down any kind of reform programme, but it is clear that Erasmus thought monasticism of little relevance to true religion.

164 Knowles (1948–59), III, 141–56.
165 Adams (1989), 62.

Yet Erasmian ideas about the religious orders, however hard-hitting, were not the most explosive to be circulating in early Tudor England. Over the 1520s, the writings of Martin Luther and his evangelical[166] supporters put forward an even more radical interpretation of the value or otherwise of the monastic life. Luther was himself an Observant friar and several of his early English adherents came from a monastic background, and so inevitably the religious life formed an important part of their manifesto. Luther (whose voluminous writings on monasticism are not easily summarised in brief), like Wyclif, stressed the lack of biblical mandate for the religious life and contended that monastic vows were a violation of the principle of Christian freedom, since love and worship should be offered to God voluntarily. Monks and nuns, he argued, followed their own rules rather than the Gospel, with these rules of life representing human efforts to improve on the teachings of Christ [cf. **51**]. Other aspects of the Lutheran programme concerned religious practices closely associated with late medieval monasticism, including his attacks on Church wealth, clerical celibacy, saint cults and intercessory masses for the dead. It followed that the only fitting remedy was the outright abolition of monasticism. This onslaught on traditional religion was brought to an English audience by a number of evangelical authors. The most systematic attack on religious houses in English was *Rede Me and Be Nott Wrothe*, probably by the ex-friars William Roye and Jerome Barlowe [**52**]. This work, and other evangelical pamphlets of the 1520s such as Simon Fish's *A Supplication for the Beggars*, blended Lutheran ideas with more traditional tenets of anticlericalism, arguing that the religious were immoral and their wealth wasted, to the detriment of the poor.

There were circulating in early sixteenth-century England, therefore, potentially explosive ideas about the monastic life. It must be strongly emphasised, however, that neither Erasmian nor Lutheran writings spread widely among the general population in early Tudor England. Erasmus wrote in Latin for an educated audience, and his more polemical works were not translated into English until the mid-1530s. Similarly, evangelicals remained a small minority in 1520s England, and their attacks on the religious life (condemned as heretical by the Church) may even have increased support for the monasteries among the orthodox majority. But it would be a mistake to dismiss entirely the impact of these ideas in early Tudor England. If they influenced only a small minority of Englishmen, this group included some of the most powerful people

166 See above, n. 5.

in the kingdom. Erasmus in particular was widely admired among the intellectual elites of early sixteenth-century England. His ideas were not accepted wholesale among this circle of admirers: Thomas More, Erasmus' friend, staunchly defended monastic observance and the practice of pilgrimage; and Robert Joseph, the humanist monk of Evesham Abbey whose letter collection survives, was able to praise Erasmus for his classical scholarship and pure Latinity without paying any heed to his writings on the reform of the Church. But the lack of respect and interest which Erasmus displayed towards the monastic life does seem to have influenced others. This is the most likely explanation for the otherwise surprising coolness shown towards monasticism by several religiously conservative humanists in the court of Henry VIII, including Stephen Gardiner, Hugh Oldham, Thomas Starkey and, most significantly of all, the king himself.[167]

Moreover, there were among those few who embraced evangelicalism in early Tudor England several highly influential figures, including Thomas Cranmer, archbishop of Canterbury from 1533, and Thomas Cromwell, arguably the driving force behind the Dissolution in the second half of the 1530s. These reformist ministers were able to play on Henry VIII's Erasmian distrust of monasticism to press forward their more radical agenda for the total termination of the religious life in England.[168] It may also be that some parts of the evangelical programme, most notably the call for clerical disendowment, potentially appealed to a wider audience. Just as the late fourteenth- and early fifteenth-century Lollard writings set out to stir up more general misgivings about ecclesiastical wealth, the works of Fish and others sought to bring the disendowment of the Church back onto the public agenda by repeatedly labouring charges of ecclesiastical greed and decadence.[169] At a time when humanists were criticising the deployment of Church wealth, when taxation was on the increase and when the price of staple goods was beginning to rise alarmingly – helping for the first time in generations to shift the economic balance of power between landholders and the masses back in favour of the former – this was a shrewd line of attack. Despite the utility and vitality of late medieval monasteries, they remained vulnerable to criticisms of this kind. The first session of the Reformation Parliament in 1529 included a petition for the disendowment of the Church (apparently presented by conservative members of the nobility),

---

167 E.g. MacCulloch (1996), 33; Bernard (2005).

168 Cf. Marshall (2003), 44–6.

169 Kaartinen (2002), 49–62.

reheating arguments which had not been aired in Parliament since the early fifteenth century.[170] The plundering of monastic property was the necessary lubricant for the Dissolution in the country at large, and the evangelicals' ability to exploit a recognisable discourse of anticlericalism was an important precondition for this course of action.[171] This, at least, is a more convincing explanation for the widespread and often sacrilegious profiteering from monastic wealth by supporters of traditional religion in the 1530s than naked greed or impiety.

## Government interference in monastic affairs

The early years of the sixteenth century therefore saw a dramatic rise in criticism of the monastic order, consisting of both novel and traditional lines of attack and sometimes blending the two together in dangerous ways. One final ingredient conspired to destabilise the position of monasteries in early Tudor England: the increasing involvement in monastic affairs by the government. This growing interventionism manifested itself in two main ways. Firstly, it can be seen in the Crown's growing willingness to interfere with monastic property. Other than the exceptional case of the alien priories, it was rare for late medieval kings to meddle with the endowments of religious houses (which were inalienable according to canon law). Tudor governments, however, appear to have had fewer scruples than their predecessors in this regard. Henry VII engineered the suppression of four smaller houses, in part to fund his and his mother's chantries; and in 1532 Henry VIII went one step further, suppressing the London priory of Holy Trinity, Aldgate and keeping the property for himself instead of granting it to another branch of the Church. The 1530s also saw several forced exchanges of monastic property, very much to the advantage of the king. Most heavily affected were those houses with desirable lands in or around London, such as Westminster Abbey, which was required in 1536 to deliver to the king several valuable manors, together with the convent's garden (or Covent Garden), in return for retaining the Berkshire lands of Hurley, its recently suppressed daughter house.[172] Monasteries also faced significantly rising tax demands over the first decades of the sixteenth century [54].

The second main signal of government interventionism in monastic affairs can be seen in the election of monastic superiors. Almost without

170 Hoyle (1995).

171 Cf. Marshall (2006).

172 Heale (2004b); Heale (2004a), 277–88.

exception, the heads of the greater monasteries of the realm were internal appointments throughout the fourteenth and fifteenth centuries. However, this trend began to change, slowly but perceptibly, in the second half of the reign of Henry VII (1485–1509), when the new superiors of several major abbeys were drawn from other houses – in at least some cases at the behest of the Crown. These external appointments became more common in the 1520s and 1530s, and the surviving correspondence of Wolsey and Cromwell makes it clear that considerable pressure was being placed on convents to appoint government nominees as their superiors.[173] Wolsey and Cromwell also sought to engineer vacancies by encouraging abbots and priors to resign [54], and pressed for the promotion of favoured internal candidates to the headship or other important offices in many houses. Indeed, in a number of cases it was superiors who owed their position to government interference of this kind, like Robert Catton of St Albans, who agreed to the unfavourable property exchanges with the Crown mentioned above: a clear indication of how superiors promoted through government patronage were subsequently vulnerable to the king's bidding.

It is apparent, therefore, that monasteries were becoming more susceptible to government interference in the early years of the sixteenth century. This need not necessarily have been cause for alarm: it could also bring benefits to a monastic order determined to prove its utility to the world. Indeed, it is probable that the increased public role accorded to abbots and priors in these same years was connected to the growth of Crown interest in monastic affairs (see above, pp. 16–17). Not only was there a sharp rise in the appointments of monk-bishops in early Tudor England, but the number of superiors called to Parliament was also raised from twenty-seven to thirty early in the reign of Henry VIII [53]. Nevertheless, religious houses can have had few illusions about their ultimate dependence on the Crown by the mid-1530s, even if it was far from obvious how this power would be used. Although plans for far-reaching monastic reforms were being discussed in government circles in these years [55],[174] the Dissolution as it unfolded was the product of a succession of contingencies and improvisations, rather than a carefully planned process. But the fact that the majority of English monasteries were in the event suppressed between 1538 and 1540 through 'voluntary' surrenders made by their superiors under severe government pressure, indicates the significance of these developments.

173 Heale (2008a).
174 Hoyle (1995).

The events of the Dissolution itself, and the motivations that lay behind it, fall beyond the scope of this book. But it is important to appreciate that they did not occur in a vacuum. Much recent scholarship has tended to present the English Reformation as a bolt out of the blue,[175] and this is perhaps true for the religious themselves and the majority of the English population. Monasticism was not losing its appeal or relevance in early Tudor England. Indeed, far from drifting into laxity or redundancy, the religious continued to offer valued services to lay society and remained receptive to new intellectual and devotional currents. Nor was there any notable disaffection with monasticism among the majority of the English people, although the inflation, falling real wages and rising taxation of the early sixteenth century may have drawn covetous eyes to monastic wealth. Nevertheless, as David Knowles commented nearly fifty years ago, 'the spectacular events of the reign of Henry VIII were rendered possible, though not inevitable, by the slow and almost imperceptible changes in outlook and opinion during the decades that preceded them'.[176] The generation leading up to the Dissolution was marked by the appearance of hostile new attitudes towards monasteries and increasing Crown dominance over monastic affairs. This did not make the wholesale suppression of religious houses between 1536 and 1540 likely, or in any way predictable. But it did make the termination of English monasticism *conceivable* by 1535, as it could hardly have been fifty years earlier to those assembled in the church of Westminster Abbey – including Abbot Eastney, attending to the king and queen, and the monks standing by in copes – for the coronation of Henry VII.

175 Duffy (1992); Haigh (1993).
176 Knowles (1948–59), III, 3.

**PART ONE:**

**MONASTIC LIFE
IN LATE MEDIEVAL ENGLAND**

# I: THE ESSENCE OF THE MONASTIC LIFE: THE BENEDICTINE RULE

The life of the monk, canon or nun was based on fidelity to a rule. The Benedictines, Cistercians, Cluniacs and many nunneries followed the sixth-century Rule of St Benedict, and other monastic orders were heavily influenced by its teachings. For those religious following it, the Benedictine Rule remained the staple of monastic reading and education throughout the later middle ages, and provided the main inspiration for their way of life [cf. **27**] – despite some late medieval modification of its precepts.

## 1. Extracts from the Rule

Translation taken from E. Henderson, *Select Historical Documents of the Middle Ages* (London, 1903), 274–314 (Latin).

## Prologue

… We are about to found, therefore, a school for the Lord's service; in the organisation of which we trust that we shall ordain nothing severe and nothing burdensome. But even if, the demands of justice dictating it, something a little irksome shall be the result, for the purpose of amending vices or preserving charity; – you shall not therefore, struck by fear, flee the way of salvation, which can not be entered upon except through a narrow entrance. But as one's way of life and one's faith progresses, the heart becomes broadened, and, with the unutterable sweetness of love, the way of the mandates of the Lord is traversed. Thus, never departing from His guidance, continuing in the monastery in His teaching until death, through patience we are made partakers in Christ's passion, in order that we may merit to be companions in His kingdom. Amen.

## Chapter 2: What the abbot should be like

An abbot who is worthy to preside over a monastery ought always to remember what he is called, and carry out with his deeds the name of a Superior. For he is believed to be Christ's representative, since he is called by His name, the apostle saying: 'You have received the spirit of adoption of sons, whereby we call Abba, Father.'[1] And so the abbot

1 Romans viii. 15.

should not – grant that he may not – teach, or decree, or order, any thing apart from the precept of the Lord; but his order or teaching should be sprinkled with the ferment of divine justice in the minds of his disciples. Let the abbot always be mindful that, at the tremendous judgment of God, both things will be weighed in the balance: his teaching and the obedience of his disciples. And let the abbot know that whatever the father of the family finds of less utility among the sheep is laid to the fault of the shepherd ... Therefore, when anyone receives the name of abbot, he ought to rule over his disciples with a double teaching; that is, let him show forth all good and holy things by deeds more than by words ...

## Chapter 5: Concerning obedience

The first grade of humility is obedience without delay. This becomes those who, on account of the holy service which they have professed, or on account of the fear of Hell or the glory of eternal life consider nothing dearer to them than Christ: so that, so soon as anything is commanded by their superior, they may not know how to suffer delay in doing it, even as if it were a divine command. Concerning whom the Lord said: 'As soon as he heard of me he obeyed me.'[2] And again he said to the learned men: 'He who hears you hears me.'[3] Therefore let all such, straightaway leaving their own affairs and giving up their own will, with unoccupied hands and leaving incomplete what they were doing – the foot of obedience being foremost – follow with their deeds the voice of him who orders ...

## Chapter 7: Concerning humility

... The sixth grade of humility is, that a monk be contented with all lowliness or extremity, and consider himself, with regard to everything which is enjoined on him, as a poor and unworthy workman; saying to himself with the prophet: 'I was reduced to nothing and was ignorant; I was made as the cattle before you, and I am always with you.'[4] The seventh grade of humility is, not only that he, with his tongue, pronounce himself viler and more worthless than all; but that he also believe it in the innermost workings of his heart ... The eighth degree of humility is that a monk do nothing except what the common rule of the monastery, or the example of his elders, urges him to do. The ninth

2 Psalms xviii. 44.

3 Luke x. 16.

4 Psalms lxxiii. 22, 23.

degree of humility is that a monk restrain his tongue from speaking; and, keeping silence, do not speak until he is spoken to. The tenth grade of humility is that he be not ready, and easily inclined, to laugh ... The twelfth grade of humility is that a monk shall, not only with his heart but also with his body, always show humility to all who see him: that is, when at work, in the oratory, in the monastery, in the garden, on the road, in the fields ...

## Chapter 16: How divine service shall be held through the day

As the prophet says: 'Seven times in the day do I praise You.'[5] Which sacred number of seven will thus be fulfilled by us if, at Matins, at the first, third, sixth, ninth hours, at Vesper time and at Compline we perform the duties of our service; for it is of these Hours of the day that he said: 'Seven times in the day do I praise You.' For, concerning nocturnal vigils, the same prophet says: 'At midnight I arose to confess to you.'[6] Therefore, at these times, let us give thanks to our Creator concerning the judgments of his righteousness; that is, at Matins, etc. ... and at night we will rise and confess to him ...

## Chapter 33: Whether the monks should have anything of their own

More than anything else is this special vice to be cut off root and branch from the monastery, that one should presume to give or receive anything without the order of the abbot, or should have anything of his own. He should have absolutely not anything: neither a book, nor tablets, nor a pen – nothing at all. For indeed it is not allowed to the monks to have their own bodies or wills in their own power. But all things necessary they must expect from the Father of the monastery; nor is it allowable to have anything which the abbot did not give or permit. All things shall be common to all, as it is written: 'Let not any man presume or call anything his own.'[7] But if any one shall have been discovered delighting in this most evil vice: being warned once and again, if he do not amend, let him be subjected to punishment.

## Chapter 48: Concerning the daily manual labour

Idleness is the enemy of the soul. And therefore, at fixed times, the brothers ought to be occupied in manual labour; and again, at fixed times, in sacred reading ... But in the days of Lent, from dawn until the

---

5 Psalms cxix. 164.

6 Psalms cxix. 62.

7 Cf. Acts iv. 32.

third full hour, they shall be free for their readings; and, until the tenth full hour, they shall do the labour that is enjoined on them. In which days of Lent they shall all receive separate books from the library; which they shall read entirely through in order. These books are to be given out on the first day of Lent ... Moreover on Sunday all shall engage in reading: excepting those who are deputed to various duties. But if anyone be so negligent and lazy that he will not or can not read, some task shall be imposed upon him which he can do; so that he be not idle.

## Chapter 66: Concerning the doorkeepers of the monastery

... A monastery, moreover, if it can be done, ought so to be arranged that everything necessary – that is, water, a mill, a garden, a bakery – may be made use of, and different arts be carried on, within the monastery; so that there shall be no need for the monks to wander about outside. For this is not at all good for their souls. We wish, moreover, that this Rule be read very often in the congregation; lest any of the brothers excuse himself on account of ignorance.

## Chapter 72: Concerning the good zeal which the monks ought to have

As there is an evil zeal of bitterness, which separates from God and leads to Hell; so there is a good zeal, which separates from vice and leads to God and to eternal life. Let the monks therefore exercise this zeal with the most fervent love: that is, let them mutually surpass each other in honour. Let them most patiently tolerate their weaknesses, whether of body or character; let them vie with each other in showing obedience. Let no one pursue what he thinks useful for himself, but rather what he thinks useful for another. Let them love the brotherhood with a chaste love; let them fear God; let them love their abbot with a sincere and humble love; let them prefer nothing whatever to Christ, who leads us alike to eternal life.

# II: RECRUITMENT AND ECONOMY

Monastic recruitment and economy were closely linked. Late medieval monasteries admitted new inmates according to their means, with both numbers and income falling after the Black Death of 1348–49. The documents in this section illustrate the realities of monastic recruitment and economy in the later middle ages. They shed light on the qualifications and commitment required from new recruits to male and female monasteries; they indicate some of the economic problems faced by religious houses in the changing conditions of the period; and they also provide a flavour of the responses adopted by monasteries in the face of these difficulties. For further material relating to the monastic economy, see also for example **6–7, 10, 31, 54**.

## 2. The recruitment of monks to Canterbury Cathedral Priory, 1330

The Benedictine cathedral priory of Christ Church, Canterbury, was one of the largest monasteries in England with a convent numbering around eighty monks in the early fourteenth century. This letter from Prior Henry of Eastry to his subprior, and the attached questionnaire, illustrates what was required in new inmates at a time when numbers of monks were around their peak.

Translated from *Literae Cantuarienses: The Letter Books of the Monastery of Christ Church, Canterbury*, ed. J. B. Sheppard, 3 vols, Rolls Series, 85 (1887–89), I, 320–2 (Latin).

### Concerning two scholars admitted by Thomas, the subprior, at the mandate of the prior

Greeting, etc. Concerning these things which you have written to us this Friday regarding two scholars, examined in the usual manner before the brethren, we commend your diligence. We will that you should examine the two scholars in turn more diligently before two senior brethren, after the scholars have first sworn an oath that they will speak the truth in the articles ordained for this matter, which you have in your possession. And if nothing canonical or notable should obstruct the said scholars, you should admit them to the monastic habit by our power and authority; enjoining them that they should thereafter conduct themselves well and honestly, as is more fully contained in the schedule of articles that you have. And, if before our coming, God willing, more scholars of similar praiseworthy condition appear before you, you should not omit to make similar proceedings. Farewell, etc.

[Articles for the examination of candidates for admission to the monastery]

Before they are received, clerks seeking the monastic habit should swear, touching the holy Gospels, that they are speaking the truth in the articles written below:

Whether they have already bound themselves by a vow or an oath to enter any other form of religion.

Also: whether they have been bound by a vow or by other means to the pilgrimage of the Holy Land or of the church of Rome.

Also: whether they have bound themselves to marry or be married, or have betrothed themselves to any woman.

Also: whether they have committed any homicide or other misdeed, or have advised or consented to homicides or other misdeeds.

Also: whether they have been present at a death-sentence, or procured a death-sentence.[8]

Also: whether they have laid violent hands on a clerk, a religious man, or a lay brother.

Also: whether they have incurred any sentence of excommunication or suspension, from which they are not absolved.

Also: whether they have been bound by oath, or any other means, to pay a debt of any money or to render account to anyone.

Also: whether they are of free condition, and of legitimate birth.

Also: whether they have incurred any irregularity, or whether they have any impediment whatsoever, public or secret, why they may not freely, without scandal and without danger to their souls, assume the religious habit and be canonically advanced to all holy orders.

Also: whether they have any incurable sickness, or any contagious illness, or whether they have been maimed in any member of the body.

When these clerks have been examined individually in all the afore-said articles, if nothing canonical obstructs them, then the prior in

---

8 Ordained clerks were forbidden to have any involvement in 'judgements of blood'.

his chapel should receive them individually by hand, with the words written below:

'In the name of the Holy Trinity we receive and admit you to the order of St Benedict, and to wearing the monastic habit in this church for the time of probation, and beyond that to solemn profession, according to regular observances and canonical sanctions.'

Also: when such clerks have been thus admitted, the prior should enjoin them, by virtue of the oath sworn, that they should say Matins and all the Hours and Vespers of St Mary every day; and that they should hear Divine Office and Mass in the church daily, unless they are hindered by a necessary cause.

Also: that they should conduct themselves soberly, modestly and honestly, just as they have done while they were in the world.

Also: that they should withdraw themselves from the company and conversation of all suspect persons.

Also: that they should wisely and prudently order and dispose all their goods, both moveable and immoveable, according to the advice of their friends; and their books, if they have any, they should place in the library of the church of Christ, Canterbury, to be inspected at a suitable time.

Also: that they should not hereafter contract marriage, nor assume the religious habit elsewhere without the advice and consent of the prior.

## 3. The ordination and profession of Benedictine nuns

This document outlines the ceremony for the reception and profession of new nuns. Composed in English so as to be readily understandable to the religious women [cf. 27], it was appended to a translation of the Benedictine Rule written in the north of England in the early fifteenth century. This document provides rather more detail about the training of new religious than 2, and offers some insight into how the vocation of a nun was understood in late medieval England.

Translated from *Three Middle-English Versions of the Rule of St Benet*, ed. E. Kock, Early English Text Society, original series, 120 (1902), 141–4 (English).

This is the manner in which a novice shall be made and received into religion.

In the beginning, when she has made her petition and asked the house, and the prioress and the convent have granted it to her, then she shall come to the prioress and kneel down before her on her knees. And the prioress shall take her hand in hers and kiss her, and she shall be received.

Afterwards, when they please to bring her into the chapter to be examined, they shall dress her in the attire that she shall use during the first year until she is professed. And then, when chapter is finished, she who shall be her mistress shall say to the prioress: 'There is a novice to be examined.'

And then the prioress shall ask for her to be brought in. And her mistress shall bring her in. And when she comes where the convent receive their penance, then she shall prostrate herself down. And then the prioress shall ask her: 'Dear daughter, what is your request?' And lying still, she shall say: 'God's mercy and yours.' And the prioress shall make her rise, and say to her in this manner: 'What is that mercy that you ask for?' And she shall say: 'To dwell in this place in the habit of religion, to serve God, and to punish my sins, and for the amendment of my life, and finally for the salvation of my soul.'

And then the prioress shall say again: 'Dear daughter, what you ask is a hard and demanding thing. Nevertheless, to those whom God inspires and gives the grace, will and power to fulfil it, and who stand stable in the purpose that they began, it is but light, meritorious and beneficial, and advantageous to the life that shall last forever. But at the beginning of this spiritual life, there are three things that befit you: to forsake your own proper will, and to live under obedience, and be obedient principally to your prioress and to your elders in the order, in all lawful and honest things. The second thing that befits you is to live in wilful poverty, owning nothing without the knowledge of your prioress, nor taking anything from any of your friends, neither gold nor silver nor any other gift, unless your prioress sees it and it is fully assigned at her will, so that you are no *proprietarius*,[9] nor fall into excessive danger against your religion. For whoever has anything, gold, silver, jewel, or any property, without the knowledge and permission of her prioress, she stands cursed.

'The third thing that befits you is to live chastely, and take God as your spouse, and forsake all your lust and the liking of your flesh; it befits you to give yourself to abstinence and to fast when others eat; it befits you to rise to the service of God when others sleep; it befits you to give yourself to prayer and devotion to purchase grace, and stand

9 An owner of illicit personal property [cf. 1].

steadfastly in the purpose that you take to yourself. And, daughter, if you say that you may fulfil with the grace of God all these points that I have rehearsed, say now here before the convent: what is your will?' And then the novice, if she will abide in her purpose, shall say in this manner: 'The good purpose that I have taken I shall fulfil to my life's end, through the grace of God and your good instruction.'

And then the prioress shall say to her: 'Dear daughter, may God, of his great grace, give you good perseverance. Go with your mistress in the name of Christ.' And her mistress shall receive her to the noviciate, and instruct her as religion requires. And when two months have passed, her mistress shall expound to her the Rule and the points and strictness of religion, concealing nothing from her. And when her mistress has expounded the Rule to her, she shall be examined again in the chapter in the same manner as aforesaid. And if she stands in her purpose after the space of six months, the Rule shall be expounded to her afterwards by her mistress. And then she shall be examined in the chapter in the manner before said.

And if she still abides fully in her purpose to her year's end, then on the day that she is professed, she shall be brought into the chapter, and examined a fourth time, as is rehearsed before. And then if she fully consents to the promise that she made before, after the Gospel on the day that she is professed, her mistress shall come to her and lead her to the step. And there she shall read her profession, with the priest who sings the Mass standing at the right corner of the altar. And when she has read her profession, her mistress shall give her a pen with ink, and the novice shall make a cross on the book of her profession, and so walk up to the high altar, with her mistress, and lay it on the right end of the altar, and kiss the altar, and bow devoutly, and going again to the step, sing there three times: *Suscipe me, Domine*, etc. The convent, all the time standing in their stalls, shall rehearse the same again three times, and *Gloria patri*. Then the novice shall prostrate herself down before the step, when *Kyrieleison, Christeleison, Kyrieleison* [is sung] ... [The prayers and psalms to be said or sung by the priest and the choir are next given] And then he [the priest] shall say four collects over her, the novice lying prostrate by the step, with the prioress and the convent standing in their stalls, their faces turned to the altar.

And when the collects are all ended, then the novice shall stand while the veil is blessed. And when the priest has blessed it, three or four of her sisters with her mistress shall come out of the choir and stand about her, while her veils are being put on, with all the rest of the convent standing in their stalls. Then, when she is dressed up in her veils, the chanter[10] shall begin solemnly this hymn: *Veni, creator*, the choir and the chanter singing verses alternately. And in the meantime the novice shall make her profession to the prioress, kneeling on her knees, saying in this manner: '*Promitto tibi obedienciam secundum regulam Sancti Benedicti.*'[11] And the prioress says then: '*Det tibi Deus vitam eternam.*'[12] And in the same manner she shall go down the prioress's side [of the choir], and then the other side. And when she comes again, there she shall prostrate and lie herself down. And then the priest who ordains her shall say or sing: *Salvam fac, Nichil proficiet* as is said before, and their collects: *Deus, qui caritatis, Acciones nostras, Fidelium deus*. When their three collects are said, the prioress shall come and lead her to her stall, where she shall stand and the priest shall go to the altar and begin the Creed. And at this she is to be given Communion.

## 4. The estates of Meaux Abbey in the late fourteenth century

The chronicle of the medium-sized Cistercian abbey of Meaux (Yorkshire) was written by Thomas Burton, a monk of the house and subsequently its abbot (1396–99). These extracts are taken from Burton's account of the rule of his immediate predecessor as abbot, William of Scarborough (1372–96), written during or immediately after Scarborough's rule. Among other things, Burton's chronicle provides much information about the abbey's estate management at a time of economic transition.

Translated from *Chronica Monasterii de Melsa*, ed. E. Bond, 3 vols, Rolls Series, 43 (1866–68), III, 182–4, 228–9 (Latin).

The said abbot [William of Scarborough] accordingly leased our grange of Salthaugh, with all the pastures there, to a certain John Franks, for a fixed term of years; and he removed from there all our sheep to Sutton, seduced by the perverse advice of the greedy, as events afterwards proved. For the first and foremost member of his council took one hundred shillings [£5] from the said John for inducing the abbot to this, and he died within a year; and another [of the abbot's council] took twenty shillings, and the others in the same manner had not a few small gifts; but the monastery, however, had nothing but the very greatest loss and injury. For firstly, we lost all our sheep that had been led away from there, namely four hundred and more, because they

10 The nunnery obedientiary responsible for leading the chant in choir.
11 'I promise obedience to you, according to the Rule of St Benedict.'
12 'May God give you eternal life.'

hated the unaccustomed pastures and died one after the other. And during the first year of the lease, in the autumn, when a very strong wind rushed in for two successive days and nights, the sheaves and stacks of corn, peas and hay were thrown by that wind somewhere into the Humber, into ditches and into the lands of others, so that scarcely anything was found undamaged on our own land. And what was found somewhere, the said John did not recognise for his own.

The River Humber at the same time flooded to such an extent that it broke its banks and, driven by the wind, washed over the coastal flood-gates opposite the grange. It drove two huge channels in the ground of the grange, so that the course of the water flowed back and forth horribly for two days and nights. As a result, the whole territory lying around, thus hidden by the waters, appeared more like sea than land. Overwhelmed therefore by these misfortunes, John hurried tearfully to the monastery and surrendered this grange, thus made destitute. Consequently, the abbot came there and assembled a very great multi-tude of workers from all parts, and at very great cost and expense he conquered the power of the waters, and blocked the aforesaid channels and had this flood-gate of the Humber repaired within a short time; so that within ten days, in the stipends of the workers alone (besides food), the expenses exceded twenty marks; and nevertheless the grange and pastures had thus been made destitute of corn and sheep and horribly flooded, and thereafter for a long time our lands there remained in a bad condition for us. The inundations of the Humber also pitiably consumed all our lands in Tharlesthorpe up to the site of our grange there. As a result, we had all our buildings in the grange and at the rectory of Keyingham removed; and we caused the grange of Ottringham and other places of ours to be rebuilt, the site of this grange, alas! having been left uninhabitable ...

The same Abbot William allowed losses in the annual value of our churches, granges and other tenements, both at the time of his election (besides the aforesaid leases, sales and grants of possessions) and in lands, tenements and rents thus sold, leased and granted, and reverting to us in the time of his abbacy, by one hundred marks and more each year – although the increases of rents should also be taken into account. And beyond such burdens still remaining from the time of his predecessors, he himself burdened the monastery with similar pensions and corrodies,[13] for the terms of lives of those retaining them, to the

---

13 The provision of board and lodging in the monastery or elsewhere, usually for term of life, in return for a gift of property or lump sum in cash.

annual value of forty marks. He ruined the grange of Tharlesthorpe, and he lost many of its lands through the inundation of waters; and he left this grange, and the other granges of Blanchemarle and Hutton Cranswick and the rectory of Easington, destitute of crops, stock of any kind or tools, besides three mules at Easington. He leased out two bovates of the rectory of Nafferton, and he diminished the crop of the same rectory. He commuted the boon-work and services of certain tenants at Nafferton, Hutton Cranswick and elsewhere to fixed money payments. He also leased out the grange of Wawne to four tenants together, and removed from there all the draught animals and other things, except three mules, sixteen oxen, some carts and ploughs and a few tools. He transferred the main buildings within the enclosed ditch at Hayholme to outside the ditch.

He took away the wealth of the horse-stud, and he enlarged the debt of the monastery by £200 and more. And welcoming too much the end of the burdens mentioned above, he introduced expenses for entertaining, ostentation and certain excesses; and he tolerated the foolishness of his servants, which seemed to those succeeding him very serious things to be curbed. However, during his time, all the lay brothers of the monastery deserted, whose number he made up with monks, and he increased the annual payment for the convent's victuals. He deprived the inhabitants and the sick of the infirmaries of the lay brothers and seculars. He demolished the kitchen of the lay brothers' infirmary, and refashioned another kitchen of the old guesthouse into a chamber above the 'polan' gate; and he built a lean-to from there up to the great gates, which he had caused to be removed from the chapel outside the gates. He caused the house called the 'Watch-house' outside the gates at Ottringham to be taken away, and the peat-stack next to the bakehouse to be transferred to near the new guest-house, and a pigsty to be established on the old site of the peat-stack.

## 5. The lease of a rectory, a close and a manor by Oseney Abbey, 1474

A great deal of monastic property, including both landed estates (temporalities) and income from parish churches (spiritualities) was leased out, or 'demised at farm', in fifteenth-century England. This characteristic lease, of both spiritual and temporal property, was made by the relatively wealthy Augustinian abbey of Oseney, near Oxford.

Translated from *Cartulary of Oseney Abbey*, ed. H. E. Salter, 6 vols, Oxford Historical Society Publications, 89–91, 97–8, 101 (1929–36), V, 170–3 (Latin).

This indenture – made between the religious men, Richard, by divine permission abbot of the monastery of the Blessed Virgin Mary of Oseney, and the convent of the same place on the one part; and William Venour' of Dinton in the county of Buckingham, husbandman, and Richard Venour' his son, of the same vill and county on the other part – testifies that the abbot and convent have delivered and leased to William and Richard their rectory of Stone next to Aylesbury in the aforesaid county, with all the rights, advantages and profits pertaining to the rectory; together with a demesne[14] close at Upton called Westcroft, with all the day-work of the customary tenants[15] of the manor of Upton ... And William and Richard may do just as they will with the customary tenants for their customary payment, excepting the tenants' chickens of customary payment, and also all kinds of mortuaries[16] from the rectory whenever arising, which are entirely reserved to the abbot and convent and their successors. The abbot and convent have also lately delivered and leased to William and Richard the whole site of the manor of Senclers in Stone, with all the lands, meadows, grazing-lands and pastures pertaining to the site of the manor.

This William and Richard, and whichever of them should live the longer, are to have and to hold the rectory with all its appurtenances together with the demesne close at Upton and all the customary tenants pertaining to it, and also the site of the manor of Senclers with its appurtenances, excepting what has been excepted above, from the feast of St Michael the Archangel, AD 1476, to the end of the term of twenty-four years next following, to be fully completed. They are to pay annually from there to the abbot and convent and their successors £20 of legal English money at four terms of the year, namely at the feast of St Thomas the Apostle, the Annunciation of the Blessed Virgin Mary, the Nativity of St John the Baptist and St Michael the Archangel by equal portions.

And the aforesaid William and Richard (and the longest living of them) shall repair, mend and maintain all the buildings of the rectory roofed

---

14 Land cultivated by the landlord or leased out, as opposed to land held by hereditary peasant tenants.

15 Tenants holding land according to the customs of the manor.

16 A payment due to the parish priest on a parishioner's death, usually either an animal or a robe.

by straw; and also all the closes as in the walls, hedges and ditches pertaining to the rectory, Westcroft and Senclers as often as shall be necessary during the term, at their own cost and expense. And William and Richard shall find carpenters, masons and tilers and any other workers and labourers, with food and drink and likewise with a bed, whenever it shall be necessary to cause any tile-roofed building of the rectory to be repaired or mended. Also William and Richard shall make and support at their own cost and expense all the costs of carriage whatsoever for the buildings and repairs of the rectory built, repaired and maintained within the aforesaid time, whenever necessary, excepting only the new building of one house.

And William and Richard shall live in the rectory with their household during the whole term. And it shall not be permitted to them to lease to anyone the rectory, close or site of Senclers nor any part of them; nor to throw down or make waste any trees in any of the aforesaid places without the special licence of the abbot and convent or the monastery's steward of that time. And William and Richard shall receive and honourably provide for the lord abbot with his men with food and drink, and hay, litter and fodder for their horses, for one day and night once in every year; and also for the steward of the monastery with his men, and the rent collector, whenever they or one of them come to hold the courts of Upton or oversee the condition of the rectory, close and manor site, or collect rent during the whole term.

And William and Richard shall have each year of the term one gown of the livery of the monastery's grooms. And they shall receive on this day eight acres of coarsely cultivated land for sowing wheat; and also twenty-seven acres of land well cultivated and manured by cart and by fold;[17] and also eleven acres of land of value, well manured by cart and fold; all of which William and Richard (or whichever of them) shall lay down and deliver at the end of their term to the use and profit of the abbot and convent and their successors. And William and Richard shall receive other tools and necessary things, as are specified on the back of this indenture; all of which they (or whichever of them) shall restore at the end of their term, as they are appraised or at face value, at the choice of the abbot and convent and the steward of that time.

And if it should happen that William and Richard are in arrears in the payment of their farm in part or in full by twenty days after any of the aforesaid terms by which they ought to have paid, then it will rightly be

---

17 I.e. manure from a cart or directly from animals in the fold.

permitted to the abbot and convent and their successors, or their proctor, attorney or deputy, to enter into and distrain[18] the rectory, Westcroft and the site of the manor of Senclers with all their appurtenances, and to take away, carry off and retain in their possession the distraints thus taken there, until such time as the farm with all the arrears (if there are any) is fully satisfied and paid to them. Moreover, if it should happen that the farm is in arrears, unpaid in part or in full for forty days after any term, as aforesaid, or if William and Richard should die within the aforesaid time, or if all of the aforesaid agreements are not completed or fulfilled, then it should rightly be permitted to the abbot and convent and their successors (or their proctor or attorney) to re-enter, recover and re-seise into their own hands the rectory, Westcroft and the site of the manor of Senclers ...

And for all these agreements to be correctly and faithfully held, observed and completed, William Venour' and Richard his son, and Richard Nasche of Edrope bind themselves to the sum of [blank] pounds of English money, to be paid to the abbot and convent and their successors if William and Richard are wanting in the above-written agreements or any one of them ... Given in our chapter house of Oseney on the feast of St Mark the Evangelist [25 April], AD 1474 ...

18 Seize, in order to force the payment of the arrears.

# III: EVERYDAY LIFE AND ADMINISTRATION

A great deal of evidence survives to illuminate the character of everyday monastic life in the later middle ages. In large part, this takes the form of administrative records, most notably accounts and inventories. Although extremely revealing, such records inevitably emphasise the financial and mundane aspects of monastic life to the exclusion of other facets. Another important source for the internal life of late medieval monasteries is the customary, which often recounts how different monastic offices (including that of the superior) ought – ideally – to be discharged. All these genres of evidence are represented below. Further material on standards of living in late medieval monasteries can be found in **12–15**.

## 6. An account from the nunnery of St Radegund, Cambridge, 1481/82

St Radegund's Priory, Cambridge, was one of the poorest nunneries in late medieval England and in 1496 was declared to be no longer viable and suppressed by the bishop of Ely [**31**]. This account was made by the receiver-general of the house a few years before the priory's closure, on behalf of her prioress, and covers only three-quarters of the year. While illuminating several aspects of life in a late medieval nunnery, it also reflects the growing financial difficulty of the priory: an earlier surviving account of 1449/50 shows annual receipts of over £80.

Translated from A. Gray, *The Priory of St Radegund, Cambridge*, Publications of the Cambridge Antiquarian Society, 31 (1898), 176–9 (Latin).

The account of Lady Joan Key, receiver-general of the house of St Radegund, Cambridge, and of the convent of the same place, from the feast of Pentecost [10th June] 1481, up to the feast of the Annunciation of the Blessed Virgin Mary [25th March] next following thereafter ... for three quarters of the year.

Arrears:

None because this is the first year of the said accountant.

Assize rents:[19]

---

19 Fixed annual payments made by freeholding tenants.

EVERYDAY LIFE AND ADMINISTRATION

EVERYDAY LIFE AND ADMINISTRATION

EVERYDAY LIFE AND ADMINISTRATION

EVERYDAY LIFE AND ADMINISTRATION

The payments of rents:

Out of this, that same accountant is allowed 15s and two chickens in rent paid to Mortymeres.

14s 4½d on similar rent paid to the mayor and bailiffs of the town of Cambridge for the hagable.[20]

7s on rent paid annually to the prior of Barnwell.

6s on similar rent paid annually to the prior of Barnwell.

6s on similar rent paid to Thomas Lovell.

3s 7½d for rent paid to Thomas Cotton.

3s 4d paid to the prior of Ely.

12d to the sheriff of Cambridgeshire.

12d paid to John Skarlett.

4d on similar rent paid to the rector of St Benedict's [Cambridge].

16d paid to the college of Corpus Christi, Cambridge.

3d paid to Walter Trumpyton

and 12d on rent paid to Thomas Pygot.

Sum: £2 14s 3d

The costs of the household:

And she seeks allowance for various recent purchases, together with stock, both live and dead, and beyond that the salted and dried fish bought there during the time of the account at various prices and consumed in the lady's household, for [blank] weeks – the details of which with their totals are fully stated in the journal of the aforesaid household and are sufficiently witnessed.

Sum: £7 14s 6½d

The purchase of corn and stock:

And 6s 8d paid for this reason to Thomas Brampton, esquire, for the price of two quarters of malt bought from him.

3s 4d, for the price of one quarter of malt bought from Master Robert Parys, esquire.

2s to the vicar of Abington for the price of four bushels of malt bought from him, together with others bought from various people for the lady's household – the details of which and their totals and names are stated in detail in the journal of the household and fully witnessed, £4 6d

20 A payment levied by the mayor and bailiffs of Cambridge on dwelling-houses in the borough.

And on three cows with their calves, together with harnesses, cords, harrows, folds and other necessities bought for husbandry, as is fully written in the oft-mentioned journal, £3 14s 8d

Sum: £7 15s 2d

The costs of the harvest:

And she reckons for Thomas Payn, William Tomson, Michael Savage and other workers there this year during the time of the account, hired at harvest time for mowing, binding, reaping, carrying and stacking, both within the nunnery and outside – as is stated separately and in detail in the journal of this household, where they are named by name.

Sum: £5 9s 2d

Necessary expenses:

And she reckons as an allowance, namely on two parcels of ling, two parcels of salted fish, two bushels of salt, 240 iron nails, paper and parchment, together with other necessities there during the time of the account, bought at the fairs of Stourbridge and St Ethel-dreda the Virgin [in Ely] for the lady's household, as appears in the oft-mentioned journal of the household in details of record.

Sum: £2 6s 1d

The costs of ploughs and carts:

And she reckons to have paid 18d on the price of one plough bought from William Dey.

8s paid for the shoeing of the lady's horses, together with the mending of all the equipment pertaining to husbandry and other necessities bought for husbandry during the time of the account – just as are stated in detail in the aforesaid journal of the household and are sufficiently witnessed.

Sum: 16s 10d

Repairs of buildings:

And she accounts for £1 11s 4d paid for various repairs made there and assigned within the church during the time of the account.

£1 9s 8d on similar repairs made and assigned at Barnwell.

And with 5s 11d on various repairs made within the town of Cambridge during the time of the account, as are fully stated in detail in the oft-mentioned journal of the household.

Sum: £3 6s 11d

The stipends of the servants:

And she accounts for <u>5s</u> on part of the stipend of Master Upgayte, chaplain; <u>20d</u> for part of the stipend of Thomas Kent, chaplain; <u>20s</u> for the similar stipend of Master Malett, chaplain; <u>8s 4d</u> for the stipend of Master Robert Burton, chaplain; <u>20s</u> for the similar stipend of Master Pek; <u>9s</u> for the stipend of the clerk and collector of garbal tithes[21] at the harvest time; <u>3s 2d</u> for part of the stipend of Thomas Baker; <u>15s 6d</u> for a similar stipend of George Geyr during the time of the account; <u>10s</u> for the stipend of the shepherd; <u>3s 1d</u> for the stipend of William Plowman, hired for husbandry; <u>5s 2d</u> for the stipend of the butler for three quarters [of the year]; <u>2s 3d</u> on the stipend of the cook; <u>20s</u> for the stipend of the vicar of All Saints [Cambridge]; <u>8d</u> for part of the stipend of John Wright; and with <u>10d</u> for part of the stipend of William Tomson; together with other stipends and gifts given by the lady, just as are fully stated in the journal of the household of the house and are sufficiently witnessed.

Sum: £7 15s 11d

The purchase of barley and other grains:

And she reckons as an allowance the £3 paid to William Pychard on the price of eleven quarters of barley bought during the time of the account.

<u>15s</u> of similar moneys paid to Walter Sergeaunt on the price of five quarters of oats bought from him during the time of the account.

<u>6s 10d</u> paid to William Barnard on the price of two quarters of peas.

<u>11d</u> on the price of two bushels of vetches.

Sum: £4 2s 9d

The sum of all the expenses and liveries: £57 5s 4½d

And thus that same accountant has £25 9s 8d in surplus [expenditure].

## 7. An account from Yarmouth Priory, 1496/97

This account illustrates the life and economy of a small male house in the late fifteenth century: the Benedictine priory of Yarmouth in Norfolk, a daughter house (or cell) of Norwich Cathedral Priory. It offers a valuable comparison with **6**, not least because poorer nunneries are generally contrasted with large and wealthy male houses rather than the many smaller monasteries of monks and canons in late medieval England. Like that of St Radegund's, the income of

---

21 Tithes taken from corn, hay and other crops.

Yarmouth Priory was falling sharply over the fifteenth century, having been as high as £205 per year in the 1380s.

Translated from St George's Chapel, Windsor, XV.55.78 (Latin).

The account of Brother Simon Folkard, warden of the cell of Great Yarmouth, of all the receipts and expenses of the cell from the feast of St Michael the Archangel [29th September] AD 1496 ... up to the feast of St Michael next coming thereafter ... in the ninth year of Lord William Spynk, the prior [of Norwich].

Remainder:

Remaining from the account of the preceding year – <u>nothing</u>.

Sum – <u>nothing</u>.

Receipts of the church, etc.

From personal tithes[22] – <u>£20 18s 3½d</u>

From offerings on the four principal feasts, with the other feasts on which parishioners are accustomed to make offerings, and the Easter collection – <u>£14 5s 3d</u>

In all masses for the dead – <u>£4 11s 7¾d</u>

From the rents offered for bellmen on the anniversaries of the dead this year[23] – <u>3s 7d</u>

From the offerings of weddings – <u>£2 7s 4¼d</u>

From purifications[24] – <u>£2 7d</u>

From certain masses – <u>£2 17s 6d</u>

From the legacies of the dead – <u>13s 2d</u>

From mortuaries[25] sold – <u>3s 4d</u>

From the chapel of the Blessed Mary of Arneburgh[26] – <u>£7 2s 7d</u>

From the pyx of St Anne – <u>5½d</u>

From the pyx of Good Henry[27] – <u>£4 11s 7¾d</u>

---

22 Tithe taken from the profits of parishioners' labour and trade.

23 I.e. those ringing bells to announce the anniversaries of the deaths of the monastery's benefactors, in order to encourage prayer for their souls.

24 The ritual cleansing of women after childbirth ('churching'), at which a payment was made to the parish priest.

25 See above, n. 16.

26 A chapel outside the precinct of the priory, housing a popular image of the Virgin.

27 I.e. King Henry VI (d. 1471), the subject of an unofficial cult in England in the decades after his death.

From the chest of St Nicholas, with other pyxes in the church – £4s 11d

From fishing and Christ's part[28] – £7 15s 5½d

From wax sold in the church and the chapel of the Blessed Mary – £2 18s 3d

From wool sold – 12d

From those dining in the monastery – £5 8s 4d

From Sir John Pennyng for his chambers – 3s

Sum – £76 6s 4¾d

Rents and farms:

From rents and farms within the town of Great Yarmouth – 20s 3½d

From the farm of the manor of Thornton with rents there this year – £8 3s 3½d

Sum – £9 3s 7d

Sum total of receipts – £85 9s 11¾d

Surplus:

On the surplus [of expenditure] from the account of the preceding year – £12 9d

Sum – as appears.

Expenses:

On the stipends of the servants with their liveries – £8

On the stipend of one parish priest – £4

On alms given to mendicant friars, to the hospital, the church and to lepers – 20s

On gifts given to preachers of the word of God and to actors – 16s 8d

On wheat and bread bought – £6

On malt and ale bought – £9 6s 8d

On oats and barley bought for the chickens and swans – 6s 8d

On the horses' hay and fodder, and horse-shoes – 13s 4d

On daily food allowances with the larder, salt, flour and spices – £23 6s ½d

On peas bought for pottage – 12d

On tallow candles for the church and the household – 11s

Also to the barber – 6s 8d

---

28 An unspecified proportion of the fishing catch which was owed to the monks as rectors of the parish of Yarmouth.

Also to the washerwoman – <u>10s</u>

On three chaldrons[29] of coal – <u>16s 8d</u>

On the carriage of the same – <u>6d</u>

On the repair and hooping of vessels in the storeroom, the brewhouse, bakehouse and the kitchen – <u>5s 3d</u>

On 1,000 pieces of furze [for fuel] bought for the household – <u>17s 4d</u>

On rushes bought for the church and the household, and for the cleaning of the church for Easter – <u>£1 1s 10d</u>

Also paid to clerks for 'lez levells' and the keeping of the Mass of the Blessed Mary – <u>8s</u>

On repairs made within the priory precinct – <u>£1 8s 7½d</u>

On repairs made at Thornton – <u>£2 2s 5d</u>

On the prior's medicine – <u>20d</u>

On the prior's necessities – <u>£2 13s 4d</u>

On twenty-six pounds of incense bought from strangers – <u>3s 3d</u>

On ropes for the bells – <u>4s</u>

Also to the warden of the bells – <u>16d</u>

On making wax for the whole year – <u>6s 8d</u>

On two thousand roofing tiles – <u>10s</u>

On wine bought for those receiving Communion at Easter, and wine for celebrating Mass for the whole year – <u>16s</u>

On stone pots for Christmas – <u>8d</u>

On wine bought for guests – <u>6s 8d</u>

On 900 faggots made at Thornton, and three hundred pieces of firewood, with their carriage – <u>16s</u>

On 950 quarters and a half of faggots bought from various men – <u>£2 5s 2d</u>

On straw bought for putting on salted fish and as bedding for the horses – <u>12d</u>

Also to Robert Sponer, steward of the court at Thornton – <u>6s 8d</u>

On the expenses of the court there – <u>3s 4d</u>

On the expenses of the prior, travelling to the monastery [i.e. Norwich] and through the neighbourhood, with the hiring of horses – <u>4s 4d</u>

On bringing in and sending back the brethren [to and from the mother house] – <u>3s</u>

On rents paid to various lords for lands in Thornton – <u>20s 10¾d</u>

29 A dry measure of four quarters or thirty-two bushels.

Also paid to the pittancer[30] for his lands in Thornton – <u>6s 8d</u>

On eight pounds of wax bought for the feast of the Purification of the Blessed Mary – <u>4s 4d</u>

On three gallons and three quarts of oil bought for lamps in the chapel of the Blessed Mary and Good Henry – <u>4s 2d</u>

On three halters bought for the horses – <u>3d</u>

On the castration of a horse – <u>4d</u>

On one shovel bought with its ironwork – <u>4d</u>

Also to the labourer in the garden – <u>10d</u>

On cords bought for the barge – <u>8d</u>

On the expenses around the pageant on the feast of Corpus Christi – <u>8d</u>

Sum – <u>£73 10¾d</u>

Pensions:

Paid to the lord prior [of Norwich] on the feast of the Holy Trinity for his pension of £3 6s 8d – <u>£3</u> and no more because <u>6s 8d</u> was pardoned out of mercy.

On the cellarer's pension – <u>£2</u>

On the convent's pension on the feast of Holy Trinity, with other expenses there – <u>£1 2s 10d</u>

On the alms of St Nicholas's day – <u>£1 1s 6d</u>

On the whole pension for two scholars, namely Brother Henry Langrake and Brother Robert Catton[31] – <u>£1 5s</u>

On half a tenth paid to the lord king on the feast of Pentecost – <u>£2 11½d</u>

On a fifteenth paid to the same lord king for our lands in Thornton – <u>20s</u>

On a feudal aid, vulgarly called 'the Aid', paid to the same lord king for our said lands – <u>15s</u>

On the expenses made towards Ralph Willoughby – <u>£1 13s 4d</u>

On paper, parchment and the writing of the account – <u>20d</u>

On the day of the account – <u>3s 4d</u>

30 The mother house obedientiary responsible for providing the monks' pittances, i.e. allowances of food, etc. often provided by benefactors to inmates in return for masses for their souls.

31 Catton was a future prior of Norwich (1504–29?) and abbot of St Albans (1531–38). Langrake was prior of Yarmouth in 1514.

Sum – £14 3s 7½d

The sum of all the expenses – £87 4s 6¼d

The sum of all the expenses with the surplus of the preceding year –
£99 5s 3¼d

The expenses exceed the receipts – £13 15s 3½d

And thus he is charged this year – £1 14s 6½d …


## 8. Pocket money and recreation at Eynsham Abbey, c. 1403/4

The following is an excerpt from the sole surviving account of the Eynsham Abbey chamberlain, the monastic officer responsible for the provision of the community's clothing. This document provides a vivid picture of how the monks of this moderately wealthy Benedictine abbey were spending their clothing allowance in the early fifteenth century. The sample of entries presented here (ten monks out of a community of twenty-two or twenty-three) includes both senior monks and new recruits.

Translated from *Cartulary of Eynsham Abbey*, ed. H. E. Salter, 2 vols, Oxford Historical Society Publications, 49, 51 (1907–8), II, xcii–xcvii (Latin).


William Henreth:

£1 15s 9¾d is owed from the preceding account; and from his portion, £2; and the responsibility of the subprior's office, 3s 4d; and from his portion of the church of Merton,[32] 8s 4d

Sum – £4 7s 7¾d

From which is delivered to him for one robe of say,[33] 8s 4d; also for half an ounce of silk, 6d; also for linsey-woolsey[34] garments, 3s 4d; also for blankets, 21d; also for one mended pilch,[35] 12d; also for leaving the monastery, 6s 8d; also for entertainment, 3s; also for spices, 8d; also for offerings given, 3s 4d; to the shoemaker, 17d

Sum – £1 10s

And £2 17s 7¾d is owed to him.


John London:

5½d is owed from the preceding account; and from his portion, £2; and

32 The proceeds from this church were set aside to pay for the monks' clothing.
33 A cloth of fine texture.
34 A cloth made from linen and wool, coarser than linen alone.
35 A leather garment, lined with fur, usually worn as an outer garment.

from his portion of the church of Merton, <u>8s 4d</u>

Sum – £2 8s 9½d

From which is delivered to him for one newly bought bed, <u>£1 10s</u>; also for one robe of say, <u>11s 8d</u>; also for linsey-woolseys, <u>2s 5¾d</u>; also for brown cloth, <u>2s 1½d</u>; also for fur bought, <u>2s</u>

Sum – £2 8s 3¼d

And <u>6¼d</u> is owed to him.


William Coggs:

<u>£2 3s 1d</u> is owed from the preceding account; and from his portion, <u>£2</u>; and from his portion of the church of Merton, <u>8s 4d</u>

Sum – £4 11s 5d

From which is delivered to him for brown cloth, <u>13¾d</u>; also for black cloth, <u>3s 11d</u>; also for one pair of shoes, <u>1½d</u>; also for silk, <u>5¾d</u>; also for a knife, <u>18½d</u>; also given to his sister by the abbot's licence, <u>13s 4d</u>; also for linen cloth, <u>8¼d</u>; also for entertainment, <u>9s 6d</u>; also for leaving the monastery, <u>6s 8d</u>; to the shoemaker, <u>4s 8d</u>

Sum – £2 2s ¾d

And <u>£2 9s 4¼d</u> is owed to him.


Thomas Meritone:

<u>7s 10¾d</u> is owed from the preceding account; and from his portion, <u>£2</u>; and from the portion of the church of Merton, <u>8s 4d</u>

Sum – £2 16s 2¾d

From which is delivered to him for one cowl of say, <u>4s 1½d</u>; for silk, <u>5½d</u>; also for linsey-woolseys, <u>2s 10d</u>; also for one cloak, <u>3s 4d</u>; also for shoes, <u>3d</u>; also for entertainment, <u>6s 8d</u>; also for a knife, <u>2s 4d</u>; also for linen cloth, <u>2s ½d</u>; also to Canterbury by reason of a pilgrimage, <u>18s</u>; also for spices, <u>13d</u>; to the shoemaker, <u>3s 2d</u>

Sum – £2 3s 2½d

And <u>12s ¼d</u> is owed to him.


Roger Clare:

<u>9s 7½d</u> is owed from the preceding account; and from his portion, <u>£2</u>; and from his portion of the church of Merton, <u>8s 4d</u>

Sum – £2 17s 11½d

From which is delivered to him for one robe of say, <u>8s 6d</u>; also for silk, <u>6d</u>;

also for black cloth, 23¾d; for linen cloth, 18d; also for entertainment, 6s 8d; also for spices, 3s 6d; also for making a chamber in the infirmary, £1 13s 2d; to the shoemaker, 2s 1d

Sum – £2 17s 10¾d

And ¾d is owed to him ...

### Richard Oxinforde:

3s 9d is owed from the preceding account; and from his portion, £1 6s 8d; and for his portion from the church of Merton, 6s 8d

Sum – £1 17s 1d

From which is delivered to him for one robe of say, 8s 3d; also for silk, 6d; also for black cloth, 23½d; also for shoes, 3d; also for mending furs, 15½d; also for one chamber in the dormitory, 8s 4d; also for leaving the monastery, 6s 4d; also for linen cloth, 8¼d; also for spices, 9d; to the shoemaker, 21d

Sum – £1 10s 1¼d

And 6s 11¾d is owed to him.

### John Radele:

9s 2½d is owed from the preceding account; and from his portion, £1 6s 8d; and from his portion from the church of Merton, 6s 8d

Sum – £2 2s 6½d

From which is delivered to him for one robe of say, 10s 3d; also for silk, 8½d; also for black cloth, 22¼d; also for one pair of bed-covers, 5s 8½d; also for linen cloth, 15¼d; also for mending one pilch, 7d; also given to his mother, 3s 4d; also for linsey-woolseys, 2s 6½d; also for entertainment, 3s 6d; also for leaving the monastery, 2s 4d; to the shoemaker, 4s 4d

Sum – £1 16s 5d

And 6s 1½d is owed to him.

### William Chyrchehylle:

6s 8d is owed here first for the term of St John the Baptist. From which is delivered to him for shoes, 9d

And 5s 11d is owed to him.

Ralph Dadyngton:

6s 8d is owed here first for the term of St John. From which is delivered
to him for six and a half yards of say, 5½d; and for silk, 6d

Sum – 5s 6½d

And 13½d is owed to him.

John Oxinford:

6s 8d is owed here first for the term of St John the Baptist.

And 6s 8d is owed to him.

Sum of all the expenses of the convent – £43 11s 11¾d

Sum owed to various brethren – £13 19s ...

## 9. Carthusian life in late medieval England: the inventory of Thomas Golwynne, 1520

The Carthusians were highly regarded in late medieval England for their
contemplative spirituality[36] and austere manner of living. The inventory of
Thomas Golwynne, a monk of the London Charterhouse, itemises the possessions he took with him when transferred to the priory of Mount Grace in
Yorkshire in 1520, and sheds much light on life in a late medieval Carthusian
monastery.

Translated from E. M. Thompson, *The Carthusian Order in England* (London,
1930), 327–8 (English).

May it be remembered that I, Dom Thomas Golwynne, monk professed
of the house of London, had with me by the licence of the honourable
father prior of the said house of London, Dom William Tynbegh, all
these things underwritten, when I departed from London to Mount
Grace, the 25th day of January, the year of Our Lord 1520.

Firstly, three habits as they come in accordance with custom.

Also, two new linsey-woolsey[37] shirts and one old.

Also, two new linsey-woolsey cowls and one old.

Also, two new hoods and one old.

Also a new coat lined; an old cloak.

Also a wide furred garment to put over all my gear, of the gift of my
Lady Conway.

36 See above, pp. 26–7.
37 See above, n. 34.

Also a new cap and an old one.

Also a new pilch[38] of the gift of Mr Saxby.

Also an old pilch and three pairs of hose.

Also three pairs of new socks and two pairs of old.

Also three old hairshirts and a belt.

Also a new pair of lined corked shoes, and a pair of double-soled shoes.

Also a pair of blankets, and two good pillows, and two little pillows, and a cushion to kneel on.

Also a new cloak by the gift of Sir John Rawson, knight of the Rhodes.[39]

Also a little brass mortar with a pestle, given by the gift of a friend of mine.

Also two pewter dishes, two saucers and a bowl and a little square dish for butter.

Also a new chafing dish[40] of latten given to us.

And two new tin bottles given by a kinsman of ours.

Also a brass chafing dish to heat water in.

Also a brass pan of a gallon given to us likewise.

Also a little brass pan with a steel handle.

Also a pair of new felt boots, and a pair of lined slippers for Matins.

Also a fair latten candlestick.

These books drawn together by cord are in vellum.

Also a fair written journal made at the cost of Master Saxby, having a clasp of silver and an image of St Jerome engraved therein: the second leaf of Advent begins *Jerusalem Alleluia*; this book cost in making £3.

Also a fair-written primer[41] with a calendar, and many other rules of our religion therein.

Also a fair-written psalter with a fair image of St Jerome therein at the beginning; the second leaf of the psalter begins *te erudimini*.

Also a large fair book written with the lessons of *Dirige*,[42] and the psalms of burying and the litany,[43] and the responses therein noted.

38 See above, n. 35.

39 A Hospitaller knight, whose order was based in the island of Rhodes at this date.

40 A vessel used for heating or warming purposes.

41 A prayer book, or book of Hours.

42 The first word of Matins in the Office of the Dead, used to refer to this service.

43 A series of petitionary prayers, mainly directed to the saints.

Also a book written containing certain masses with the canon of the Mass and a calendar at the beginning of the book with a fair image of Jesus standing before.

Also a little penance book written.

Also a written book of prayers of various saints with images painted, and *Dirige* written therein.

Also a written book of paper with various stories, and of *Ars Moriendi*[44] therein.

Also a printed breviary[45] by the gift of Master Rawson.

Also a journal and a printed primer given by Master Parker.

Also a little Golden Legend[46] in print.

Also the Shepherds' Calendar[47] in print.

Also Aesop's fables in print.

Also a *Directorium Aureum*[48] in print.

Also a complete frame to weave with strips of thread, with nine pulleys of brass, and nine plummets of lead, with two swords of iron to work with in the frame.

Also a double still to make aqua vitae, that is to say an alembic with a serpentine closed both in one.[49]

## 10. Administration in a late medieval nunnery: the cellaress of Barking

Barking Abbey (Essex) was one of the wealthiest nunneries in medieval England, and the cellaress – the officer responsible for the provisioning of the house – its most important obedientiary. This fifteenth-century description of the cellaress's duties reveals much about the nuns' administrative activities, as well as the economy and lifestyle of a wealthy female monastery.

Translated (with corrections of transcription from British Library, Cotton MS

44 'The Art of Dying Well': a fifteenth-century treatise providing advice on how to approach death in a Christian manner.

45 A service book containing the Divine Office.

46 A thirteenth-century collection of saints' lives by Jacobus de Voragine, printed in English translation by William Caxton in 1483.

47 A popular late medieval almanac containing astrology and Christian instruction.

48 A mystical treatise written by the fifteenth-century Observant Franciscan Henry Herp.

49 I.e. distilling apparatus. The spirits may have been used for drinking, medicine or alchemy.

Julius D.viii) from W. Dugdale, *Monasticon Anglicanum*, ed. J. Caley, H. Ellis and
B. Bandinel (London, 1846), I, 442–5 (English).

This is the charge belonging to the office of the cellaress of the
monastery of Barking, as hereafter follows.

The arrears:

First she must look when she comes into her office at what is owing to
the office by various farmers and rent-gatherers, and see that it is paid
as soon as she may.

The collection of rents and farms:

Great Warley: And then she must receive yearly from the collector of
Great Warley, at the feast of St Michael, £2 10s and from the same
collector yearly, at the feast of Easter, £2 10s

Bulphan: And also from the collector of Bulphan, yearly at the feast of
St Michael, £2 10s. And also from the same collector there yearly, at
the feast of Easter, £2 10s

Mucking: And also from the collector of Mucking, at the two terms
aforesaid, £4. And also from the farms there, at the said two terms,
£3

Hockley: And also from the collector of Hockley, at the feasts of
Michaelmas and Easter, in even portions, £10

Tollesbury: And also from the collector of Tollesbury, at the said two
feasts, in even portions, [blank]

Great Wigborough: Also from the collector of Great Wigborough, at
the said two feasts, in even portions, £10

Ingatestone: And also from the collector of Ingatestone, at the said two
feasts, in even portions, £2 8s

Slapton: And also from the collector of Slapton, at the said two feasts,
in even portions, £9

Lidlington: And also from the farmer of Lidlington, at the said two
feasts, in even portions, £16

Uphall: And also from the farmer of Uphall, per year, £6 13s 4d

Downhall: And also from the farmer of Downhall, per year, £2 16s 8d

Wangley: And also from the farmer of Wangley, per year, £4 10s

Barking: And also from the collector of the rents and farms of Barking
and Dagenham, belonging to the said office, per year, £12 18s

London: And also from the canons of St Paul's in London, for a yearly rent, £1 2s per year. And from the prior and convent of St Bartholomew's in London, per year 17s. And from John Goldington, for a yearly rent from various tenements at St Mary-Sherehog in London, per year 22d. And she should receive yearly £1 13s 4d from a tenement in Friday Street in London; but it is not known where it stands. And she should receive yearly £1 10s from the rent of the Tyburn; but it is not paid.

The issues of the larder:

And also she must be charged with all the ox skins that she sells; and of all the entrails of the oxen; and with all the tallow that she sells, coming from her oxen: and also of every portion of beef that she sells: and all these are called the issues of the larder.

The foreign receipt:

And also if she sells any hay at any farm belonging to her office, she must charge herself with it, and it is called a foreign receipt.

Sum total of all the said charge [blank]

Grain:

From this with part of the said sum she must purvey yearly three quarters of malt, for the tuns of St Ethelburga[50] and Christmas, twelve bushels for each of them, and then she must pay to the brewer for each tun, 20d. And then she must purvey a quarter and seven bushels of wheat for the pittances[51] of William Dune, Dame Matilda Loveland, Dame Alice Merton, Dame Matilda the king's daughter:[52] and for rissoles[53] in Lent, and to bake with eels on Maundy Thursday. And then she must pay to the baker for the baking of every pittance, 6d. And she must also purvey two bushels of green peas for the convent in Lent every year. And then she must purvey one bushel of green beans for the convent for Midsummer.

Store:

And she must purvey twenty-two good oxen per year for the convent.

50 The first abbess of Barking Abbey (fl. 664), whose tomb was venerated in the abbey. This entry refers to drink brewed for this feast and for Christmas.
51 See above, p. 100 n. 30.
52 Matilda Loveland, Alice Merton and Matilda, the daughter of King John, were all thirteenth-century abbesses of Barking.
53 Balls or cakes fried in breadcrumbs with a sweet or savoury filling.

Provision for Advent and Lent:

Also she must purvey two barrels of red herring for the convent in Advent and seven barrels of red herring for the convent in Lent; and also three barrels of white herring for the convent in Lent; and she must also purvey 1,200 [sic] pounds of almonds for the convent in Lent; and eighteen salted fish for the convent in Lent; and fourteen or else fifteen salted salmon for the convent in Lent; and three portions and twenty-four pounds of figs: and one portion of raisins for the convent in Lent; and also twenty-eight pounds of rice for the convent in Lent and eight gallons of mustard for the convent.

Rissole money:

And also she must pay to every lady of the convent, and to the prioress, the two cellaresses and the kitchener for their double allowance, for their rissole money, payable sixteen times a year to every lady, and the doubles at each time, ½d; but it is paid now only at two times, that is to say, at Easter and Michaelmas. Also she must pay to every lady of the convent, and to the aforesaid four doubles, to each lady and double, 2d for their crisps and cramcakes,[54] always paid at Shrovetide.

Anniversaries:

And also she must pay for five anniversaries, that is to say, those of Sir William Vicar, Dame Alice Merton, Dame Matilda the king's daughter, Dame Matilda Loveland, and William Dun; and also to purvey twelve gallons of good ale for the pittance of William on the day of his anniversary.

The offerings and wages, and the gifts of the cellaress:

And also she must pay as an offering to the two cellaresses per year, 12d; and then she shall pay to the steward of the household at the time he brings home money from the courts, on each occasion, 20d; and then she shall give to the steward of the household at Christmas, 20d; and to my lady's [i.e. the abbess's] gentlewoman, 20d; and to every gentleman, 16d; and to every yeoman as it pleases her to do, and grooms in the same way. And then she must buy a sugar loaf for my lady at Christmas; and also she must pay to her clerk for his wages, 13s 4d; to her yeoman cook, £1 6s 8d; and she shall pay for a gown to her groom cook and her pudding wife, 2s a year.

---

54 A kind of pastry and a loaf of unleavened bread, respectively.

The pittance of the convent:

And also she must purvey three carcasses of mutton for the convent, for the pittance of Sir William Vycar. Also she must purvey a measure of wheat, and three gallons of milk for free meat[55] on Saint Ethelburga's day. Also she must purvey four bacon hogs for the convent for the pittances of Dame Alice Merton and Dame Matilda the king's daughter, at two times in winter; and she must buy six young pigs, six sows for the convent and also six entrails and one hundred eggs to make white puddings; also bread, pepper and saffron for the same puddings; and also to purvey three gallons of good ale for her needs. And also to purvey marrowbones to make white worts[56] for the convent; and then she must purvey at St Andrew's-tide a pittance of fish for my lady and the convent.

And then she must pay at Shrovetide to every lady of the convent, and to the four doubles, for their crisps and for cramcakes to every lady and double, 2d; and then she must purvey for my lady abbess for Shrovetide eight chickens; and also buns for the convent at Shrovetide; and also four gallons of milk for the convent at the same time; also two gallons of red wine for the convent at the same time. And then she must purvey for every Sunday in Lent pittance fish for the convent; and also to be sure of twelve stub eels and sixty shaft eels to bake for the convent on Maundy Thursday; and also half a gallon of Tyre wine for my lady abbess on the same day, and two gallons of red wine for the convent on the same day. And also to purvey three gallons of good ale for the convent every week in Lent, and to have one gallon of red wine for the convent on Easter eve; and also to purvey three carcasses of mutton for the convent for the pittance of William Dune; and also to purvey for every lady of the convent and the five doubles, to every lady and double half a goose delivered at the feast of the Assumption of Our Lady.

Egg money:

And also she must pay to thirty-seven ladies of the convent for their egg money from Michaelmas until All Hallow's day, to every lady each week, 1½d; and then to every lady each week from All Hallow's day until Advent, 1¾d; and then to every lady each week from Advent Sunday until Childermas day, 1¼d; and then to every lady for the same egg money each week from Childermas day to Ash Wednesday, 1¾d; and then from Easter to Michaelmas, to every lady each week, 1½d.

55 I.e. for distribution to the poor.
56 A broth seasoned with herbs.

And then she must pay to each lady for the egg money for each vigil[57] falling within the year, ½d And then she must pay to the convent each week in the year, except Lent, thirty-two eggs, or else 2¾d in money for them every week, except the four weeks in Advent, when she shall pay only sixteen eggs each week. And also she must pay to the convent for every vigil falling within the year eight eggs, or else ½d and half ¼d, and the fourth part of ¼d in money for the same.

Butter:

And then she must purvey for the feast-butter of St Ethelburga for thirty-seven ladies, and the four doubles (that is, to the prioress, the two cellaresses and the kitchener), to every lady and double one portion, every dish containing three portions. And then she must pay to the ladies and doubles for their store butter five times per year, that is to say, in Advent, and three times after Christmas, to each lady and double at every time, ½d; and also she must purvey for the ladies and doubles for the feast-butter at Easter and Whitsun, the same as she did at St Ethelburga's-tide. Also she must purvey for the ladies of the convent, and the four doubles, and the convent for their fortnight butter from Trinity Sunday to Holy Rood day, that is to say, to every lady, double, and convent, at each fortnight between the said two feasts one portion of butter, three portions making a dish. And also she must purvey to the ladies with their doubles for the feast-butter of the Assumption of our Lady, to every lady and double one portion of butter.

The hiring of pasture:

And then she must be sure of pasture for her oxen at the appropriate time of year, as her servants can inform her.

Mowing and making hay:

And also to see that her hay is mown, and made at the appropriate time of the year, as the season requires.

The costs of repairs:

And then she must see that all kinds of houses within her office are sufficiently repaired both outside at her farms and manors, and within the monastery …

---

57 The evening before a feast-day, when the services for the celebration would begin.

## 11. The role and status of the monastic superior: the Barnwell Observances

The customary of the medium-sized Augustinian priory of Barnwell (near Cambridge), written in the late thirteenth century, provides an account of the roles and responsibilities of different monastic officers, including the house's prior. The activities and lifestyle of the monastic superior are illuminated in several other documents in this collection, including **1, 13–14, 22, 26, 33–4, 40, 53–4**.

Translated from *The Observances in Use at the Augustinian Priory of St Giles and St Andrew at Barnwell, Cambridgeshire*, ed. J. W. Clark (Cambridge, 1897), 36–43, 50–1 (Latin).

### Chapter 6. Concerning the reverence due to the prelate

… The prelate therefore should in all places be honoured by everyone with the utmost reverence. Accordingly in the first chapter that he shall hold after he has been installed, all the obedientiaries, lying prostrate, should place their keys at his feet. He shall order them that they take them up again until he has more fully investigated whether anyone ought to be removed from their obediences or to be changed. In whatever place the prelate may be, whether standing or sitting, except in the dormitory, none should pass before him without bowing reverently. If the brethren are seated anywhere and he arrives, they ought to rise and not sit until he himself sits down or orders them to sit; wherever he passes before them they should rise and bow, and remain standing until he has passed through, unless they are writing or occupied with such works. Then while sitting, they shall humbly bow to him from their seats.

In chapter, when he is passing through the midst of the convent, they should rise and bow, and stand until he sits. If, however, they are facing downwards when he enters, that bow is sufficient. Whoever brings him a book or anything else should bow. If in the church or the chapter house anyone places in his hand or receives from him a holy water sprinkler or a censer, a seal, a letter, a vestment, a cruet of wine or water or any other such thing pertaining to divine service, he ought to kiss his hand. If anyone wishes to communicate anything secret to him while he is seated, or ought to hear anything secret from him, he should do it with bended knee unless he is a priest. If anyone ought to kiss him, while he is standing or sitting, he should first bend the knee, and then, wherever he is sitting, raise himself up for his [the abbot's] kiss. No-one, except priests, should presume to sit next to him, but he should sit at his feet, unless ordered that he sit next to him. Then, having bowed, he should sit next to him.

All should also watch that they conduct themselves properly in all their manner of living, especially before him, and never presume to bring forth words contrary to modesty or discipline. If perhaps anyone in speaking has exceeded the limit, and been ordered by him to be silent, by no means should he presume to speak any more.

It should rest to the abbot alone that whenever there are any more serious things to be punished, they should be reserved to his judgement. While he himself is seated he ought to rise to no brother coming to him. Anyone writing or doing any work who is called to him should come without delay. Anyone called to lunch with him should not excuse himself falsely, nor depart after lunch, unless he has received his permission. If there is dispute over any custom, his prescription should be binding.

Whenever he is at Prime or Compline, he says the confession and makes the absolution. At private masses also, if he is present, he does the same; and he who is celebrating the Mass receives the blessing from him before [the reading of] the Gospel.

To him alone, when he eats in the refectory, is it permitted to send out whatever he pleases. No outsider, secular or religious, should be introduced without his permission. When eating outside the refectory, if he sends his charity to any brother, that brother should bow deeply as if he sees the prelate himself present. If anyone else sends this, that brother should send what is bestowed on him to the one presiding in the refectory.

If the prelate wishes to confer an office on anyone, although the brother selected may truly assert his inadequacy, he should not however decline it stubbornly if the prelate persists in his opinion. His command ought to be of such authority to all that no-one should presume to neglect or put off anything he orders, provided that it is not against God. He alone appoints and deposes the obedientiaries. He receives and clothes the novices; he has them professed, and he assigns a master to them, and when their service has been heartily rendered, he absolves them and has them ordained. His name is not written on the table for keeping an entire week in convent.[58]

A graceful vestment should be prepared specially for him for his private Mass, and the altar at which he wishes to celebrate should be adorned

---

58 I.e. as a hebdomadary, the member of the community whose turn it was to officiate in choir and at other services for that particular week.

more gracefully than usual. Moreover, two tapers should burn at his Mass, unless he is celebrating for the dead, and then one should suffice. When he goes forth outside, if it pleases him, he should have carried with him a full set of vestments with all the apparatus necessary for Mass, which is not permitted to the subprior or to any inferior unless perhaps he has been called to bury any friend.

In his presence, no brother should exit the enclosure of the monastery without his permission. Brethren going about within the enclosure either to the granges, the tailor's workroom, the garden, or to the other offices, although having received leave from the subprior, at the prelate's appearance they should bow to him, and to seek permission from him, and to show to him the permission previously obtained.

Therefore, with these and the like reverences, the prelate ought to be honoured with humility by his subjects. However, with fear before God, he should be set beneath their feet.

### Chapter 9: How the prelate is to be reproached if he transgresses

It is certain that prelates, if they ever do wrong, are worthy of as many deaths as they have set examples of perdition to their subjects. For the higher the station, the greater the fall. If the prelate therefore transgresses in anything, or incurs a stigma which cannot be tolerated or hidden (for which he should not be judged or reproached by his subjects), first he should be secretly and humbly admonished by the more devout brethren concerning his correction, but not reproached or judged. If, having been warned, he neglects to be corrected, he should be admonished again and again in a spirit of humility, and if he is wise and fears God, he will afterwards love more readily those who have been concerned for his salvation. However, just as a more serious fault should not easily be believed of a prelate nor rashly alleged against him, thus, when it is certain, it should by no means be tolerated. In this case, therefore, what cannot be amended by his subjects, ought to be referred to the pope or the bishop.

# IV: BUILDINGS AND ADORNMENT

The late medieval period is not renowned as a great age of monastic building, with far more investment ploughed in these years into parish churches. Nevertheless, surviving remains, archaeological excavation and documentary sources indicate that the construction and adornment of monastic buildings continued apace over the later middle ages. This section illustrates the kinds of projects commonly undertaken in monasteries of different sizes, their cost and something of the impression they made on contemporaries. For further material relating to monastic building, see in particular **4, 35, 40, 52**.

## 12. The buildings of Wilberfoss Priory, *c.* 1539

This description of the site of Wilberfoss Priory was produced around the time of the nunnery's dissolution in August 1539, and is preserved alongside a list of the Yorkshire priory's eleven nuns, their pensions and a survey of their lands (valued at only £21 16s 10d in 1535). Although little is recorded about the use or contents of the buildings described, a clear picture of the nuns' material surroundings emerges.

Translated from W. Brown, 'Description of the buildings of twelve small Yorkshire priories at the Reformation', *Yorkshire Archaeological Journal*, 9 (1886), 204–6 (English).

The church contains in length sixty feet and in breadth twenty-two feet within, and it is ceiled above with good substantial boards, and covered with slates. It has sixteen good stalls in the choir for the nuns, and the high altar with a fair new altar covering, all gilded, which contains by estimation ten pounds, two altars in the choir and one beneath, and nine glass windows containing by estimation seventy feet of glass.

Memorandum that the parish church is adjoining to the nunnery church at the lower end.

Also the cloister on the north side of the church contains in length sixty feet square, and in width six feet without any glass, and there are chambers over three parts of it, with the fourth part covered with slates.

Also the chapter house in the east part of the cloister is newly made, twenty feet long and sixteen feet wide, ceiled above and plastered, and with good substantial timber walls, white-limed, and a glass window containing eight feet of glass.

Also the milk house, twelve feet long and eight feet wide, and timber walls without glass.

Also another little chamber or storehouse, eight feet square.

Also the gile-house[59] eight feet square, without glass, timber walls.

Also a fair new chamber over the chapter house, twenty feet long and sixteen feet wide, good substantial timber walls, ceiled and plastered above; a bare glazed window, containing twelve feet of glass and covered with slates; a chimney.

Also a little closet by the same chamber in order to look into the church to hear divine service.

Also the dormitory over the chapter house and cloister and elsewhere [blank] feet long, [blank] feet wide, timber walls, covered with slates. Also the kitchen in the north-east corner of the cloister, seven feet square, with a chimney, timber walls, and covered with slates.

Also one new larder house by the kitchen under the granary, fourteen feet long and nine feet wide, timber walls.

Also another inner larder house, fourteen feet long and eleven feet wide, with new timber walls, white-limed and under the granary.

Also the low hall in the north part of the cloister, twenty-four feet long and eighteen feet wide, timber walls without any glass.

Also a buttery eighteen feet long and eight feet wide.

Also a fair new chamber over the hall, thirty feet long and twenty-one feet wide, well ceiled and plastered above and covered with slates, two glazed bay windows containing twenty-four feet of glass, and a chimney.

Also a little buttery by the same chamber.

Also a low parlour in the north-west corner of the cloister, sixteen feet square, with a glazed bay window containing twelve feet of glass, a chimney, the floor boarded, ceiled above and plastered and painted, and timber walls.

Also a little buttery by the same parlour.

Also another buttery at another side of the same parlour.

---

59 A room for the fermentation of wort (similar to a brewhouse).

Also a little kitchen by the said parlour with a fair chimney.

Also a chamber over the said parlour, sixteen feet square, ceiled and plastered above, covered with slates, a glazed bay window containing six feet of glass, and a chimney.

Also another chamber by this chamber, sixteen feet long and twelve feet wide, ceiled above and covered with slates.

Also another chamber over the west part of the cloister, sixteen feet long and twelve feet wide, covered with slates, timber walls, without glass.

Also three other chambers over the west part of the cloister, covered with slates, without glass.

Also three little houses under the same chambers, to lay wood in.

Memorandum that all the said houses are about the cloister.

Also the new granary by the great kitchen in the east part of the inner court, forty-four feet long and fifteen feet wide, timber walls, white-limed, and covered with slates.

Also a workhouse and a storehouse under the same granary, besides two larder houses, timber walls.

Also the bakehouse in the north part of the court, twenty feet long and sixteen feet wide, timber houses covered with slates.

Also a little bulting-house[60] by the same bakehouse.

Also a poultry house sixteen feet long and ten feet wide.

Also a granary over the same poultry house, eighteen feet long and sixteen feet wide, covered with slates.

Also a new parlour on the west part of the court, twenty-four feet long and sixteen feet wide, a chimney, timber walls, a glazed bay window containing [blank] feet of glass, and ceiled above.

Also two chambers over the same parlour with one chimney, one glass window of ten feet of glass, and covered with tiles.

Also the priest's chamber outside the gates, twenty feet long and twelve feet wide, daubed walls, covered with thatch.

Also an ox-house and two stables under one whole roof, seventy feet long and sixteen feet wide, daubed walls, covered with thatch.

Also an old swine-cote, twelve feet long and eight feet wide, broken

60 A building used for the sifting of flour.

walls, covered with thatch, decayed.

Also a corn barn, ninety-six feet long and eighteen feet wide, daubed walls, covered with thatch.

Also an old barn to lay turfs in, twenty-four feet long and twenty feet wide, broken walls, covered with thatch, decayed.

Also a dovecote, ten feet square, mud walls, covered with thatch.

Also a kiln house,[61] sixteen feet long and ten feet wide, daubed walls, covered with thatch.

Also an orchard where the dovecote stands.

An acre and a half, full of ash trees.

Also gardens.


## 13. Construction and adornment at St Albans Abbey, 1420–40

The great Benedictine abbey of St Albans (Hertfordshire) is one of the best documented of all English monasteries, thanks to its long and rich tradition of chronicle writing. This document is taken from the lengthy account of the rule of Abbot John Whethamstede (1420–40, 1452–65), and details (apparently in the abbot's own words) his material legacy to the community – and its cost – during his first abbacy. Another version of the document survives, itemising Whethamstede's expenditure more fully, and this is the source of the additional notes provided.

Translated from *Annales Monasterii S. Albani, a Johanne Amundesham, monacho*, ed. H. T. Riley, 2 vols, Rolls Series, 28.5 (1870–71), II, 197–200 (Latin).


Firstly, therefore, that abbot, so that he might begin from the sanctuary of the Lord, caused the chapel of the Blessed Virgin to be painted anew; and on its painting and various other ornamentations he spent over £40.

Also in the church, he built anew a certain little chapel against the shrine [of St Alban]; on whose building and fine adornment for the celebration of Mass, he is read to have spent more than £74.

Also, in the church, in the western part of the choir, he built a certain new wooden construction for the reading of the Gospel; on whose building he is read to have set out over the sum of £43.


61 A building containing a furnace or oven for burning, baking or drying.

Also, he caused four large graduals[62] to be made in the same choir; on whose making he spent over the sum of £20.

Also, for the making, or writing, of a certain large antiphoner[63] for the same choir, newly made by the brethren in his time, he contributed over the sum of £4.

Also he caused a certain suitably dignified pair of organs to be newly made for the same choir; on whose making he is read to have spent over £17.

Also, for the west end of this church, he caused a certain stone window to be cut in the north parts; on whose cutting and carriage costs he is read to have spent over the sum of £27.

Also, so that his church might stand on the right of its bridegroom [i.e. Christ], just like the other queen in gilded clothing, surrounded by variety,[64] he is read to have spent on copes and chasubles, on fonts, chalices and censers, on the mitre and crozier,[65] and various other ornaments for the same church, over £640.[66]

Also, that abbot in his time endeavoured to have dignified windows newly made on either side in the church; for whose making he himself is read to have bestowed over the sum of £10.

Also, he caused entirely new chambers to be made for the sick in the infirmary; on whose making, together with the repair of the chapel there, he is said to have spent over the sum of £564.

Also, he caused to be made there that dignified chamber which extends from the said chapel up to that passage which leads from the conventual kitchen to the prior's chamber; and on its making he spent nearly £300.[67]

Also, within the refectory and the oriel,[68] he spent on plate and salt-cellars, on one maple-wood cup and six spoons, over £26.

---

62 A service book containing antiphons, i.e. short passages sung alternately by both sides of the choir, for Mass.

63 A service book containing antiphons for divine service.

64 A reference to the heavenly queen of Psalms xlv. 9, generally associated in the middle ages with the Virgin Mary.

65 The hat and staff of a bishop, also permitted to 'mitred' abbots by papal grant.

66 Over £500 of this sum was devoted to the purchase of lavish suits of vestments for the community's worship.

67 Built for the abbot's hospitality, and specifically for the visit of the king.

68 A dining room in which (unlike the conventual refectory) meat could be eaten.

Also, within the conventual guest-house, for its improvement and adornment, he spent on three coverlets for the beds there over the sum of 5 marks.

Also, on the abbot's part,[69] on various repairs made there, as – consider – on the improvement of the chamber situated between the [abbot's] chapel and hall, on the renovation of the gallery which leads from that chamber to the hall, on the enlarging of the abbot's study, on the strengthening of the wardrobe, and on the extending of the inner court, he spent over the sum of £126.

Also, within the wardrobe there, on basins, plate and ewers, and on pots, spoons, and salt-cellars, he spent nearly £100.

Also, within the abbot's chapel he caused one new pontifical[70] to be made for the use of the abbot himself, on whose making he spent over the sum of 7 marks.

Also, within the town of St Albans, in various repairs made there, as – consider – on the renovation of the stone gate situated there opposite the Great Cross, on the building of six tenements in the wine market, and on three others newly built opposite the Great Gate, together with three others situated in Fishpool Street, he is said to have spent over the sum of £565.[71]

Also, within the manors, on various repairs made there, as – consider – on two barns and one dovecote newly built at Winslow; on a third barn, and one large building for putting malt in, newly built at Newnham; on a fourth barn, and the other building for putting horses in, built at Leggats; on a fifth barn, built at St Machutus; on a sixth barn, and the other building for putting cows in, newly built at Harpesfield; on a seventh barn newly built at Newland Squillers, together with various other repairs made at Tyttenhanger, Threehouses, Radwell, Rickmansworth, and elsewhere, the said abbot spent over the sum of £580 from his own purse, beyond the expenses on various other small repairs made by him on either side, and beyond that which was spent by his officials in their offices, on useful and necessary repairs to those offices.

Also, in the city of London, on various repairs made there, as – consider – on the improvement of the [abbot's] hostel there, and on the repair

---

69 I.e. the property and buildings of the monastery set aside for the abbot, as opposed to that accorded to the convent.

70 A service book containing the ceremonies performed by a bishop.

71 The new gate and the set of new tenements in the wine market each cost over £240.

made on a certain brewery, situated in Aldersgate Street, he is said to have spent over the sum of £85.

Also, at Oxford,[72] on various repairs made there, as – consider – on the making of one library for the order, and on the building of a certain little chapel for the future students of the monastery there, together with a close around its garden, he spent over the sum of £108.

Also, at Redbourn,[73] on various repairs made there, as – consider – on the close of the outer court, on the fine adornment of the chapel, on the improvement of the altars, and on the aid spent on the making of a chamber built over the nave of the church, and for the renovation of the kitchen, together with various ornaments bestowed on this place, he is believed to have spent over the sum of £40.

## 14. Building at late medieval Glastonbury Abbey

The antiquarian John Leland journeyed around England in the 1530s and early 1540s, describing the main sites he visited and often including miscellaneous information gleaned during his travels. His description of the very wealthy Benedictine abbey of Glastonbury in Somerset is one of his fullest, and includes the following account of the main building works carried out by the monastery's late medieval abbots, both within the abbey precinct and on their country retreats.

Translated from *The Itinerary of John Leland in or about the Years 1535–1543*, ed. L. Toulmin Smith, 5 vols (London, 1907–10), I, 289–90 (English).

Walter [sic] Fromond, abbot [Geoffrey Fromond, 1303/4–22], began the great hall. Walter Monyngton, the next abbot to him [1342–75], finished it.

Walter Monyngton made the chapter house to the middle part.

John Chinnock, abbot [1375–1420], his successor, completed it, and is buried there in a tomb with an alabaster image.

This John Chinnock built the cloister, the dormitory and the refectory.

Abbot Adam [of Sodbury, 1323–34] gave seven great bells.

Richard Bere, abbot [1494–1525], built the new lodging by the great chamber, called the king's lodging, in the gallery.

---

72 I.e. at Gloucester College, the general house of studies of the Benedictine Order in Oxford.

73 A daughter house of St Albans, used for the monks' recreation.

Bere built the new lodgings for the secular priests and clerks of Our Lady.[74]

Abbot Bere built [King] Edgar's chapel at the east end of the church. But Abbot Whiting [1525–39] completed some part of it.

Bere arched on both sides the east part of the church that had begun to cast out.

There are six goodly windows in the top of each side of the east part of the church. There were four of old time, with two since added, and the presbytery lengthened by Walter Monyngton, abbot.

Bere made the vault of the steeple in the transept, and underneath two arches like St Andrew's cross,[75] or else it would have fallen.

Bere made a rich altar of silver and gilt, and set it before the high altar.

Bere, coming from his embassy out of Italy made a chapel of Our Lady of Loreto,[76] joining to the north side of the body of the church.

He made the chapel of the [holy] sepulchre in the south end of the nave of the church, by which he is buried under a flat marble in the south aisle of the body of the church.

He made an almshouse in the north part of the abbey for seven or ten poor women with a chapel.

He made also the manor place at Sharpham in the park, two miles west of Glastonbury: it was before a poor lodge.

Wyrrall Park lies close to Glastonbury to the west.

Northwood Park a mile to the east of Glastonbury. John Selwood [1456–93], abbot, built a place there.

Pilton Park about six miles from Glastonbury to the east. John Chinnock, abbot, built a manor place there.

Weston, a little manor place [ ... ] mile west of Glastonbury.

Meare, a fair old manor place, two miles from Glastonbury to the north.

South Damerham, a mean manor place seven miles west-south-west from Salisbury in Wiltshire.

74 Employed to sing the Lady Mass and other services [cf. **20**].

75 A reference to the scissor arches at nearby Wells Cathedral.

76 A replica of the Holy House of Loreto, a shrine believed to be the cottage in Nazareth in which Christ grew up, transported to Loreto in Italy by angels.

East Brent, ten miles north-north-west from Glastonbury, a fair manor place.

Sturminster Newton castle in Dorset, four miles from Shaftesbury. [King] Edmund Ironside gave it to Glastonbury.

## 15. A Venetian observer's impressions of English monasteries, c. 1500

The well-known account of a Venetian traveller's description of England around the turn of the sixteenth century includes the following passage (often quoted, but rarely cited in full) about English monasteries and their material splendour. The identity of the author is unknown, but it is likely that he was a nobleman in the company of the Venetian ambassador.

Translation taken from *A Relation; or rather a True Account of the Island of England ... about the Year 1500*, ed. C. Sneyd, Camden Society, old series, 37 (1847), 29–31, 40–1 (Italian).

But above all are their [the English's] riches displayed in the church treasures; for there is not a parish church in the kingdom so mean as not to possess crucifixes, candlesticks, censers, patens, and cups of silver; nor is there a convent of mendicant friars so poor, as not to have all these same articles in silver, besides many other ornaments worthy of a cathedral church in the same metal. Your Magnificence may therefore imagine what the decorations of these enormously rich Benedictine, Carthusian, and Cistercian monasteries must be. These are, indeed, more like baronial palaces than religious houses, as your Magnificence may have perceived at that of St Thomas of Canterbury.[77] And I have been informed that amongst other things, many of these monasteries possess unicorn's horns, of an extraordinary size. I have also been told that they have some splendid tombs of English saints, such as St Oswald, St Edmund and St Edward, all kings and martyrs. I saw, one day, being with your Magnificence at Westminster, a place out of London, the tomb of the saint king Edward the Confessor, in the church of the aforesaid place Westminster; and indeed, neither St Martin of Tours, a church in France, which I have heard is one of the richest in existence, nor any thing else that I have ever seen, can be put into any sort of comparison with it. But the magnificence of the tomb of St Thomas [Becket] the Martyr, archbishop of Canterbury, is that which surpasses all belief. This, notwithstanding its great size, is

---

77 I.e. Canterbury Cathedral Priory.

entirely covered over with plates of pure gold; but the gold is scarcely visible from the variety of precious stones with which it is studded, such as sapphires, diamonds, rubies, balas-rubies, and emeralds; and on every side that the eye turns, something more beautiful than the other appears. And these beauties of nature are enhanced by human skill, for the gold is carved and engraved in beautiful designs, both large and small, and agates, jaspers and cornelians[78] set in relief, some of the cameos[79] being of such a size, that I do not dare to mention it: but every thing is left far behind by a ruby, not larger than a man's thumb-nail, which is set to the right of the altar. The church is rather dark, and particularly so where the shrine is placed, and when we went to see it the sun was nearly gone down, and the weather was cloudy; yet I saw that ruby as well as if I had it in my hand; they say that it was the gift of a king of France ...

Although the church of England is so rich, there are not more than two archbishops, Canterbury and York. In the province of the former, there are thirteen English and four Welsh bishops; in that of the latter, only two. But the number of religious houses in England, both for men and women, is prodigious, and the greater proportion are of royal foundation. Nor can I omit to mention here, that in the diocese of Bath there are two convents, not above twelve miles distant from each other; the one for monks, named Glastonbury, and the other for nuns, named Shaftesbury, both of the order of St Benedict. The abbot of the former has an annual income of more than 25,000 crowns, and the abbess of the other above 10,000; and the English say amongst themselves that 'the finest match that could be made in all England, would be between that abbot and abbess'! However, there are few of the monasteries of England that send to Rome for their Bulls ...

78  A reddish-white quartz.
79  A jewel with two layers of different colours.

# V: REFORM AND VISITATION

Monastic observance evolved over the later middle ages, moving away from earlier practice in a number of ways. In part, this reflected a conscious decision to 'modernise', as with the Cistercian Order's modification of the isolationism of its founding fathers. This tendency brought some opposition, and both Henry V and Cardinal Wolsey sought (unsuccessfully) to impose a return to older practices in the later middle ages.[80] More regular initiatives for the reform of individual houses took place in the form of visitations, inspections conducted by bishops and internal visitors of each order. A large number of visitation reports survive, giving the most vivid picture of late medieval monastic life – warts and all – that we have. For further perspectives on monastic reform and observance, see for example **20**, **48**, **51**, **55**.

## 16. The Cistercians and women: access to Kirkstall Abbey church

Although the early statutes of the order forbade women from entering male Cistercian monasteries for any reason, the late medieval Cistercians were more closely integrated with their lay neighbours. The following letter, concerning female access to the monastic church, was written by the abbot of Fountains to the abbot of his daughter house of Kirkstall in Yorkshire.

Translated from *Memorials of the Abbey of St Mary of Fountains*, ed. J. Walbran and J. Fowler, 3 vols, Surtees Society, 42, 67, 130 (1863–1918), I, 205–6 (Latin).

To all whom these present letters shall reach, Brother Robert, abbot of the monastery of the Blessed Mary of Fountains, the father abbot of the monastery of the Blessed Mary of Kirkstall, having full jurisdiction in the same house, sends greeting and trusting faith in the underwritten. Although by the institutes of our order, the entry of women within the precinct of the abbeys of the aforesaid order is prohibited under severe penalties, we however – unhesitatingly seeking the salvation of souls, of both the men and women who happen to visit the church of the monastery of Kirkstall in person on certain days in the year, as has been inserted more plainly in certain indulgences granted by Pope Boniface

---

80 For a translation of Henry V's 1421 statutes for Benedictine reform, see Myers, ed. (1969), 787–90.

IX – wish to tolerate for a time the entry of women on prescribed days, to the said church only. On the condition, however, that they are introduced to no other buildings within the precinct of the monastery, either by the abbot or by any monk of the monastery, under the penalties appointed in the institutes of the order. These penalties we wish and determine to uphold irrevocably by the present letters, for the abbot and the monks of the monastery alike, if they are found guilty in the aforementioned matters. In witness of all of which, we affix our seal to the present letters. Given at our monastery of Fountains, the 5th day of March, AD 1402.

## 17. The Benedictine response to the proposed reforms of Cardinal Wolsey, 1520

One hundred years after Henry V's abortive attempts to return the Benedictines to a closer observance of their Rule, Cardinal Wolsey sought to make similar reforms. The statutes presented to the Benedictine Order in November 1519 are not extant, although we do have Wolsey's contemporaneous ordinances for the reform of the Augustinian canons which propose only moderate changes [cf. **20**]. However, the obsequious Benedictine response to Wolsey's statutes, composed during the chapter meeting either of November 1519 or February 1520, does survive; and it indicates unambiguously the black monks' attitude to the prospect of turning back the clock.

Translated from *Documents Illustrating the Activities of the General and Provincial Chapters of the English Black Monks, 1215–1540*, ed. W. A. Pantin, 3 vols, Camden Society, 3rd series, 45, 47, 54 (1931–37), III, 123–4 (Latin).

Most reverend father in Christ and lord, deservedly worthy of deference, we have read with all due reverence the little book of statutes for the order of the holy father Benedict, from start to finish, presented to us by your holy lordship the previous week. Although we perceived in this many things which are to be embraced by good monks with all enthusiasm and delight of mind, some however occurred in the course of reading which seemed to us to be of greater austerity than can be observed by monks in this unhappy age of ours. Without doubt, so great a number of monks are contained in England, and so great and so abundant are their monasteries and sites, that it would be an altogether difficult deed (at least by human diligence) that such a multitude may suddenly be recalled to the austerity of regular observance, without murmur and a great rebellion of spirit. For that reason we – humble and most unworthy ministers of the same order, most devoted dependants and most obedient sons of your most holy fatherhood – falling down at your holy knees with all prayers, seek most entreatingly and beg, that your most clement lordship will turn the eyes of your accustomed piety and compassion to us and our aforesaid order kindly and with mercy; so that by your holy and most wise diligence, by your divine ability so much greater than that of other men, and finally by your most super-abundant wisdom, everything in this future reformation of the monks may be modified; and thus the hard and more difficult things may be taken in hand, so that the weak monks of our religion may not be turned to flight and apostasy, nor suddenly rise up against their pastors by any diabolical impulse (which God forbid), nor also those who have decided to enter our order either shrink from excessive austerity and rigour, or flee the same religion.

Because it is beyond doubt that if everything in the reformation of the order should tend to excessive austerity and rigour, we should not have the monks (at least not a decent and sufficient number) to inhabit so many and so great monasteries of our order. For if there were in England as many monasteries either of the sacred order of the Carthusians, or of the order of St Bridget, or of the Friars Minor of the Observance, as there are monasteries of Benedictine monks, certainly we do not see from where could be gathered such a multitude, that their sites could be sustained by them. Since in this our age (with the world now drawing to its close), those who seek austerity of life and regular observance are very few and very rare. Whatever we have said in these matters, most holy father, we do not say because we could suggest anything needing to be done that was not before sufficiently foreseen, and sufficiently recognised, by your holy lordship; but rather, stirred by our disposition, we have plainly disclosed how greatly we require the consolation and the help of your most reverend lordship in all these things. To whom, most holy father and lord, deservedly worthy of deference, we commend us all and all our need, with all the humility, obedience and reverence that we shall be able to offer so holy a father, always and in supplication, with our perpetual services and prayers.

Most faithful intercessors for your perpetual salvation, the humble dependants and most unworthy ministers of the order of black monks in England, now assembled in London by your command.

## 18. The visitation of St Helen's Bishopsgate, 1439

Late medieval visitation records survive in large numbers from houses of all sizes. This example, relating to a medium-sized London nunnery, lists the injunctions thought necessary for reform by the external visitor, following his inspection of the convent. It is revealing not only about the state of religion in the monastery, but also about the ecclesiastical authorities' attitudes to female monasteries in fifteenth-century England.

Translated (with minor corrections of transcription from British Library, Cotton Charter V. 6) from W. Dugdale, *Monasticon Anglicanum*, ed. J. Caley, H. Ellis and B. Bandinel (London, 1846), IV, 553–4 (English).

Reginald Kentwood, dean, and the chapter of the church of St Paul's [Cathedral, London], to the religious women, prioress and convent of the priory of St Helen's of our patronage and immediate jurisdiction, and every nun of the said priory: greeting in God, with desire of religious observances and devotion. Forasmuch as in our ordinary visitation in your priory, both in the head and in the members, recently exercised, we have found many defaults and excesses which need manifest correction and reformation; we, willing virtue to be cherished and holy religion to be kept, as in the rule of your order, ordain and make certain ordinances and injunctions, which we send you, written and sealed under our common seal, to be kept in the form that they have been specified and written to you.

First, we ordain and enjoin you, that divine service is done by you duly, night and day; and silence duly kept in due time and place, according to the observance of your religion.

Also we ordain and enjoin you, prioress and convent, and each of you individually, that you make due and full confession to the confessor assigned by us.

Also we enjoin you, prioress and convent, that you ordain a convenient place for an infirmary, in which your sick sisters may be honestly kept and relieved with the costs and expenses of your house accustomed in your religion during the time of their sickness.

Also we enjoin you, prioress, that you keep to your dormitory, and lie there at night, according to the observance of your religion, unless it is the case that the law and the observance of your religion allow you to do the contrary.

Also we ordain and enjoin you, prioress and convent, that no secular person is locked within the bounds of the cloister [i.e. at night], and that no secular person come within after the Compline bell, except female servants and girl pupils. Also that you admit no women lodgers without our licence.

Also we ordain and enjoin you, prioress and convent, that neither you nor any of your sisters use or haunt any place within the priory by which evil suspicion or slander might arise. These places, for certain reasons that move us, we do not write about here in our present injunction, but will notify to you, prioress; nor should you have any means of looking or seeing outward, by which you might fall into worldly affection.

Also we ordain and enjoin you, prioress and convent, that some sober and discreet woman of the said religion, honest and of good name, be assigned to the shutting of the cloister doors and keeping the keys, so that no person may have entry or issue into the place after the Compline bell, or at any other time, by which the place may be slandered in the future.

Also we ordain and enjoin you, prioress and convent, that no secular women sleep at night within the dormitory, without a special grant given in the chapter house, among you all.

Also we ordain and enjoin you, that none of you speak or commune with any secular person, or send or receive letters, missives or gifts from any secular person, without licence of the prioress; and that there should be another of your sisters present, assigned by the prioress to hear and record the honesty of both parties in such communication. And such letters or gifts sent or received may thus turn into honesty and worship, and not into villainy, or slander of your honesty and religion.

Also we ordain and enjoin you, prioress and convent, that none of your sisters should be admitted to any office, except those who are of good name and reputation.

Also we ordain and enjoin you that you ordain and choose one of your sisters, honest, able and knowledgeable in discretion, who can, may and shall have the charge of the teaching and instruction of your sisters who are ignorant, in order to teach them their service and the rule of their religion.

Also, forasmuch that various perpetual fees, corrodies[81] and liveries have been granted before this time to various officers of your house and other persons, which have hurt the house, and because of dilapidation

81 See above, p. 87 n. 13.

of the goods of your house, we ordain and enjoin you that you receive no officer to a perpetual fee of office,[82] or grant any annuity, corrody or livery, without special assent from us.

Also we enjoin you that all dancing and revelling should be utterly given up among you, except at Christmas and other honest times of recreation used among yourselves, in the absence of seculars in all respects.

Also we enjoin you, prioress, that there may be a door at the nuns' choir, so that no strangers may look on them, nor they on the strangers when they are at divine service.[83] Also we ordain and enjoin you, prioress, that there should be made a hatch of suitable height, crested with spikes of iron, before the entry of your kitchen, so that no strange people may enter, with certain latchkeys provided by you and by your steward to such persons that you and he think honest and suitable.

Also we enjoin you, prioress, that no nuns have any keys for the postern door that goes out of the cloister into the churchyard except the prioress, for there is much coming in and out at unlawful times.

Also we ordain and enjoin that no nun has or receives any children with them into the house, unless the profit of the board turns to the aid of the house.

These ordinances and injunctions and each of them, as they are rehearsed above, we send to you, prioress and convent, charging and commanding you, and each of you all, to keep them truly and wholly in virtue of obedience and upon pain of contempt; and that you cause them to be read and declared four times a year in your chapel before you, so that they may be had in mind and kept, under pain of excommunication and other lawful punishments to be given to the person of you, prioress, and to individual persons of the convent, which we intend to use against you if you disobey us. Reserving to us and our successors the power to change, declare, add and diminish these aforesaid ordinances and injunctions, and to dispense with them, as often as the case requires and it is needful. In witness of which we set our common seal, given in our chapter house the 21st day of the month of June, the year of Our Lord 1439 ...

82  I.e. a hereditary grant of office.

83  The church of St Helen's Bishopsgate was shared between the nunnery and the parish: cf. **12**.

## 19. The visitations of Cockersand Abbey, April and December 1488

Exempt from the jurisdiction of the bishop, the Premonstratensian Order operated their own system of inspection. These two visitations of the abbey of Cockersand (Lancashire) were made by the commissary-general of the order, the abbot of Shap, Richard Redman. Redman's injunctions exhibit a willingness to praise as well as chide, unusual in visitation records, and so provide a more rounded impression of observance in the house.

Translated (with corrections of transcription from Oxford, Bodleian Library, MS Ashmole 1519, provided by Brother Anselm Gribbin) from *Collectanea Anglo-Praemonstratensia*, ed. F. A. Gasquet, 3 vols, Camden Society, 3rd series, 6, 10, 12 (1904–6), II, 114–17 (Latin).

### The visitation of April 1488

The names of the brethren of the monastery of Cockersand of our Premonstratensian Order.

Lord William Bowland, abbot

*Priests:*

Brother Miles Chatburn, prior

Brother John Woddes, subprior

Brother John Bordforde, vicar of Garstang

Brother John Banke, vicar of Mitton

Brother George Lyndisley, warden of the chantry of Tunstall

Brother Hugh Fausett, warden of the chantry of Middleton

Brother John Preston, procurator of Garstang

Brother Matthew Kyrkeby, procurator of Mitton[84]

Brother Thomas Pulton, circator[85]

Brother Robert Syngleton, external provisor[86]

Brother James Skypton, granger and cantor[87]

Brother Henry Staynynge, sacrist

Brother William Bowland

---

84 Apparently companions provided for the vicars of these churches, in accordance with canon law.

85 The official responsible for discipline and regular observance in the house.

86 The official responsible for provisioning the monastery.

87 The official responsible for leading the services in choir (often known as the precentor), assisted by the succentor.

Brother Robert Burton, succentor

Brother Edward Becrofte, sacrist and refectorian

Brother William Bentham, cellarer

*Novices:*

Brother John Lancaster

Brother William Hoton


AD 1488, the 28th day of the month of April, we, Richard etc., taking with us our brother Robert Bedall, prior of our monastery of Shap, have visited the monastery of Cockersand, of our said order, of the diocese of York, just as we are held by our right and by the custom of religion. In this, indeed, we have found there nothing known that was savouring of crime, but a bond of mutual love and charity between head and members happily flourishes, so that we have found nothing at all worthy of our correction or needing to be referred to the general chapter. But we have found everything governed laudably, both in spiritualities and in temporalities, through the most prudent circumspection of the abbot of the same monastery. However, for greater tranquillity and security, we strictly order, on pain of greater excommunication, that no professed canon of the monastery should dare or presume to reveal in any way the confidential matters of our order or the counsels of the brethren or servants of the monastery to magnates, lords or any other secular persons; or to engage them by entreaty or payment, so that through them they [the canons] might be advanced to any offices or other dignities. Nor should anyone presume themselves to be suitable for any internal or external office, except those whom the abbot has acknowledged to be worthy for such by his discretion.

And we order all officers that they should assemble for divine service as much as they are able. But chiefly we enjoin more strictly and order the brethren, both seniors and juniors, who are not deputed to exterior offices by the abbot, that they should be present at the Hours both day and night, and also at all the Hours of the Blessed Mary day and night; and sing them right through most devoutly together, running about nowhere at that time nor wandering anywhere, on pain of the greatest contempt. And if, under the same penalty, anyone should ever presume to send across for meats, bread or drink to the officers deputed to the same, or to transfer anywhere at the hour of dinner or supper what has been served up before them, they should be sent away, having discharged the necessity of nature. In order that they should be rendered to the utility and advantage of the monastery, we have also given as a command to the lord abbot that he should receive no-one to the profession of our religion whom he has recognised to be joined by affinity or consanguinity.[88] We order, moreover, by the authority of the lord of Prémontré that the feast of St Margaret the Virgin should in future be venerably celebrated as a double feast, as a virgin and martyr, in perpetuity. We excommunicate the apostates[89] John Barton and John Presaw and we declare them excommunicated. We also absolve the other brethren being members of the chapter there from all sentences of law and order, and we declare them absolved in these writings. In the last visitation, the monastery owed nothing, nor indeed do they at the present; in produce and other necessaries it is excellently provided. Given etc.

And in the same monastery they have consumed in expenses for each week sixteen bushels of wheat and four of flour oats. And twenty-four bushels of malt. And fifty oxen and one hundred and twenty sheep, and they have consumed these things per annum.

## The visitation of December 1488

AD1488, the 17th day of the month of December, we Richard, etc., taking with us our beloved co-brother, Dom Robert Bedall, canon and prior of our monastery of Shap, have visited the monastery of Cocker-sand of our order, of the diocese of York, not by the due course of the revolution of years, but having been requested by frequent entreaties to this, and indeed compelled by the infamy of the places spread every-where. We have found there Brother William Bentham in many ways defamed of a lapse of the flesh with a certain woman, called Margery Gardener. Concerning this, having been accused before us, he did not deny the crime but declared himself guilty, and therefore we have enjoined to him the penalty of more serious guilt of forty days, and to be sent out to the monastery of Croxton for three years.

Brother James Skypton,[90] also detected concerning the same vice, which was charged to him by us with such a woman, Ellen Wilson by name, absolutely denied himself to have carried out that shameful act in any way; but having been summoned he was not able to purge himself

88 I.e. no new recruits should be related to one another or to the existing canons.

89 I.e. canons who have left the monastery without permission.

90 A future abbot of the house, 1502–5.

lawfully by purgation,[91] because none of the brethren wished to stand up to be called to witness to this with him. We therefore impose on him for such wickedness a worthy penance of forty days, and moreover to be sent out for seven years to the monastery of Sulby.

For avoiding such and similar enormities we strictly prohibit drinking after Compline, on pain of fasting for three days on bread and water. And we command more strictly to the lord abbot, and to the other presidents, that they should not license anyone in any way to do this. We strictly prohibit moreover to all the brethren of the church, on pain of contempt, that they should not use white nor especially black pointed hoods. And we order to the prior and the subprior that they should at no time allow women into the infirmary, refectory or the building called the 'Jordan chamber' to carry pots, since through this no little loss and scandal can arise. And the prior of the said monastery, because of the weight of the customs and the weakness of nature, we have completely exonerated from the burden of choir and cloister day and night. It is by no means the case that we have not found further things to be reformed at the present time, which we leave to the wholesome discretion of the abbot. Given, etc.

---

91 The process, according to canon law, by which a defendant proved his innocence, consisting of a denial corroborated by the oaths of several of his peers.

# VI: LITURGY AND SPIRITUALITY

The liturgy – the regular round of services in worship of God – was the core of the monastic life. Numerous liturgical manuscripts survive, mainly from larger houses, detailing for the inmates' benefit how these services should be ordered. The study of liturgical books is a highly complex and specialist field, and as a result this section makes use of more circumstantial evidence to illustrate the importance of the liturgy and some of the ways it was changing in the later middle ages. As the biography of Thomas de la Mare indicates, the liturgy was also an important component in monastic spirituality. This facet of the religious life is not easy to recapture, partly because of the limited and often inaccessible evidence for it, and partly (as emerges below) because monastic spirituality was far from uniform. For further material relating to the liturgy, see in particular **1**, **3**, **19**, **32**, **43**; and for other facets of monastic spirituality, see **3**, **9**.

## 20. The provision for the liturgy of the Augustinian canons: Wolsey's reforming statutes, 1519

Cardinal Wolsey's 1519 statutes for the reform of the Augustinian canons set out to restore certain traditional practices of the order and to remove unwanted innovations. The following chapter on the order's liturgy reflects this concern about novelty, but also indicates that the Augustinians were responding to the most current musical developments in early Tudor England.

Translated from W. Dugdale, *Monasticon Anglicanum*, ed. J. Caley, H. Ellis and B. Bandinel (London, 1846), VI, 851–4 (Latin).

## Concerning the canonical Hours to be sung and heard uniformly and devoutly by all the canons together

We have also determined that each and every regular canon, according to the custom of individual places, should distinctly, plainly and devoutly sing the psalms and the other things pertaining to divine worship, without great haste or too much hesitation, with perfect expression of words, and with a moderate pause after the middle point. Indeed, each and every regular canon who is an obedientiary, besides the prelate, should be devoutly present at all the canonical Hours, especially Matins and High Mass, ceasing from any lawful hindrance, or be subjected to regular discipline if they are elsewhere for a reason which may not be dispensed by their superiors. And since among all churchmen, and especially the religious, that method of singing is deservedly to be approved in which wanton melodies do not flatter the ears of bystanders, nor is the favour of human praise desired in the division of notes [i.e. polyphony], but plain chant and the modest dignity of psalm-singing, with sweet and quiet modulation, incites and invites the souls of the listeners to spiritual delight and the desire for the melodies of heaven; we therefore more strictly prohibit that polyphony, called 'prick-songs' in English, should from now on be sung in the choirs of canons or be permitted to be sung.

We prohibit moreover, that layfolk, or even singers who are secular clerks, whether men or boys, should be admitted in the choir with the canons at the time of divine service to sing psalms in any way. We do permit however that they should be able to perform masses of the Blessed Virgin, or of the name of Jesus and the like – which are accustomed to be solemnly sung outside the conventual choir, as in all the monasteries of this kingdom, by secular men, even laymen and boys – with polyphony, and to be sung with organs: provided that none of the canons, except he who will celebrate this Mass at the altar, is present. We also permit that the canons among themselves, with lay and secular singers excluded, should be able to perform some other melodies beyond the simple and daily chant on Sundays and saints' days and other great solemn feasts, at masses and Vespers and the other divine offices; on the condition that the integrity of the chant and the expression of words is not disregarded. Truly since the continual and immoderate labour of singing not only hurts the voices of those singing psalms, but also weakens their souls for the service of God (especially since in some monasteries of this realm the canons are few, and sometimes three or more sung masses, over and above the canonical Hours, are to be celebrated every day); for this reason we, sympathising with their labours in this regard, do not deny that in all those monasteries they should be able to use the melodies of organs in their choirs and elsewhere for their relief, and that they should be able to retain in their household for playing these organs some man of honest behaviour, a layman or a secular clerk, provided that he should not mix with the canons with too much familiarity.

## 21. Public liturgy in a monastic church: the Rites of Durham

The Rites of Durham was written in the late sixteenth century by a knowledgeable and sympathetic observer, who may have been employed at Durham
Cathedral Priory around the time of this large Benedictine house's suppression
in 1539. It provides many details about the routine and ceremonial of the monks,
and about the more public side of their liturgy – including, in this section, the
performance of the weekly Jesus Mass in the nave of the cathedral.

Translated from *The Rites of Durham*, ed. J. Fowler, Surtees Society, 107 (1903),
32–4 (English).

In the body of the church, between two of the highest pillars supporting
and holding up the west side of the lantern, over against the choir door,
there was an altar called the Jesus altar where the Jesus Mass was sung
every Friday throughout the whole year. And on the rear side of the
altar there was an attractive high stone wall, and at either end of the
wall there was a door which was locked every night, called the two rood
doors,[92] for the procession to go out and come in at. And between those
two doors the Jesus altar was placed, as is aforesaid, and both ends of the
altar were closed up with fine wainscot, like a porch adjoining both rood
doors, very finely varnished with fine red varnish. And in the wainscot
at the south end of the altar there were four fair cupboards, to lock up
the chalices and silver cruets, with two or three suits of vestments and
other ornaments belonging to the altar for the holy days and principal
feast-days. And at the north end of the altar, in the wainscot, there was
a door to come into the porch, and a lock on it to be locked both day
and night.

Also there was standing on the altar against the aforesaid wall a most
curious and fine table[93] with two parts to open and close again [i.e.
a triptych], with all of the whole Passion of Our Lord Jesus Christ
most richly and skilfully set out in the most lively colours, all like the
burnishing gold, as He was tormented and as He hung on the cross,
which was a most lamentable sight to behold. This table was always
locked up, except only on principal feast-days. Also in the front part of
the porch from one end to the other, there was a door with two broad
parts to open from side to side, all of fine joined and fair carved work.
The height of it was something above a man's breast and at the top of
the door it was all struck full of iron spikes, so that no man should climb

92 The doors in the rood screen which divided the public portion of the church (the
   nave) from the monks' choir and the high altar in the presbytery.
93 A wooden altarpiece.

over ... And on the principal feast-days when any of the monks said Mass at that altar, then the table which stood on the altar was opened, and the door with two parts which stood in the front part of the said closet or porch was set open also, so that every man might come in and see the table in the manner and form aforesaid.

Also there was at the summit of the said wall, from pillar to pillar, the whole story and Passion of Our Lord fashioned in stone, most skilfully and most finely gilt; and also above the said story and Passion was all the whole story and pictures of the twelve Apostles, very ingeniously set out and very finely gilt, continuing from one pillar to the other, fashioned very skilfully and ingeniously in the stone. And at the top above all these stories, from pillar to pillar, was set up a border very ingeniously fashioned in stone with marvellously fine colours, very skilfully and finely gilt with branches and flowers. The more that a man looked at it, the greater his affection to behold it: the work was so finely and skilfully fashioned in the stone that it could not be more finely done in any kind of metal. And also above the height of all upon the wall stood the most handsome and famous rood in all this land, with the image of Mary on one side and the image of John on the other, with two resplendent and glistening archangels, one on the side of Mary and the other on the side of John. So what with the fairness of the wall, the stateliness of the images, and the vividness of the painting, it was thought to be one of the handsomest monuments in that church.

Also on the rear side of the rood, before the choir door, there was a loft, and at the south end of the loft stood the clock; and under the loft by the wall there was a long bench, which reached from the one rood door to the other, where men sat to rest themselves and to say their prayers and hear divine service.

Also every Friday at night, after Evensong was performed in the choir, an anthem was sung in the body of the church before the Jesus altar, called the Jesus anthem. This was sung every Friday at night throughout the whole year by the master of the choristers and the deacons of the church. And when it was done, then the choristers sung another anthem by themselves, kneeling all the time their anthem was sung before the Jesus altar, which was very devoutly sung every Friday at night at the tolling of one of the Galilee bells.[94]

---

94 I.e. the bells in the western end of the church (known at Durham as the Galilee).

## 22. The spirituality and asceticism of Abbot Thomas de la Mare

Thomas de la Mare, abbot of St Albans 1349–96, was the most prominent Benedictine monk of his day, a friend to kings and for many years the president of the provincial chapter of the black monks. This extract from the biography of the abbot, apparently written by his monk-chaplain, provides a rare glimpse of the inner life of a Benedictine monk (albeit a remarkable one) in late medieval England.

Translated from *Gesta Abbatum Monasterii S. Albani*, ed. H. T. Riley, 3 vols, Rolls Series, 28.4 (1867–69), III, 400–3 (Latin).

This abbot, a special lover of divine service, was accustomed to attend this with his convent as often as he properly could, and especially on Sundays and feasts celebrated among the people, retaining from memory the offices pertaining to him and carrying them out with alacrity, and animating and instructing others by his example.

At Mass, indeed, he was neither slow nor hasty, but moderate, tearful and devout; and in the intervals of the Mass, principally celebrated by himself, he either conferred the first tonsure on clerks under his jurisdiction (according to the tenor of his privileges), blessed vestments or was wont to say holy meditations or some other divine service with his chaplains or alone. He busied himself in like manner when going to the church, robing himself or walking abroad or riding, when he was not otherwise occupied with important persons, business or discussions. Indeed he used to observe the time and times of divine service so strictly that he would be hindered by the presence of no temporal lord and the abundance of no worldly business; but in his own time he would perform or prepare for divine service and those things which are proper for religion. In the middle of the night and in the morning he would rise before the convent, and complete Matins, the Hours and masses. Every day he was wont to hear three or four masses and to celebrate first himself masses for the dead, or of St Mary – especially for the dead. In the intervals, he used to ruminate alone either on the psalter or on holy meditations, or chant the seven psalms with the litany, or the fifteen psalms,[95] or the Office of the Dead, alone or with a companion. He used to devote his time to reading or to the orderly arrangement of public affairs and those of the monastery and religion, always busy in these things which are pleasing to God and were useful to his neighbours.

95 I.e. the seven Penitential Psalms and the Gradual Psalms (nos 120–34).

Hawking, hunting and all kinds of games, both public and private, he fled from like poison, and abhorred; so that he would turn his face away from such things and, in the manner of St Martin, permit to go away unharmed hares and birds put to flight by the power of dogs and hawks and flocking to his sanctuary. He had, however, outstanding hunters and hawkers, among both his esquires and his other servants, for supervising his warrens, for capturing harmful beasts and birds, and for giving recreations to his lords and friends. However, he would by no means permit them to practise their art in his presence or permit his monks to be present, except the officers assigned to this. This in fact seemed more difficult for him, but also more meritorious, because when he was a young and secular man, he was well practised in such things, and as if by nature inclined to this pursuit out of custom and his nobility of flesh.[96]

He was also admirable in his abstinence, so that he would never eat until he was full, and would dine rarely, and then moderately; he would often abstain from drinking from dinner of one day to dinner of the next; he would abstain from fish even on Fridays; and he would be content with one kind of fish even on Saturdays. On Wednesdays and Fridays in Lent, he would sit at dinner, eating either a little bread or nothing, but holding his fast until the next day. On the vigils of the feasts of St Mary and St Mary Magdalene, St Katherine, and All Saints, he would enjoy a moderate portion of bread after Vespers. On the vigils of the Passion of St Alban he used to fast on fish; and if, because of the arrival of visiting magnates or the recreation of his co-brethren, he would break his own usual abstinence, he either made up for this afterwards by more severe fasting or made amends with generous almsgiving.

Having prohibited reading aloud at table by monk or clerk, and thus preserving the seriousness of religion, he was cheerful, bountiful and courteous; he used to distribute his tastier delicacies quite abundantly and courteously to guests, strangers and his servants – although he did not permit his alms to be diminished on account of this. And the more sumptuously and abundantly he served them, the more he abstained from food and drink. Being a strict tamer of his flesh, several times twice or more often in the week he summoned a companion to him in a certain place of privacy, and received suitably harsh bodily disciplines; blaming the foolishness and sloth of his giving, if ever he wanted to strike [himself] more mildly. These things seemed slight to him, unless he put on a harsh hairshirt, and mortified the delicate flesh.

96 Thomas de la Mare was related to several noble families.

He was accustomed to taste or snatch sleep in bed with his cowl and footwear taken off, and other garments or cloak put on. He appeared to sit upon soft cushions and warm furs and cloaks, when hard stones and the nettles with which he rubbed down his body were in between. For he never, as was supposed, used to sleep up to the middle of the night, but was often wont to say the entire psalter before the vigils of the convent, as well as his other accustomed prayers contained in books produced by him.

## 23. Carthusian spirituality and sanctity: Dom John Homersley of the London Charterhouse

The Carthusians, more than any other late medieval monastic order, were renowned for their spirituality, following as they did a daily routine based more on contemplative reading and prayer than collective ritual. This account of a venerated monk is taken from the early sixteenth-century register of the London Charterhouse, compiled by an inmate of the house.

Translated from W. St John Hope, *The History of the London Charterhouse from its Foundation until the Suppression of the Monastery* (London, 1925), 82–4 (Latin).

In AD 1393, Dom John Homersley was received into the order in this house of London. And there were also in my time, Dom John Nevyll, Dom Thomas Gorwey and Dom William Hatherley, formerly prior of Hinton, monk-priests and professed of this house, who saw the afore-said John Homersley in the flesh, and each of them much commended his praiseworthy manner of living. And especially, however, the afore-said Thomas Gorwey, who was his novice, was accustomed to recount these things which are written below. Moreover, certain things which the same Thomas Gorwey related about himself, I have also heard from the aforesaid Dom W. Hatherley.

Truly this venerable father Dom John Homersley was a very simple and gentle man, walking without reproach in the way of God's command-ments and of the observances of the Carthusian Order. For he loved his cell and solitude, he closed his mouth from evil things and, so that he would not offend in his tongue, he would speak rarely and briefly even about good things, although he would preach the word of God with his hands. For he was incessantly copying sacred books for the church, for the refectory and for the cell; and, carrying what had been written to the prior's cell, he would not procure that they should be lent to anyone nor placed anywhere, but leaving them there with the prior, he would return to his cell in silence. Soberly contented with the food and clothing of the order, he would drive far from him the desire of all unstable things; and not lightly, but as if under compulsion, would he receive gifts. And if sometimes he had received money or some such thing, through the excessive importunity of the offerer, he would go immediately to the prior's cell and entrust it to him; but if he did not find the prior, he left the money on the ground next to the prior's cell, having placed a tile over it, and not caring any more about it, if it was found.

On a certain occasion, when he was tempted by the spirit of fornication with a vehement ardour of lust, he gravely wounded his own flesh, so that, in the words of the blessed Gregory[97] about St Benedict, 'through wounds of the skin, he might heal the wounds of the mind'. He never forsook the church because of sickness, unless the sickness was so great that he could not walk. Asked from this why he had come into the church when he was sick, he replied thus: 'It is as good for me to be sick in the church as in the cell.' He lived in the cell which Sir W[illiam de Ufford], earl of Suffolk, founded in the eastern range of the cloister,[98] on whose door are the verses beginning with the letter T. Indeed that spiritual man deserved to have various visitations of good spirits, but the servants of darkness also appeared to him, intending to overthrow him with malign temptations; but God, who does not desert those who trust in Him, protected him.

At a certain time, after Compline, the spirits of his father and mother (who had died previously) stood by him unseen, with three other good spirits talking to him about his passing away from this present world to eternal rest; but he, being very pious and afraid, said nothing to them. Moreover, he remembered how a certain of the Fathers had once been deceived in the desert by tricking visions. Satan was also present in a horrible and visible form, having with him the soul of a certain boy, a relative of the same John Homersley who had previously died. For those other blessed spirits and especially the spirit of his mother advised him that he should speak to them, asserting that if he did this they would take the boy's soul with them to heaven, because they had been sent to him to do this. But he remained silent. The Lord and Saviour Jesus Christ then appeared to him, comforting him and advising him to speak, saying, 'Remember, my son, my Passion, and you will have help.' And

97  Pope Gregory the Great (d. 604), who wrote an account of the life and miracles of St Benedict.
98  Cf. below, p. 162.

still he said nothing, his aforesaid enemy standing terribly near the soul of the boy, compelling him to act shamefully before Christ. Then He, our most loving saviour Jesus Christ, merciful and just in all his ways, benignly correcting and not handing over to death this John Homersley, enjoined on him for that taciturnity a perpetual penance: namely, that because he did not dispose himself in the accustomed way to receive the gifts of the Holy Spirit freely offered, he should fast on every vigil of Pentecost on bread and water, and on every Friday he should say a certain prayer of St Augustine. And he faithfully fulfilled these things, even in his last servitude, when it was not permitted to him by the prior to keep the other abstinences of the order.

On a certain occasion when he erred in writing, there appeared to him Our Lady and patron, the mother of God, and with her the spirit of a certain priest previously dead, who while he lived used to supply parchment for writing books to the same John Homersley from his own means. Then our most blessed Lady showed to him his error where he defaulted in writing and sweetly warned that he should amend the book, and then disappeared ...

On a certain night he saw the soul of King Henry V immediately about to enter the kingdom of eternal blessing, having been completely delivered from the places of Purgatory. A certain anchorite of Westminster, enclosed next to the [parish] church of St Margaret, also saw the same vision, which he related to a certain lay brother of our order. Truly the same anchorite agreed in all things with John Homersley himself concerning the hour of the aforesaid deliverance. Hearing of this, the executors of the king caused a silver tomb to be placed over his buried body.

At a certain time, Dom J. Mapulsted of good memory, the third prior of this house [from its foundation], being sick, came to the cell of the aforesaid Dom J. Homersley. When Dom J. Homersley had seen his face, with his sickness swelling up, he warned him reverently that he should provide himself with medicine. The prior replied to him, 'I wish to have no other medicine but your prayers.' And on the following day the prior appeared perfectly healed.

Within a few days after the death of this Dom Jo. Mapulsted, the prior, Dom Thomas Gorwey, came to the cell of the said John Homersley and sought from him whether he knew if the soul of this lord prior had yet been received into everlasting glory. But he answered, no. The same T. Gorwey said to him again, 'How is it that the soul of one who was so holy of life is so far separated from the supreme reward?' And he again replied, 'Truly he was of holy life with regard to himself, but because he did not act perfectly towards his subjects, the door of the heavenly kingdom is not yet open to him.' And he added, 'Sans doute' – for he used to have this for an oath – 'Sans doute', he said, 'he takes to himself a dangerous work, whoever takes up the office of prelate.'

The same J. Homersley was buried according to his desire, at the feet of Dom J. Luscote, the first prior, whose clerk he was before his entry into religion.

## 24. Monastic devotion at Godstow and Missenden

Glimpses of late medieval monastic devotional life are relatively rare, and it is characteristic that the prayers which follow were written on spare pages of fifteenth-century registers recording monastic business. The first two verses are found in the English register of the medium-sized nunnery of Godstow (Oxfordshire), and the remainder from that of Henry Honor, abbot of the Augustinian priory of Missenden in Buckinghamshire (1462–c. 1506). All these verses are characteristic of vernacular religious lyrics popular among the laity in late medieval England, and versions of each can be found in lay collections of devotional material from this period.

Translated from *The English Register of Godstow Nunnery, near Oxford, Written about 1450*, ed. A. Clark, 3 vols, Early English Text Society, 129–30, 142 (1905–11), I, 4–5 (English); and from British Library, Sloane MS 747, fos 46v, 49v, 65v (English).[99]

## (a) Invocation to the cross (Godstow)

> The cross of Jesus Christ be ever our aid,
> And keep us from peril of sins and pain.
> Blessed be that lord who on the cross did bleed,
> Christ, God and man, who for us was slain:
> Dead he was and rose up again.
> Ever help us, cross! with him to arise
> From death to life, and sin to despise.
>
> Gracious cross! now grant us that grace
> To worship him with all our mind,
> In words, in works, and in every place
> Kneeling and kissing you, where we you find.
> Let us never be to him unkind

Mercifully who made us to be men
No more to keep but his commands ten.

O blissful cross! teach us all virtue
Pleasing to God for our salvation,
Quenching all vices in the name of Jesus
Ransom paying for our damnation.
Send us such grace of conversation
That we may ascend and glorified be
Where Christ is king who died on the tree.

Christ, who died on the holy rood!
I pray you, good lord! with all my might,
Send us some part of all your good,
And keep us from evil every day and night,
Continue in your mercy preserving all right.
By the title of your passion make us saved
So to your cross reverence we may have.

## (b) In the name of the Father and Son and Holy Spirit, Amen (Godstow)

In the name of the blessed Trinity
The Father, the Son, and the Holy Ghost,
I make this cross[100] to defend me
From my enemies and their boast.
Bless me, Lord Jesus, that I be not lost,
Through the virtue and grace of this cross holy sign
Whereon you suffered your passion pain.

## (c) Missenden register, fo. 46v

Jesus, for your Holy Name
And for your bitter passion
Save me from sin and shame
And endless damnation

Five Pater Nosters, five Ave Marias and a Credo. 5,000 days of pardon.[101]

---

100 I.e. the sign of the cross.

101 An indulgence, granting 5,000 days' remission from Purgatory to the devout reciter
   of this prayer, along with five Our Fathers, five Hail Marys and the Creed.

## (d) Missenden register, fo. 49v

When your head aches, *Memento*
And your lips blacken, *Confessio*
And your heart pants, *Contricio*
And your wind wants, *Satisfactio*
And your limbs enfeebled lie, *Libera me Domine*
And your nose waxes cold, *Domine Miserere*
And your eyes hollow, *Nosce te Ipsum*
For then your death follows, *Veni ad Iudicium*.[102]

## (e) Missenden register, fo. 65v

| | |
|---|---|
| Arise early | and arise temperately |
| Serve God devoutly | and to your supper soberly |
| The world busily | and to your bed merrily |
| Go your way sadly | and be there jocundly |
| Answer demurely | and sleep surely |
| Go to your meat eagerly | |

---

102 The Latin terms relate to confession and the sacrament of penance, an important
  part of one's preparation for death.

# VII: LEARNING

Learning was always a central component of the monastic life, but the involvement of monks and canons in university studies from the late thirteenth century (with considerable papal encouragement) signalled a significant change of emphasis. Although only a small minority of religious ever attended university, this intellectual elite tended to dominate monastic affairs in the later middle ages. Moreover, learning within the cloister was adapted to correspond with and provide an introduction to the university curriculum, thereby bringing monastic education in general closer in line with that of the outside world. This development did not affect the nuns, who were excluded from university study and generally lacked a Latin education, although literacy in English and French remained common in nunneries. See **1**, **2**, **9**, **22**, **41–2** for further material concerning monastic learning and study.

## 25. Benedictine constitutions for university study, 1363

Pope Benedict XII's 1336 constitutions for the Benedictine Order required that one in twenty monks should be sent to university to study theology or canon law, and that all Benedictine monasteries should contribute to the maintenance of the order's house of studies in Oxford. The 1343 statutes of the Benedictine provincial chapter in England included practical provisions for the implementation of this programme,[103] and further statutes were issued in 1363, focusing particularly on the problems that had arisen in this process. It is clear from these latter statutes that the new papal and capitular demands had provoked a range of responses among Benedictine houses in England.

Translated from *Documents Illustrating the Activities of the General and Provincial Chapters of the English Black Monks, 1215–1540*, ed. W. A. Pantin, 3 vols, Camden Society, 3rd series, 45, 47, 54 (1931–37), II, 76–82 (Latin).

### Concerning those to be sent to a university

Since it would be in vain to make any constitutions unless they are afterwards observed by men, it is thus fitting to fortify constitutions with penalties, so that men may be compelled to the observance of these constitutions by the fear of the penalties. And if there should be so great

---

103 For a translation of relevant sections of Benedict XII's constitutions and the provincial chapter's 1343 statutes, see Myers (1969), 779–81.

a revolt by anyone that they do not wish to be easily turned to what is to be observed, it is proper to add penalties onto penalties, so that those whom certain penalties do not turn, an additional multitude will bend.

Since therefore Pope Benedict XII of happy memory formerly decreed, to no little honour of our religion, that from individual monasteries of our order out of every number of twenty monks, one suitable for acquiring the fruit of greater learning should be sent to a university, and established very severe penalties against those not sending them; and, as we have learned from the report of many, there are still certain prelates of our religion whom neither papal statute nor the fear of these penalties soften, so that they would send of their monks to a university according to the appointed number; we, seeking to confound their rebellion as much as we can, have constituted that all the prelates of our order whosoever – who are bound by virtue of the aforesaid papal constitutions to send any of their monks to university, but are not doing this as they are obliged – beyond the penalties constituted by the supreme pontiff against such things, should also pay in the name of punishment every year for each person whom they are bound to send to university by virtue of the aforesaid statute and do not send, £10 to the lord presidents [of the provincial chapter] for the time being, to be converted to the common uses of the order ...

And since many suppose that they are not bound by virtue of the Benedictine constitutions to send to a university any scholar or scholars from convents of any number fewer than twenty, the same Benedict XII – in a certain explanatory bull for this constitution, which expresses his intentions more fully – makes rejoinder to their erroneous opinion in these words: If there is a church, monastery or other principal place in which there are not twenty monks, but there is a number greater than six, the visitors appointed by the provincial chapter, when they exercise the office of visitation in these houses, are bound to enquire about the means and charges of the same houses. And if, with such charges having been borne, they should find the means to provide for one or more monks to be sent to the said studies, they should report this in the subsequent provincial chapter; at which the presidents, with the advice and consent of the greater part of the chapter, should make an ordinance by apostolic authority concerning one or more monks to be sent to the said studies, according to the house's resources.

Also, since although wisdom flourishes in the old, and old men are venerable, they are however as a whole more dulled of ability than the young, and less suitable for study in the philosophies; and since it is stated in the Benedictine constitutions that those who are teachable and more suitable for acquiring the fruit of knowledge should be chosen to be sent to a university; we have constituted that in future times the old and the advanced in age should not be sent to a university to learn more philosophy.

To this we add also, stating that those who by election ought to be sent to a university, namely one out of every twenty, should be chosen according to the form laid down in the Benedictine constitutions; but others beyond the number required in the said constitutions should by no means be sent, unless according to the chapter *Ut periculosa*: namely that licence to go to university should first have been granted to each of them by their prelate, with the advice of their convent or the greater part of it; excepting, as the aforementioned explanatory bull itself expresses in these words, any place [i.e. monastery] from which out of custom, ordination or statute (which we decree is to be observed inviolably) more monks are to be sent to such studies than is ordained in our ordinances ...

Since the monk by reason of his profession should stick to the tracks of he who had come before, not that he might do his own will but the will of He who sent him, and not to be served but rather to serve;[104] it seems absurd in a monk, whose place it is to be subjected to his prelate's will and to flee worldly honours, to procure, against or beyond the will of his prelate, the entreaties or letters of magnates so that they may come to the study of letters, or remain in that activity, or attain any degrees in a university, or ascend to the summit of the degree of master. And for this reason we strictly forbid by the present letters that any monk of our religion procure or cause to be procured, against or beyond the will of his prelate, entreaties or letters from any secular person whatsoever, so that he may be sent to a university, or be detained there, or advanced to any university degrees whatever, against the knowledge or even the will of his prelate.

And we state that if anyone of our order presumes to procure entreaties or letters as mentioned above by themselves or by another, and is convicted of this, without any appeal whatsoever by him, he should be rendered unfit to be sent to a university, if he has not yet been sent there; but if he has already been established in a university, he should be recalled by his prelate, not to be returned there hereafter ...

104 Cf. Matthew xx. 28; John iv. 34.

## 26. Learning in the cloister: Winchcombe Abbey under Richard Kidderminster

Richard Kidderminster, abbot of Winchcombe (1488–1527), was one of the most renowned monks of his day and a celebrated preacher, who had won the favour of popes and of King Henry VIII. This well-known account of learning in a larger Benedictine abbey was written by Kidderminster himself towards the end of his abbacy, looking back with nostalgia on the earlier years of his rule.

Translated from W. A. Pantin, 'Abbot Kidderminster and monastic studies', *Downside Review*, 47 (1929), 199–200 (Latin).

The congregation of Winchcombe at that time, by the patience of God, numbered twenty-eight monks, of whom many were devoted both to reading and to regular observance, so that there was scarcely one complete day in the week which did not have, one way or another, one bachelor in holy theology expounding the Old Testament, or another bachelor expounding the New Testament. And indeed I in my person, twice a week, would explain something out of the Master of the *Sentences*[105] for my own part; so that it was so beautiful to see how the men were devoted to the study of sacred literature, and how they used Latin conversation among themselves even in their recreation; and the cloister of Winchcombe at that time conducted itself no differently than if it had been another new university (although a small one). And in fact among all these things, regular observance was so ardent among us, and brotherly charity so enlarged, that you would scarcely believe there to have been a cloister of such unity and concord in England, at least among so small a number. Certainly only merciful God knew how much at this time I took delight to be occupied with sacred literature with the brethren in the cloister; where, having built a certain little study (if only I had permitted it to stand to this day!), I committed myself both day and night to the work of reading; and such was this diligence, that I would have had nearly no learning in sacred literature and sacred theology, without all that I drunk in there in the cloister.

I have accordingly said all these things for this reason, so that those coming after may learn the profit to be had of sacred literature in universities, but also in cloisters; something the incredible learning of the Venerable Bede plainly proves, who is testified to have dedicated himself nowhere else other than in the cloister and in regular observance. If

105 The *Sentences* of Peter Lombard (d. *c.* 1160) was the standard textbook of theology in medieval universities.

only the monks of our time, who think there is no place of learning besides the universities, would embrace this more closely as a more vigorous example.

## 27. The preface to Bishop Fox's translation of the Benedictine Rule, 1517

Numerous sources make it clear that Latin – the language of most intellectual discourse – was rarely known among nuns in late medieval England. A great deal of devotional and other literature was now available in English and French, but monastic rules and statutes (as well as liturgical services) were written in Latin. Bishop Richard Fox of Winchester here outlines his reasons for making a translation of the Benedictine Rule, published (at Fox's own expense) in 1517.

Translated from *Letters of Richard Fox, 1486–1527*, ed. P. S. and H. M. Allen (Oxford, 1929), 86–8 (English).

Forasmuch as every person ought to know the thing that he is bound to keep or accomplish, and ignorance of the thing that he is bound to do cannot nor may not excuse him; and forasmuch also as the reading of the thing that a person is bound to do and execute, unless he understands it, is not at all advantageous to its execution, but only something useless, labour in vain and time lost:

We, therefore, Richard, by the permission and sufferance of our Lord God bishop of Winchester, turning over in our mind that certain devout and religious women, being within our diocese and under our pastoral charge and care, have not only professed themselves to the observance of the Rule of the holy confessor St Benedict, but also are bound to read, learn and understand the same Rule when they are novices and before they are professed; and also after their profession they should not only in themselves keep, observe, execute and practise the Rule, but also teach their other sisters the same; so that for the same purpose they daily read and cause to be read some part of the Rule by one of the sisters among themselves, both in their chapter house after the reading of the martyrology,[106] and some time in their refectory at the time of refreshment and repasts. All of these readings are always done in the Latin tongue, of which they have no knowledge or understanding, but they are utterly ignorant of the same; whereby they do not only waste their time, but also run into the evident danger and peril of the perdition of their souls.

106 A register of deceased benefactors and inmates owed prayer by the community.

We the said bishop, knowing and considering the above, and remembering that we may not without the peril of our soul allow the said religious women, of whose souls we have the care, to continue in their blindness and ignorance of the Rule, to the knowledge and observance of which they are professed; and especially to the intent that the young novices may first know and understand the Rule before they profess themselves to it, so that none of them shall any more afterwards probably say that she did not know what she professed, as we know by experience that some of them have said in times past.

For these causes, and especially at the pressing request of our right dear and well-beloved daughters in our Lord Jesus, the abbesses of the monasteries of Romsey, Wherwell, St Mary's outside the city of Winchester, and the prioress of Wintney, our very religious people of the diocese, we have translated the said Rule into our mother tongue: common, plain, round English, easy and ready to be understood by the said devout religious women.

And because we would not have there to be any lack amongst them of the books of this translation, we have therefore – above and besides certain books of it, which we have given to the said monasteries – caused it to be printed by our well-beloved Richard Pynson of London, printer, the 22nd day of the month of January, the year of Our Lord 1517 ...

**PART TWO:**

**MONASTERIES AND THE WORLD**

# VIII: MONASTIC FOUNDATION AND SUPPRESSION IN THE LATER MIDDLE AGES

The number of monasteries in medieval England remained remarkably stable over the later middle ages. Only a small number of new foundations were made after 1300, mostly lesser houses of Augustinian canons (like Maxstoke) or the fashionable priories of the Carthusians which could be endowed collectively. Similarly, the only major dissolution of these years involved the anomalous alien priories, closed because of their dependence on French monasteries. The suppression of small houses did become a little more common from the late fifteenth century, and a more far-reaching dissolution of lesser houses was under discussion in early Tudor England (cf. **55**). But despite their rarity, new foundations and suppressions reveal much about late medieval attitudes to monasteries.

## 28. The foundation statutes of Maxstoke Priory, 1337

On his foundation of Maxstoke Priory (Warwickshire) for Augustinian canons in 1337, William de Clinton issued a lengthy charter specifying how the monastery should function. These ordinances – reminiscent of those made for several contemporary secular colleges – provide a good impression of what late medieval founders expected from their religious houses.

Translated (with corrections of transcription from National Archives, C66/192) from W. Dugdale, *Monasticon Anglicanum*, ed. J. Caley, H. Ellis and B. Bandinel (London, 1846), VI, 524–6 (Latin).

… In honour of the holy and indivisible Trinity, Father, Son and Holy Spirit, and the glorious blessed Virgin Mary, St Michael the archangel and All Saints, I have newly founded, built and endowed from my own property a certain monastery or priory of regular canons, of the order of St Augustine, in a certain site of mine in Maxstoke, close to the manor of the same vill, in the diocese of Coventry and Lichfield; with the express agreement and assent of the most serene prince the lord Edward [III] by the grace of God most illustrious king of England, and of the venerable father the lord Roger, by the same grace bishop of Coventry and Lichfield, of brother Henry, prior of Coventry, master Richard, dean of Lichfield and the chapters of the said churches, and of all others whose consent is required in this matter. This I have done for my healthy state, and that of Juliana my wife, and our lord, the lord Edward, by the grace of God now illustrious king of England, of Laurence of Hastings, of the lord Roger the aforesaid bishop, of brother Henry the aforesaid prior, of the aforesaid dean Richard, monks of Coventry and the canons of Lichfield now being, while we live; and for the salvation of our soul, and of Juliana my wife, our aforesaid lord king, Laurence, Roger, Henry, Richard and the monks and canons, when they have died: and also for the soul of the lord John de Clinton my father, of the lady Ida my mother, the lord John my full brother, and for their children, living and dead; and for the souls of the kings of England, of all the lords of Hastings, the bishops of the churches of Coventry and Lichfield, of the said prior and dean, monks and canons, parents, and our other benefactors, and of all the faithful departed, wishing, establishing and ordaining as is contained below.

Namely, that in this priory there should henceforth be one elective prior, and one convent of twelve canons besides the prior, who should lead a religious, honest and regular life, pleasing to both God and men, according to the rule and order of the blessed Augustine. And perpetually by day and night they should worship Him, glorify Him, praise Him and worthily and laudably serve Him alone, who made me and them out of nothing, just as He made every other creature. And they should perform with sincere affections and pure minds that venerable sacrament of the precious body and blood of Jesus Christ, the redeemer of humankind, who left his body to be given as food and his blood as drink to his faithful.

Also I will, establish and ordain that the aforesaid prior and canons and their successors should use for over-garments, both in winter and summer, a regular black cloak and hood, and under the cloak a linen garment and other clothing, both day and night, just as other regular canons of the order use. And that, out of their property, the prior should not have a portion distinct from the convent, nor the convent from the prior; but just as they are God willing one body, and ought to have one heart and one soul, not false in love, so all their property should be distributed in common, according to the state and degree of each, preserving the aforesaid order and rule.

Also I will, ordain and establish that whenever the priory is in any way publicly vacant, there shall be an election of the prior of the monastery to be held, immediately within five or six days after this vacation in the priory is publicly known. When the Mass of the Holy Spirit has been solemnly celebrated in choir, the subprior and the convent of the church should proceed freely to the election of the future prior, doing just as will be proper by the holy institutes, requiring no licence to elect from me, my heirs or my successors.

Also, I establish and ordain that whenever and however often the priory happens to be vacant, no-one should have custody or the administration itself of the same priory or its property during the vacation, unless only the subprior and convent and any others whom the subprior and convent themselves shall wish to appoint to the administration of the property; who should be bound to render a faithful reckoning or account of such administration to the future prior and the convent of the same place, or to others, whom they shall think fit to be assigned to this, when they have been legitimately forewarned.

Also, that no-one should be admitted as a canon in this priory, unless he is free at the time of his entry, and known as a free man, and publicly reputed to be of good and honest behaviour, suitably literate for the position of a regular canon; and he should have a suitable voice for singing divine service, or at least he shall excel so much in other things that he ought deservedly to be preferred to all other men of the aforesaid condition in his admission to regular status, for the improvement of the state of the monastery. And he shall have attained eighteen years of age, and should truly be considered suitable and fit to receive the sacred order of the priesthood when he reaches the lawful age. Also at the end of his first year, when he ought to profess, before his profession he should read or cause to be read in his presence openly and publicly in common each and everything contained in these letters of my foundation; and then he should immediately promise in good faith that he shall observe and cause to be observed each and every one of them, insofar as they concern or can concern him and shall be in his power.

Also since I have already made provision to the said prior and convent of £100 of yearly rent in churches, lands and rents in the vills of Maxstoke and Long Itchington for the number of twelve canons and a prior, as aforementioned, I will and ordain that when by me, or by another, or by their own industry, they have been supplemented by ten marks of annual rent in lands or other rents, they should be bound to increase their number immediately within the following month, by one suitable person to be admitted into the brotherhood as a canon, if within the space of a month one worthy to be admitted may be found or otherwise as soon as they can find a suitable person. And while there are thirteen canons with a prior, nine shall always be priests, as far as that is possible. And as the property of the priory shall happen to be increased by ten marks a year, thus the number of canons should rise, and the number of priests should be increased without delay in proportion to the number of canons added.

Also that it should not be permitted to the said prior and convent to sell, grant or give any corrody[1] or annual pension to any persons at all, or otherwise burden this monastery perpetually for any reason, or bind it in any way, unless because of evident utility or inevitable necessity arising at any time. And this utility and necessity should first be approved, after sufficient examination, by the then bishop of the same place.

Also that each and every officer, obedientiary, and others holding the administration of the property of the said priory or church should be bound to render a faithful reckoning or account concerning their receipts, expenses and their administration of the priory's property four times every year before the prior and convent, or before three suitable and discreet people chosen by the prior and convent. And besides this let a clear indenture be made, which should be read before the convent, so that besides this the whole convent may be able to know the state of the monastery; and then the indenture should be placed in the treasury of the monastery and should be observed faithfully.

Also I ordain that when I have gone the way of all flesh, each year in perpetuity on the day of my obit, the prior and convent (and the subprior and convent when the priory is vacant) should be bound to say solemnly in the convent *Placebo* and *Dirige*,[2] and a solemn Mass in choir, and the whole Office of the Dead for my soul and the aforesaid souls, and all the faithful departed. And that on this very day of my obit, there should be made a distribution to one hundred paupers from the parish of Maxstoke, to each namely one loaf weighing fifty shillings.[3] And to paupers coming from other places and on whatever day in perpetuity, there should be brought at the hour of dinner in the presence of the prior or his deputy in the refectory, beyond the customary loaf, one white conventual loaf; and one dish from the kitchen or other things, which should be assigned and given to the poorer members of the parish of Maxstoke every day by the discretion of the prior or the almoner, with one flagon of conventual ale, for the benefit of my soul and the souls named above, and all the faithful departed.

1 See above, p. 87 n. 13.

2 See above, p. 105 n. 42. *Placebo* was the first word of Vespers in the Office of the Dead, and used like *Dirige* as a shorthand to signify that service.

3 Weights of bread were usually expressed in pounds, shillings and pence in the later middle ages.

Also that the Mass of the Blessed Virgin Mary, the chapter Mass and the Mass of the day, should be celebrated communally, at the due hours and places, as has been accustomed in other priories of the same order. On condition that in all the masses to be celebrated solemnly in choir, except on major festivals, commemoration should be made for me and Juliana my wife, our lord the king and the others named above, while we are in the present life; and when we have died, commemoration should be made for us and for all the people having died named above, as is accustomed for the dead.

Also I will and ordain that every prior, having been confirmed or made, before he may govern in spiritualities or temporalities, should cause to be recited openly and publicly in the presence of the convent and him who shall install him, when he is to be installed, each and everything contained in these letters of foundation of my aforesaid monastery; and immediately afterwards he should promise in good faith that he shall observe them insofar as they concern him and shall be in his power, and that he shall cause them to be fulfilled and observed.

Also I will and ordain that at no time, nor for any reason, will I, my heirs or successors, be able by any means to seek, demand or have anything whatsoever other than as I have ordained above, from the aforesaid prior and convent, or subprior and convent, when the priory is vacant or full, by reason of patronage or lordship or of any other right whatever. Nor should the monastery be liable to any payment through me or my heirs or successors, or through my family or theirs. Nor should anything be seized from the property of the said monastery for any reason in my name or theirs, or by any artificial excuse; and whoever shall do differently or otherwise shall incur thereby the curse of Omnipotent God the Father and of the glorious Blessed Virgin Mary, and Blessed Michael the archangel, and of all the saints of the court of heaven, unless he will have made agreeable satisfaction for the aforesaid. Amen.

Also inflamed by the zeal of pious devotion, like all the faithful of Christ, towards the mother of grace, the glorious Virgin Mary, and for the sake of the Virgin herself, towards the most blessed Anne mother of the same Virgin: I will, ordain and establish, that after the office of the Matins of the Blessed Virgin Mary has been completed in choir, and after the Mass of the Virgin, and after the individual Hours, the priest who has celebrated Mass, and the celebrant of the office, in the same voice with which he has completed the office, should say the Angelic Salutation, and the commendation of her mother, in the future in perpetuity, in this manner: 'Hail Mary, full of grace, the Lord is with you, you are blessed among women, and blessed is the fruit of your loins, Jesus, Amen. And may your venerable mother Anne be blessed, from whom your virginal and immaculate flesh proceeded.' And the choir should respond, Amen ...

## 29. The endowment of the London Charterhouse

The London Charterhouse was established in 1371, one of seven Carthusian priories founded in late medieval England. The following document, written as a summary of the house's most important benefactions and entered into an early sixteenth-century register of the priory, illustrates the process of the monastery's collective endowment, and the reciprocal benefits received by those granting money and property.

Translated from W. St John Hope, *The History of the London Charterhouse from its Foundation until the Suppression of the Monastery* (London, 1925), 84–8 (Latin).

### Concerning the chantries

In the name of God, Amen, the year 1431. We have examined carefully the indented deeds by which we and our successors are bound and obliged to certain fixed chantries perpetually to be continued in this house by our brothers who are priests, on behalf of certain of our great benefactors, who have built cells in that cloister at their own cost, and have liberally given other property to us. And so that the tenor and effect of the same deeds in an abbreviated form of words, avoiding the prolixity which is wont to engender boredom for those listening, may be more briefly recited before the convent once or twice a year, we have inserted the full effect of these deeds in this document, as follows in this form.

Firstly, by the charter of King Richard II, sealed under the great seal, by which he gave to us the advowson of the church of Ellesborough, with licence to appropriate it, and by the papal bull concerning the appropriation of the same church, we are perpetually bound that one of our brethren shall celebrate specially and pray for the souls of the said lord King Richard and the lady Anne, formerly his wife the queen; of the lord Edward [the Black Prince], formerly prince of Wales, his father; of the lady Joan, lately princess [of Wales], his mother; of the lord Edward, the brother of the said King Richard; and of the lord Edward III, formerly king of England, his grandfather; and of all the faithful departed.

Also by one indenture sealed with the seal of the reverend father the lord Thomas Hatfield, formerly bishop of Durham [1345–81], who built two cells in the east range of the cloister – for whose construction and endowment he gave to us, so it is said, 600 marks – we are perpetually under the obligation that two monk-priests inhabiting the aforesaid cells now and always in the future should celebrate divine service, and should pray specially for the souls of the said reverend father the lord Thomas the bishop, King Edward III, John the bishop's father, Margery his mother, William his brother, Joan and Margaret his sisters, and all the faithful departed; and conditions and grave penalties are there laid down if that celebration shall cease for one month or for one year without just cause, as is expressed more fully in the said indenture.

Also by another indenture made in the same form and under the same conditions and penalties, we are similarly under the obligation that one monk shall celebrate in perpetuity and pray for the souls of Sir Richard Rouhale, priest, of Gervase and Margery his parents and of all the faithful departed. And the executors of the said Richard have given £40.

Also by a third indenture we are under the obligation that one monk shall in perpetuity celebrate specially and pray for the soul of the lady Mary de St Pol, formerly countess of Pembroke [d. 1377], who built one cell in the north part of the cloister, and beyond this gave for the endowment of the house £200 and very many other gifts. The said monk shall also celebrate similarly for the souls of the lord Aymer, formerly earl of Pembroke the husband of the said countess; of the lord Guy de Chastellon and the lady Mary her parents; the lord William de Valence, and the lady Joan, the parents of the said Aymer; and for the souls of their friends and benefactors, and all the faithful departed.

Also by a fourth indenture, we are under the obligation that one of our monks shall celebrate and pray for the souls of Frederick Tilney and Margery his wife, and Philip their son, which Margery indeed gave 260 marks for the building and endowment of one cell in the north range of the cloister; and the said monk shall dwell in the said cell. It is also granted to the said souls a special association in a perpetual trental[4] for the dead and in the collect *Omnipotens qui vivorum* in the Mass of the Blessed Virgin.

Also by a fifth indenture under the same form and for a similar benefaction we are under the obligation in all respects that one monk shall

4 A series of thirty masses for the soul.

celebrate in perpetuity and pray for the souls of Thomas Aubrey and Felice his wife, and all the faithful departed. And the said monk shall dwell in the cell which they themselves have built in the north range of the cloister, adjoining the other cell.

Also by a sixth indenture we are under the obligation that one monk shall celebrate in perpetuity and pray for the souls of the lord William de Ufford, formerly earl of Suffolk [d. 1382]; of his wives Joan and Isabella; Robert and Margaret the parents of the said William; and for the souls to whom they themselves were bound. And the monk shall dwell in the cell that the executors of the said earl have built in the east range of the cloister; and they gave 420 marks of the property of this earl for the fabric of that cell and for the maintenance of the said monk.

Also for the souls of William Stowe and Alice his wife. This William indeed gave to this house his tenements built in St John's Street, and he also built new tenements on our land outside the great gate towards Smithfield, and did many other good things for this house. Also besides this he sustained many labours and toils for this house in the early days of its foundation. One of our brethren who is a priest shall celebrate for all future times; and to this we are deservedly obliged, as appears more fully in the indenture then made. And the said monk shall receive one pound of ginger and one pound of sugar every year from the aforesaid rents.

Also by another indenture we are under the obligation that one of our brethren shall celebrate divine service in perpetuity for the souls of Roger Wolferston, Beatrice his wife, Richard, Alice and Benedict and for those to whom they are bound, etc. And the said Roger gave £80.

We are also bound, although not by any sealed deed, that one of our brethren who is a priest shall inhabit the cell that Richard Clitheroe built at his own expense, and gave up for its endowment the lease granted to him by us of our inn at Rochester. And the brother shall pray specially for the souls of this Richard and Alice his wife and for those to whom they were bound and all the faithful departed.

Also those inhabiting the cells which William Symmes caused to be made from his own property, and Robert Chamberlain from the property of Dame Margery Nerford and Christian Ipstones made to be built, are specially bound to pray for these very benefactors here named and for all their friends living and dead.

Also by the will of John Gulforde who left to us 10 marks of annual and quit rent, to be paid by the prior of St Bartholomew [Smithfield], we are under the obligation by the same will that one of our brethren who is a priest shall celebrate specially and in perpetuity for the soul of this John and the souls for which he was bound during his life.

Also by the will of John Northampton, formerly citizen of London [d. 1398], who left to us his tenements in Pentecost Lane, we are similarly obliged that one altar in our church should be assigned, where two monks should celebrate daily, having in special memory the soul of this John; and the souls of James, Andrew and his wife Matilda; his parents Thomas and Mariot; his former wives Joan and Parnel; and the souls of all to whom the said John was bound; and that these names should be written and placed on a certain table[5] on the said altar, before the face of the priest. Also he charged us that we should keep the anniversary day of his obit every year, and that on that day half a mark should be spent on a pittance;[6] and every monk should then have half a pound of ginger, and every Lent one pound of dates, one pound of figs and one pound of raisins out of the profits of the same tenements and rents. And all these charges he imposed on us merely by pleading.

It is also to be committed to perpetual memory that Sir William Walworth, knight and formerly mayor of London [d. 1386?], gave to us 1,000 marks sterling from his property and from the property of John Lovekyn, his master, and formerly mayor of London, for the construction of five cells in the great cloister. And he bestowed many other good things on this house both in his life and in death. Also Adam Fraunceys, formerly citizen and mayor of London [d. 1375], gave to us 1,000 marks sterling out of his property for the construction of five cells. And although neither of them bound us by any deed, all the same out of good conscience those inhabiting the said cells that they built with their own property are bound to pray specially for them as their founders.

Also William Symmes, citizen and grocer of London, whose memory shall be blessed to that generation that is to come, was received as our brother the first Sunday in Lent, AD 1418. This William indeed built one cell in the south range of the cloister, for whose construction and for the paving of the great cloister, and the repair with hard stone around the walls of our church in their summits, he paid 300 marks and more.

Also the same William Symmes first of all began our aqueduct, and on part of the construction of the same aqueduct he paid over 300 marks.

5 See above, p. 137 n. 93.
6 See above, p. 100 n. 30.

Also the same William Symmes, after the building and construction of the same aqueduct, gave 220 marks to us to buy certain rents for its repair and conservation, so that Christ's faithful and poor might more openly and freely enjoy the benefit of water, and so that this house should be perpetually exonerated from the repair of this aqueduct. And he willed that out of the profits of these rents half a mark should be spent annually on the day of his obit on a pittance for the convent, and another half a mark on alms for the poor. And for this good deed, may his name not be deleted from the number of the saints, but be written in the book of life among the saints and the elect. Amen.

William Symmes also gave 220 marks besides the aforementioned to this house and convent on various occasions and for various reasons. And he also bestowed on this house many other good things and benefits both in books and in ornaments of the church, for all of which may God, the bestower of all good things, reward him, and according to his merits multiply the same one hundred times in the life everlasting. Amen.

The sum of all these things extends to 1,040 marks and beyond.

Also it is to be committed to memory that John Peke and Joan his wife have perpetual commemoration with certain others at Mass at the altar of St Agnes where they are buried, and they have given 100 marks of their goods to this house.

## 30. A petition for the confiscation of alien priory property, 1414

The alien priories, daughter houses of French monasteries, were a subject of controversy throughout the extended, but intermittent, period of conflict between England and France between the 1290s and the 1450s. This is the last in a series of parliamentary petitions from the lay elites to the king, lobbying for the permanent confiscation and redistribution of alien priory property. The resulting Statute of Leicester commenced a process which led to the suppression of many alien houses.

Translation taken from C. Given Wilson, ed., 'Henry V, Parliament of April 1414, text and translation', in *The Parliament Rolls of Medieval England*, ed. C. Given-Wilson et al., item 21. CD-ROM. Scholarly Digital Editions (Leicester, 2005) (French).

Concerning alien possessions. Also, the commons pray that if a final peace is made between you, our most sovereign lord, and your adversary of France in the future, and if consequently all the possessions of

alien priories situated in England are restored to the mother houses of
the religious overseas to whom such possessions belong, loss and harm
will befall your said kingdom and your people of the same kingdom,
because of the great farms and consignments of money which yearly
and forever after will be rendered from the same possessions to the
aforesaid mother houses, to the very great impoverishment of your
same kingdom in this matter, which God forbid.

May it please your most noble and most gracious lordship to consider
that at the beginning of the war which arose between the said kingdoms,
they were, from all the possessions which your lieges then held by
gift of your noble progenitors in parts overseas within the jurisdiction of France, forever ousted and disinherited by a judgment rendered
in the same kingdom of France. And thereupon to graciously ordain
in this present parliament, by the assent of your lords spiritual and
temporal, that all the possessions of alien priories located in England
should remain in your hands, belonging to you and your heirs forever;
with the intention that divine services in the aforesaid places might be
more properly carried out by Englishmen in future, this not having
been done previously at these places by Frenchmen; except the possessions of conventual alien priories and of priors who are inducted and
instituted;[7] and except that all the alien possessions given by the most
gracious lord the king, your father, whom God absolve, to the master
and college of Fotheringhay and to their successors – which is of the
foundation of our said lord the king, your father, and of the foundation of Edward duke of York – notwithstanding the peace to be made,
should there be one, with all kinds of franchises and liberties granted
by our said lord the king, your father, to the said master and college
and to their successors, and confirmed by you, shall remain perpetually, by authority of this present parliament, with the said master and
college and their successors, for their use and disposal in accordance
with the tenor and purport of the letters patent of our said lord the
king, your father, concerning the foundation of the said college, without
any charge or outgoings to you, most sovereign lord, or your heirs, or
any outgoings to any other persons or person; saving the services owed
to lords of English fees,[8] if there are any; and notwithstanding that the
same grant made by our aforesaid lord the king, your father, to the said

7 I.e. priors who were formally instituted by a bishop and could subsequently only be
removed from office by the ecclesiastical authorities, as opposed to a 'dative' prior
who could be appointed and removed by the mother house at will.

8 Heritable estates held in return for service to a lord, who remained the owner of the
property.

master and college and to their successors shall only apply during the war between you, most sovereign lord, and your adversary of France; and saving also to each of your lieges, both spiritual as well as temporal, the estate and possessions which they have at present in any such alien possessions, either purchased or to be purchased, in perpetuity, or for the term of life or a term of years, from the mother houses overseas, by licence of our lord the king, your most noble father, whom God absolve, or of King Edward III, your great-grandfather, or of King Richard the second since the conquest, or of your own gracious gift, grant, confirmation or licence received in this matter. Paying and supporting all the charges, pensions, annuities and corrodies[9] granted to any of your lieges by you, or any of your noble progenitors, to be taken from the aforesaid alien possessions or priories.

*Answer*

The king wills it; and also that the said master and college of Fotheringhay shall have an exemplification of this petition from the king under his great seal for their greater security in this matter; and this by the assent of the lords spiritual and temporal attending this present parliament.

## 31. The closure of St Radegund's Priory, Cambridge, 1496

From the late fifteenth century, a growing number of small and apparently decayed English monasteries (both male and female) were suppressed in favour of academic colleges. The nunnery of St Radegund, Cambridge was particularly vulnerable to such a transformation both because of the financial problems it was experiencing [cf. **6**] and because of its prime location just outside the king's ditch in Cambridge. The college founded in its place by Bishop Alcock of Ely, following Henry VII's favourable response to his petition, quickly became known by the catchier name of Jesus College.

Translated (with corrections of transcription from National Archives, C66/579) from W. Dugdale, Monasticon Anglicanum, ed. J. Caley, H. Ellis and B. Bandinel (London, 1846), IV, 217–18 (Latin).

The king to all whom, etc. greeting. You should know that we have heard – from both the trustworthy report of the reverend father in Christ, John, bishop of Ely, and from public repute – that the house or priory of religious women of St Radegund (of the bishop's foundation

9 See above, p. 87 n. 13.

and patronage according to the right of his church of Ely) and the lands, tenements, rents, possessions, buildings, as well as the properties, goods, jewels and other ecclesiastical ornaments, that have been given and bestowed piously and charitably to the same house or priory from ancient times; these things – through the negligence and the thoughtless and dissolute conduct and incontinence, by reason of the closeness of the university of Cambridge, of the prioresses and religious women of the aforesaid house – are so dilapidated, destroyed, devastated, alienated, diminished and taken away, and the religious women are reduced to such want and poverty, that they are not able to maintain and support divine service, hospitality, and other accustomed works of mercy and piety there, according to the first foundation and ordination of their founders; nor in any way to sustain or relieve themselves, who are only two in number, of whom one was professed elsewhere and the other is a minor, but the aforesaid women would be compelled to abandon the house or priory as if desolate. As a result, the bishop, for the sake of greater devotion and the increase of divine worship and of virtue, has most humbly entreated us that we should graciously deign to grant to him our royal licence, so that he may be able to remove and expel totally the aforesaid women from the house or priory, and to make anew, found, raise up, create and establish there a certain college, to endure for all future time in perpetuity.

We, therefore, considering deeply the above matters and the pious and devout intention of the bishop, in the sight of God and from the sincere devotion which we bear and have to the holy and indivisible Trinity, and to the most blessed Virgin Mary mother of God, St John the Evangelist and the holy virgin Radegund, and all the saints; we have granted from our special grace and given licence to the same reverend father and his successors … that he and his successors as bishops of Ely, and his executors, deputies and assigns, or any of them, be able to make, found, raise up, create and establish out of the aforesaid house or priory, to endure for all future time in perpetuity, a certain college of one master and six fellows, and with a certain number of scholars to be educated in grammar and to pray and perform divine service every day within the college for our prosperous condition – and for that of Elizabeth, queen of England, our most dear consort, and for our most dear mother, Margaret, and our very dear sons, Arthur prince of Wales, the first born, and the duke of York, the second born, and for all our children, while we live, and for the good condition of the bishop himself similarly while he lives; and for our souls when we have died and also for the soul of our very dear father Edmund of Richmond, and for the soul of the bishop himself when he has likewise died, and besides to celebrate in perpetuity for the souls of the previous founders of the house or priory and for all the faithful departed; and to perform the other works of mercy and piety there according to the ordination and ordinances in this regard to be made, ordained and constituted by the bishop himself or by his executors or assigns.

And that the aforesaid college, when it has been thus made ... should be named, called and pronounced in perpetuity the college of the most blessed Virgin Mary, St John the Evangelist and the glorious virgin St Radegund next to Cambridge in the county of Cambridge. And that the master, fellows and scholars of the college and their successors ... should be nominated, named, called and pronounced the master, fellows and scholars of the college of the most blessed Virgin Mary, St John the Evangelist and the glorious virgin St Radegund next to Cambridge. On condition that by this name they should be able to sue and be sued, to answer and be answered, and to prosecute, defend and be defended in any courts and places whatsoever and before any judges or justices whatsoever, spiritual or temporal;[10] and that they should be one body and one corporate community in name and deed, and they should have perpetual succession and a common seal for settling the business of the college. And also that there should be people able and capable in law to inquire and receive the lands, tenements, rents, reversions, pensions, annuities and other possessions of any kind from whatever person or persons who wish to give, leave or assign those things to them. And that they themselves should be able to grant, make, ordain and establish as is necessary the ordinations, statutes and ordinances for the good and sound rule of the college ...

10 I.e. in the secular or church courts.

# IX: PATRONAGE

Every monastery had an official patron, the legal (and sometimes hereditary) descendant of its first founder, with particular rights and responsibilities regarding the house. In return for prayers, hospitality and perhaps some say in the monastery's affairs, the patron was expected to provide protection and support at times of need. Although many houses found it difficult to maintain their patrons' interest throughout the later middle ages, monasteries might also attract support and patronage from other benefactors. This section illustrates the interaction between monasteries and their patrons and benefactors in this period. Other documents of relevance to the subject of monastic patronage include **6, 28–9, 36, 38**.

## 32. The induction of new patrons at Marrick Priory

The following description of the ceremonial reception of new patrons of the small Yorkshire nunnery of Marrick is a rare survival of its kind. It summarises neatly the reciprocal benefits to be gained (at least in theory) from the relationship between patron and priory, and the significance of the founder – here a synonym for patron – to the house.

Translated from Oxford, Bodleian Library, MS Ch. Yorkshire a.1 26b (English).

### The form of taking the founder

The Lady Prioress:

He shall be met at the outer gate with a solemn procession with cross, tapers[11] and incense and holy water, where a seat shall be provided, and first the prioress shall say to him thus: 'Sir, what is your desire and my lady's at this time?'

The Founder:

'I desire to be the partaker of your prayers and to be taken and admitted founder of this monastery, as my ancestors have been here before.'

(The bells shall be rung at his coming.)

---

11 Wax candles used for devotional purposes.

The Lady Prioress:

'Monsieur, you are most heartily welcome to us and inasmuch as we have assured knowledge that your mastership by lineal descent has come of the honourable stock whose predecessors have obtained and enjoyed by right title to be founders of this place, from H. the first esquire of the worshipful name of Aske unto your mastership now present by you. In consideration of which, we grant to you this your request, so that your mastership may make a promise to us to defend, maintain and help us in all business, troubles, disquiet and just causes against our adversaries; not only in word or by giving counsel, but also in effect and deed, as your ancestors have done here before, with as diligent labour taken as if it were your own cause. And to perform this you must place your hand on this book and kiss it.'

(The sign of the cross is to be made.)

'Sir, by this you shall be the partaker of all our prayers, suffrages and good deeds done and to be done not only in this place but also in all places of our order, as we shall cause you to be admitted at the next visit; that is to say of all masses, Matins, Primes, Hours, Evensongs, Complines, *Diriges*,[12] commendations, fastings, prayers, alms-deeds, vigils, disciplines, corrections, readings, meditations and contemplations with all other devout and meritorious acts done and to be done in the whole order.'

That done, then the lady prioress shall cast holy water and cense them with the subprioress. Then the lady prioress and the subprioress shall lead them into the church with a procession, singing *Honor virtus* for the founder, and *regnum mundi* for the foundress. And in the church a seat is to be prepared for them and *Te deum* is to be sung solemnly; after *Te deum* the chanter shall begin an anthem of the patron and so enter into the choir and up to the altar, and after the anthem *Kyrieleison Christeleison Kyrieleison; Et ne nos; Salvos fac servos tuos; Mitte eis domine auxilium de sancto; Nihil proficiet inimicus in eo; Esto domino dominus turris fortitudinis; Domine exaudi; Dominus vobiscum oremus.*[13]

Then *De profundis*, in a low voice, with the collects *Inclina* and *fidelium*.

---

12 See above, p.105 n. 42.

13 Liturgical prayers, psalms and responses to be sung by the community.

## 33. The Founders' Chronicle of Tewkesbury Abbey

Among the services provided by monasteries for their patrons was the production of dynastic histories. The following account is an extract from one version of a Tewkesbury Abbey chronicle which recounts the history of this wealthy Benedictine monastery's patrons, the Despensers, emphasising the family's connections with the abbey.

Translated (with corrections of transcription from British Library, Cotton MS Cleop. C iii) from W. Dugdale, *Monasticon Anglicanum*, ed. J. Caley, H. Ellis and B. Bandinel (London, 1846), II, 59–65 (Latin).

In AD 1359 the lady Elizabeth le Despenser, the daughter of William de Montacute formerly earl of Salisbury, and the wife of Guy de Bryan knight, and the widow of Hugh III le Despenser, died at Astley in the county of Hampshire on the last day of May, that is on St Petronella the virgin's day. She lies buried with her noble husband by her first marriage in a suitably illustrious tomb with images of white marble. That Guy de Bryan appropriated certain rents in the town of Bristol for the benefit of his soul, and that of his wife the lady Elizabeth, and he assigned them to the office of the sacrist of Tewkesbury and to he who celebrates the first Mass for the said Guy daily in our church at the altar of St Margaret ... And he who celebrates as hebdomadary[14] shall receive for his labour 1s 9d; and if the abbot celebrates Mass on their anniversary, he shall receive 5s; if the prior, 3s 4d; and the monk who reads the Gospel, 8d; he who reads the epistle, 8d; he who holds the paten, 8d; and the precentor[15] with his two fellows, 8d each; and to the prior, 12d; and to each of the monks 4d.

Therefore Edward I [le Despenser], the brother of Hugh III, begot Edward II, Thomas, Henry and Gilbert II by Anne the daughter of the lord of Ferrers, and by the fortune of war died before his brother. He was earl of the Isle of Wight and was afterwards made earl of Devon. Edward II [le Despenser], the son of that Edward, succeeded Hugh III and joined himself in marriage to the lady Elizabeth, the daughter of the lord Bartholomew Burghersh, by whom he begot Edward III [le Despenser] – who died aged twelve at Cardiff, but is buried at Tewkesbury in the chapel of St Mary – and Hugh IV, who died soon after he had been born and who is buried with his brother. He then begot four daughters, whose names are these: Cecily, who died young and was buried with her brothers; then Elizabeth, lady of la Zouche and the widow

14 See above, p. 113 n. 58.
15 See above, p. 131 n. 87.

of the lord John de Arundell; and the lady Anne who was espoused to Hugh Hastings and afterwards Thomas Morley; and Margaret who was given in marriage to the lord Robert de Ferrers. And the aforesaid Edward in his old age bore Thomas le Despenser, earl of Gloucester. He succeeded his father as his heir and joined to himself in matrimony the lady Constance, daughter of the lord Edmund de Langley, duke of York, the son of King Edward III; and by this Constance Thomas begot Richard, Elizabeth and Isabella. And the aforesaid lady Margaret, wife of the lord Robert de Ferrers, died the 3rd November, AD 1415 and was buried at Merevale [Abbey]. She was the mother of the lord Thomas, Edmund and Edward de Ferrers.

And Edward II [le Despenser] died in Wales, at Llanbleddian on St Martin's day the year 1375, and was buried at Tewkesbury before the doors of the vestry next to the presbytery, where his wife built the stone chapel crafted with marvellous skill, which was dedicated in honour of the Holy Trinity. That man, among other goods that he bestowed on us, gave to us the richest chalice of the purest gold, and another very precious jewel crafted with marvellous skill, in which the body of the Lord is placed on solemn feast-days. And the lady Elizabeth his wife remained in her widowhood after the death of her husband for nearly thirty-three years. And she died on St Anne's day AD 1409 and was buried within the choir of Tewkesbury on the left of her husband under a stone of marble. That woman, among other goods that she bestowed on the monastery, presented one set of red vestments with gold lions: namely, one chasuble with three dalmatics and ready-made albs, with fifteen copes. After the death of Edward II, Thomas his son and heir succeeded, the earl of Gloucester, who was wickedly killed at Bristol by the common people, on the third day after the feast of St Hilary, AD 1400. He was buried at Tewkesbury in the middle of the choir under a lamp which burns perpetually before the body of the Lord; and he died the tenth year before his mother.

In AD 1414 the lord Richard III le Despenser, his son and heir, died in his eighteenth year at Merton, while he was in royal custody five miles from London, on the 7th October; but he was buried at Tewkesbury on the left of his father … And the lady Elizabeth, the first daughter of the lord Thomas and Constance his wife, and the sister of the said Richard, died at a youthful age at Cardiff, and was buried in the church of the blessed Mary there.[16] And in the seventh month after the lord Thomas le Despenser died, the lady Constance his wife bore him an

16 I.e. in the church of Cardiff Priory, a daughter house of Tewkesbury Abbey.

excellent daughter, named Isabella, at Cardiff on St Anne's day, AD 1400. And afterwards the lady Constance was given in marriage to the lord Thomas, earl of Arundel, by whom she bore a daughter named Eleanor, who was afterwards married through the lady Isabella her sister, then countess of Warwick, to Hugh lord of Audley, by whom she bore a son named James; to whom the lord William Bristow, abbot of Tewkesbury, was godparent.

After the death of the lord Richard III le Despenser, the lady Isabella his sister took up the le Despenser lordship, and was espoused to the lord Richard IV de Beauchamp, son and heir of the lord William Beauchamp, and lord of Abergavenny, on the day of the Seven Sleepers in the year 1411. The lord Thomas Parker, eighteenth abbot of this place, officiated at their wedding at Tewkesbury ... While the lord king Henry V was attacking the French, the lord Richard IV de Beauchamp was made earl of Worcester at London. And the lady Isabella his wife conceived from him and bore to him a daughter named Elizabeth, who was born at Hanley the 16th day of September, the year of grace 1415 ... The lord abbot Thomas Parker was godfather to her, and she was afterwards given in marriage to the lord Edward Neville the younger brother of the earl of Westmorland, from whom was born the lord George, their heir.

And that Richard IV de Beauchamp, afterwards earl of Worcester, in the time of King Henry V, on the 18th March AD 1421, in France at Meaux en Brye, was struck in the side by a catapulted stone and died there soon afterwards. He was buried the 25th day of April at Tewkesbury, at the end of the choir, between the choir and the chapel of the founder, between two columns where afterwards the lady Isabella his wife ordained a beautiful chapel crafted with marvellous skill, which she caused to be consecrated in honour of the blessed lover of Our Lord Jesus Christ, Mary Magdalene,[17] of St Barbara the virgin, and St Leonard the abbot. This chapel was dedicated on the 2nd day of August AD 1438. A year and ten months after the lord Richard IV earl of Worcester died, the lord Richard Beauchamp V (the earl of Warwick, and the cousin of Richard IV, earl of Worcester) having had papal dispensation, espoused the lady Isabella, countess of Worcester and widow of the aforesaid lord Richard, and took possession of her in the county of Warwick, AD 1423, on the 26th day of November. After a year and three months and a few days, on the 22nd day of March, AD 1425, the lady Isabella bore to Richard V her husband an excellent boy and their heir, named

17 A phrase with no *Da Vinci Code*-like connotations.

Henry, at the castle of Hanley. But Master John de Fordham, prior of Worcester, officiated at the aforesaid wedding, when the lord William Bristow, abbot of Tewkesbury was present in the same castle ...

### 34. Durham Cathedral Priory and Sir Robert Ogle: the exchange of patronage between monastery and aristocracy

As well as maintaining good relations with their legal patrons, it also benefited religious houses to win the favour of other local notables. As one of the dominant families in fifteenth-century Northumberland, where the Benedictine monks of Durham owned much property and two daughter houses, the Ogles were worth courting. These two letters – taken from the voluminous letter-books of the late medieval priors of Durham – shed light on how the relationship between large monastery and influential local landowner could work in practice.

Translated from Durham Cathedral Muniments, Reg. Parv. III, fos 13, 28v (English).

### Letter directed to Robert Ogle, knight:

Right worshipful Sir, I recommend myself to you in my most special manner, thanking you with all my heart for your good help, support and effectual favour shown and done to me. The time I was staying with you in the north country, I was beseeching God for His sovereign mercy to reward you where I do not suffice. And may it please you to remember how my brother, the bursar, showed to you at Norham certain evidence of a portion of ground lying between Norham and Shoresworth, called Whiterig, given to St Cuthbert[18] and his ministers by Hugh, sometime bishop of Durham – in which portion we are disturbed against right and good conscience by the freeholders of Norham, to our great hurt and nuisance to our tenant at Shoresworth. For this reason, I beseech you as heartily as I can, and as my singular trust is and has been for a long time in you more than any knight living, that it may please you to rule and govern this matter as you best can, so that St Cuthbert and his ministers may have their right, and our tenant at Shoresworth rejoice in our name and occupy the aforesaid portion of ground. Since we and no others have right in this, as our evidence openly shows, furthermore I beseech you that when you come to our district you will dispose yourself to visit St Cuthbert so that we may talk together about this and other matters, both for your hearty ease and mine as I trust fully to God, who

18 The patron saint of Durham Cathedral Priory.

may have you evermore in His gracious keeping, and send you much worship in this world and heavenly bliss at your ending. Written at Durham the 6th day of March [1447].

Letter sent to Robert Ogle, knight:

Worshipful, right trusty and well-beloved Sir, I recommend myself to you in the most special manner, thanking you for your great gentleness and kindness always shown to me and my brethren, and having you to know that I have received your letter and I will with good heart attend to your desire in receiving that child into our almshouse and school for whom you have written; praying you, as my trust is in you, that you will favour, support and defend the proctor of our church of Norham in the execution and raising of the profits which belong to it by due and right, so that he is not oppressed or vexed therefore against that, as right and law will determine. And also that you will remember and have in mind to support and put in peace the right of St Cuthbert in that portion of ground called Whiterig, lying between Shoresworth and Norham, in order to increase your reward in everlasting bliss, in which, after worship had in this life, may our Saviour Christ Jesus keep you by his mercy and grace. Written at Durham the [blank] day of February [1448].

## 35. An unheralded benefactor of Hatfield Regis Priory, 1329

In 1324, in return for his financing a major rebuilding programme in the priory (a house of modest wealth), the Benedictine monks of Hatfield Regis in Essex granted Robert Taper and his wife the same spiritual services as were accorded to the original founder of the house. Five years later, however, a new and sceptical cohort of monks questioned whether their benefactor truly deserved such fulsome commemoration. In the following inquisition, Taper describes – with remarkable patience – his benefactions to the priory.

Translated (with minor corrections of transcription from British Library, Harley MS 60) from W. Dugdale, *Monasticon Anglicanum*, ed. J. Caley, H. Ellis and B. Bandinel (London, 1846), IV, 434–5 (Latin).

Memorandum that when brother Roger de Crishale, formerly prior of the monastery of Hatfield Regis, William de Sabrichford, the subprior, and certain other senior monks of this monastery related that Robert Taper of Hatfield had raised up at his own expense the greater part of the new fabric of their conventual church, and had bestowed many other goods on this monastery, nevertheless some of their brethren were uncertain whether or not these things were true as related. Therefore, brother John of Hatfield, then subprior there, wishing to be informed for his benefit and for the benefit of the other brothers about these matters, called the below-written brothers, namely Hugh of Hatfield, Geoffrey of Crowland, Godfrey of Chelneston, Alexander of Berdefeld and William of Dunmow, then the conventual clerk, who came together before Robert Taper himself on the 8th day of the month of July, AD 1329, in the choir of the conventual church, to inquire more truly from the same Robert about the aforesaid benefactions.

Asked therefore by brother John, the subprior, if, as had been related, he had caused the chapel of the cross in the said church to be built at his own expense, together with the new fabric of the oratory then adjoining the chapel, he answered yes; except however for the food of the workers, for part of the cost of the carriage of materials, and for a certain pile of stones gathered in the church. Asked also if he had caused the chapel of the Blessed Virgin Mary to be built at his own expense, together with the new fabric of the oratory then adjoining the chapel, he answered yes, except for part of the cost of carriage and the food of the workers; and he added that his wife caused the ceiling of the same chapel to be painted at her own expense.

Asked also if he had caused the glass of the new presbytery to be made at his own expense, together with the ironwork, he said yes, except for the window that John de la Lee had caused to be glazed. Asked also if he had caused the great window to be made from the south side at his own expense, together with the glass and ironwork, he said yes, and to the assessment. Asked also if he had caused the great window at the west end of the parish church to be made in the same way, he answered yes, for he handed over £20 sterling for the construction of that window, as William who was then subprior said.

Asked also if he had caused the great bell to be made, he said yes, and it cost £20 beyond half a mark. Asked also if he had found at his own expense one stone-cutter for the construction of our dormitory, he said yes, beyond the food; and he furnished much more for this work, so he said, and did not know how to mention everything individually. Asked also if he had formerly made the improvement of the old wooden structure of the old presbytery, together with the lead roofing, he said yes. Asked also if he had appropriated the tenement of Philip Bush to the monastery at his own expense, he said yes, and it cost all together 190 marks. And he made mention, just as was before revealed to brother John himself, that he formerly received the manor at Nosterfield not in recompense for his expenses in the acquisition of the said Bush tenement, but at the request of brother William, then subprior, for the restoration of the manor which was itself nearly destroyed – and after its restoration it rendered from there 20 marks a year to the monastery. Indeed he had conferred his own tenement in Hatfield to the monastery a little before, which the brethren themselves have seen with their own eyes.

Asked moreover if he paid on the monastery's behalf to Nicholas de Storteford 27 marks for a certain obligation they had made to him, he said yes. And the same Robert immediately after the inquiries and these responses voluntarily offered himself to swear over the high altar that each and every one of the aforesaid things was true. This Robert also conferred many other things in proportion to the time and places involved that were little touched on in the aforesaid inquisition.

# X: THE RELIGIOUS SERVICES OF LATE MEDIEVAL MONASTERIES

Donations of new property may have been difficult to acquire for late medieval monasteries, but rather more common were benefactions made in return for specific religious services provided by the monks, nuns and canons. These services consisted principally of intercessory prayers and masses for the souls of benefactors, in order to shorten the time they would need to spend in Purgatory. Monastic prayers were quite often requested in wills, but they could also be secured by joining a convent's confraternity. Another important religious service provided by the religious was the saint cults they sponsored, which often formed a focus for local (and sometimes national) devotion. The documents in this section illustrate the nature of these religious services, provided by a variety of houses, as well as the demand for them among the monasteries' lay neighbours. Other material relating to saint cults and confraternities can be found in **7, 15, 40**.

## 36. Testamentary bequests to late medieval monasteries

Wills are the most plentiful source of information about lay benefaction to the Church in the later middle ages. Many make no mention of monasteries, but a significant minority remember houses of nuns, canons or monks in their bequests. The two examples given below, both from Yorkshire, are representative examples of the kinds of provision made by townsmen and knights respectively, and illustrate something of the different religious tastes of these two groups.

Translated from *Testamenta Eboracensia*, ed. J. Raine, J. Raine and J. Clay, 6 vols, Surtees Society, 4, 30, 45, 53, 79, 106 (1836–1902), I, 133–4, II, 181–3 (Latin).

## (a) The will of Roger de Moreton of York, 1390

In the name of God, Amen. On the 20th day of November AD 1390, I, Roger de Moreton, citizen and mercer of York, make my testament in this manner. Firstly, I leave and commend my soul to God Omnipotent, the Blessed Virgin Mary, and to all the saints, and my body for burial in the church of St Martin in Coney Street in York. Also I leave for my mortuary[19] my better garment tailored for my body. Also I leave

19 See above, p. 89 n. 16

for my forgotten tithes and offerings, 6s 4d. Also I leave to the fabric of the aforesaid church for having my burial there, 13s 4d. Also I leave twenty pounds of wax, to be made into five candles and to be burned around my body on the day of my burial. Also I leave two torches of wax, of 13s 4d in price, for burning at Mass on the day of my burial, and then for burning and serving in the church at the high altar. Also I leave to my parish chaplain, 2s. And to Sir Adam Fournyvall, chaplain there, 12d; and to Sir Robert de Clifford, chaplain there, 12d. And to Sir Roger de Malton, chaplain, 6s 8d. And to the parish clerk, 12d and to the sub-clerk there, 6d.

And I leave for funeral expenses and for the wake of my friends and neighbours, £5. Also I leave for distribution to paupers where the alms will best serve for the salvation of my soul, £5. Also I leave to a certain honest and worthy chaplain for celebrating divine service for the salvation of my soul, for the souls to which I am obliged, and those from whom I have anything justly or unjustly, and for the souls of all the faithful departed, for two whole years in the aforementioned church, £10. And to the fabric of Great St Peter's, York, 13s 4d.

Also I leave to the Carmelite friars of York, 20s. Also to each house of the other three orders of mendicant friars in York, the sum of £2. Also I leave to the poor nuns of the house of St Clement next to York, for dividing between them, 20s. Also I leave to the poor inmates of the hospital of St Leonard, York, 10s. And to the poor in the maison dieu[20] in Fossgate in York, 6s 8d. And to the four houses of lepers in the suburbs of York, in equal portions, 8s. Also I leave to the work of the fabric of the hospital of St Thomas the Martyr outside the Micklegate, 3s 4d. And to the poor in the maison dieu on the Ouse bridge in York, 12d. Also I leave to poor prisoners in the castle of York, 2s. Also I leave to the poor men and women in the maison dieu of Thomas Howm in Hertergate, 2s. Also I leave to the nuns of Keldholme, eight pounds of wax. Also to the nuns of Rosedale, eight pounds of wax, and to the nuns of Basedale, eight pounds of wax. And to the monks of Rievaulx, twelve pounds of wax. Also I leave to the poor in the maison dieu of John de Derthyngton in Peter Lane, 12d.

Also I leave to Roger, the son of Thomas my brother, 20s. Also I leave to Agnes del Berry, my servant, 6s 8d. Also I leave to Robert de Kyrkeby, my servant, 20s. And to John de Oswaldwyk, my servant, 20s. Also I leave to Isabella my daughter, nun of St Clement's of York, for her

20 A hospital for the poor.

black garments to be bought, according to the deliberation of Agnes, my wife, and my other executors, at suitable times according to her need, 4 silver marks. Also I leave to sister Elena of the same house of St Clement, 13s 4d. Also I leave to my daughter, Beatrice, 12d. And to Denyse, my servant, 12d. Also I leave to each of my godchildren, 12d. Also I leave for the improvement of the chapel of Moreton, 3s 4d. Also I leave to the children of Agnes, the wife of Robert Gudbarn of Haxby, for dividing between them in equal portions, 13s 4d. Also I leave to Master Roger son of Thomas de Moreton, 20s. Also I leave to Joan, the wife of William de Moreton, flax-hewer, 3s 4d.

## (b) The will of Sir John Stapleton, knight, 1455

In the name of God, Amen. On the 21st day of the month of February, AD 1455. I, John Stapleton of Wighill, knight. Firstly, I leave and commend my soul to Omnipotent God and to the glorious Blessed Virgin Mary and to all the saints of the court of heaven, and my body to be buried wherever God intends me to die. Also I give and leave 5 marks for purchasing one vestment in the parish church of Wighill, to serve as long as it is able to last, on which vestment I want the form of my arms to be made. And I leave for the fabric of the said church, 20s. To the vicar of the same church for my forgotten tithes and offerings, £2. To the prior of Healaugh Park, 20s; and to each canon-chaplain there, 13s 4d. And to each novice who is not a chaplain there, 3s 4d. To the fabric of the church of the said house of Healaugh Park, 40 marks. To the prioress of Sinningthwaite, 13s 4d; and to each nun there, 6s 8d; and to the fabric of the same house, £5. Also I leave to each order of friars mendicant in York, 13s 4d. To the fabric of the church of St Peter, York, 20s. To the guild of St Christopher, York, 6s 8d. To the prior of the house of Holy Trinity, York, 20s. To the convent of the same house, 20s; for the fabric of the said house's church, £2. To each house of lepers in York, 6s 8d. To be distributed among poor men and women lying in bed in York, £2.

I leave an adequate salary to one worthy and honest chaplain to celebrate divine service in the church where my body will be buried for my soul and the souls of my parents, and of all those from whom I have any goods unjustly, and all the faithful departed, for three whole years following my death. And if it happens that I am buried within any abbey or place of the religious, then I wish that the said chaplain be assigned by my executors to celebrate in the church where my body will be buried, as mentioned above. I leave for distribution to the poor, the blind, the lame and the impotent, for my soul on the day of my burial, <u>28 marks</u>.

[There follow bequests to his family, including a long list of personal possessions and valuables left to his wife, Margaret and to his son, William.]

To each anchorite within York, <u>13s 4d</u>. To the convent of the abbey of the Blessed Mary, York, for one obit, namely *Placebo* and *Dirige*[21] and a Requiem Mass to be said for my soul and for the souls of my parents and all the faithful departed, £2. I leave to my wife, Margaret, one gold ring with a ruby set and one chest bound with iron, being in the abbey of the Blessed Mary. And to William my son, two other gold rings called signets. And to Brian, my son, two other gold rings recently made in London, my three best furred robes and two other robes not lined with fur, my two best hoods and my two best doublets and one chest of spruce wood. I leave to the convent of nuns of Moxby, <u>20s</u>. Also I wish that my mortuary should be disposed according to the discretion of my executors and that the law of the church should be entirely kept. Also I leave to William Norton, esquire, <u>£2.</u> To Ralph Reresby, £2 for his labour. To William Castley, my servant, <u>20s</u>. To John Roueslay, my servant, <u>20s</u>. To Robert Dalby, my servant, <u>10s</u>. The residue is to be disposed by my executors for my soul as they see fit. I appoint as my executors Margaret my wife, William Norton, esquire and Brian my son, and Ralph Reresby as supervisor. With these witnesses, William Bramham, vicar of Helay and William Barwyke, vicar of Wighall.

## 37. A letter of confraternity from Hailes Abbey

Monastic grants of confraternity, such as this fifteenth-century example from the Cistercian abbey of Hailes (Gloucestershire), were widespread in late medieval England. They generally offered the recipient the same spiritual benefits on death as a member of the community – although some more important benefactors might be granted fuller forms of commemoration [cf. **35**] – and seem to have attracted considerable interest among the laity.

Translated from British Library, Royal 12 E xiv, fos 37–37v (Latin).[22]

William, by divine permission abbot of the monastery of Blessed Mary of Hailes and the convent of the same place, of the Cistercian Order and the diocese of Worcester, to our beloved in Christ, Sir William Peyto and Sir Thomas Gryseley, knights, and the lady Katherine, the wife of

21 See above, p. 158 n. 2.
22 © The British Library. All rights reserved.

the said Sir William: greeting in the embraces of the saviour. The affection of your sincere devotion and love, which you bear to us and our monastery, and especially your devotion to and reverence for the most precious blood of Our Lord Jesus Christ – a small part or drop of which is honourably and decently preserved in our monastery[23] – moves us to give to you in exchange for such transitory things a special recompense, spiritual compensations and things which concern the salvation of souls. We therefore admit and receive you by the present letters, in life and death alike, the aforesaid Sir William and Sir Thomas, knights and the lady Katherine into the fraternity of our monastery and of our entire order, and to participation in all the intercessions and spiritual good works which should happen to be made in our monastery and in our universal order of whatever land, by day and night, in masses, fasts, prayers, vigils, alms, disciplines and other good deeds, public and private. Adding as well and granting besides that when the day of your death should happen to come to pass, and has been communicated to us or our successors, that on the following day in our chapter there should be made a special absolution just as has been accustomed to be made for our brethren, sisters and benefactors, to endure in perpetuity. In witness of which, we have affixed our common seal. Given etc.

### 38. Entrants into the confraternity of St Albans Abbey in the 1420s

Alongside letters of confraternity, a small number of lists of new entrants to confraternities also survive, from large and small houses alike. These records, such as the St Albans example below, provide a valuable indication of the numbers and kinds of people joining confraternities – although the St Albans book of benefactors (British Library, Cotton Nero D vii) makes it clear that the following document does not give an exhaustive list of entrants to the house's confraternity in the 1420s.

Translated (with minor corrections of transcription from British Library, Harley MS 3775) from *Annales Monasterii S. Albani, a Johanne Amundesham, Monacho*, ed. H. T. Riley, 2 vols, Rolls Series, 28.5 (1870–71), I, 65–9 (Latin).

The names of those who received fraternity in the time of Abbot John VI [Whethamstede], AD 1421:

Sir Roland Lenteshale, steward of the lady Katherine the queen, and Sir John Styward, knights, and Lewis John were received into the

---

23 The celebrated relic, the Holy Blood of Hailes, given to the monastery by its patron, Edmund, earl of Cornwall in 1270.

fraternity of this monastery on the 10th day of March; on which day they bestowed on the convent 20s.

Sir Thomas More, formerly dean of St Paul's London, whose executors bestowed for the works of this church, £1 6s 8d.

John Shawe, formerly vintner of London, whose executors, by the legacy of the same John, gave to his son, Dom William Shawe, monk of this church, £20.

William Otes, citizen and mercer of London, for whose soul Robert Newtone gave for the new window at St Michael's altar, £2.

Sir John Chilterne, canon of St Paul's London, for whose soul Master Reginald Kentwood, dean of the same church, gave for the work of the infirmary and for other works of this monastery, £8 of gold.

Sir John Beule, formerly warden of the chapel of St Andrew, and afterwards vicar of St Peter's [St Albans], who left to the fabric of the church, 2 marks; and to the convent, £1 10s; and for the hall of the new infirmary, one large basin.

Sir John Trylle, warden of the chapel of St Andrew, who distributed to each claustral monk, for the salvation of his mother Helen, 4d.

Lady Katherine, anchorite of the Holy Martyr, Joan Parys, Christiana Browne, Sabina Femme, of London, having been devoted to God and to this monastery, were received into the fraternity on St Gregory's day; and they bestowed 20s.

On the feast of St Luke the Evangelist, William Bourghe and Katherine his wife, Peter Harchelle and Sir Henry Howe, chaplain, received fraternity of this church with a pious mind and with devotion.

AD 1424, on the day after the Epiphany of the Lord, the lord Humphrey, illustrious duke of Gloucester, with his wife, the lady Jacqueline, duchess of Holland, received fraternity of this church most devoutly. And on the same day they bestowed on the convent two pipes of good red wine, after they had spent their Christmas splendidly in this monastery.

John Hastelere and his wife received fraternity the first week of Lent. And in the same Lent William, master of the scholars, John Clobbe, and his wife, received fraternity, and they gave to the convent a pittance[24] of 13s 4d.

John Crosby, Juliana Huet, Henry Glasiere and Cecilia his wife received fraternity of this church, and they gave 20s.

24 See above, p. 100 n. 30.

John Croftone and his wife, and the prioress of the nuns of St Margaret's, received fraternity on the 27th January. They bestowed on the convent a pittance and wine, and £1 6s 8d.

On the Friday before the feast of St Michael, there were received into the fraternity John Barbour with his wife, John Bledlowe, previously deceased, and the wife of John West, recently deceased. They bestowed on the convent on the said day, £1 6s 8d.

On the vigil of the feast of St Alban there were received into the fraternity of the chapter our devout neighbours of this monastery, namely John Peryen', with his daughter, and the prioress of the Meadows,[25] with a nun; and they bestowed on the chapel of St Mary one frontal for the high altar there; and also Sir Henry Halsame.

AD 1428, on the day of the Holy Trinity, Master Thomas Aschwell, doctor of Sacred Theology, and William Flete were made brothers of our chapter; on whose reception resounded the new canticle, *Diligamus nos invicem, quia caritas ex Deo est*, etc.

And on the feast of Corpus Christi, a man of venerable life and devoted to God and to our patron [i.e. St Alban], the illustrious commander Richard, earl of Warwick, with his wife, Isabella, and with very many others, received in the chapter the benefit of fraternity of this monastery. On their solemn reception the canticle, devoutly uttered by the abbot following the chapter, resounded, *Albanus dum*, with the versicle, *Ora pro nobis, Beate Albane*, with the prayer *Deus, qui Beatum Albanum* by the abbot. And the same lord Richard bestowed on the convent, £5 of gold.

The lord Henry de Beauchamp, son and heir of the earl of Warwick, the lord Despenser, Emma Porter, John Pereys and Hugh le John were received into the fraternity.

On the day after Corpus Christi, the household of the said earl, devoutly inclined to devotion to God and his mother, received the benefit of fraternity devoutly, giving gifts of gold and silver. The sum of these gifts, both from the lord Richard and his wife, and from all their household, whose names here follow, extended to £10 11s 11d –

---

25 St Mary de Pré, a nunnery dependent on St Albans.

Names of the gentlemen:

Ralph Mountfort
Thomas Porter
Richard Middelmare
John Denyssch
William Menstone
John Waldyewe
Richard Thornes
Master Thomas Duncan
Ralph Mullyng
John Coliet
John Halfhyde
Ralph Lichefeld
John Bramtone
Richard Verney
William Warde
John de Bosse
John Stacy
John Pedulle
Thomas Maylston
William Lane
John Porkys
Alice Lythfott
Cecily Paynel and Margaret Euer, nuns of Sopwell

William Wythman, esquire, and the lord king's cook, bestowed on each claustral monk, 12d in the eighth year of the reign of King Henry VI [1429/30]. And Henry Dyper reverently received fraternity in the chapter, around the feast of St Martin. Taking leave of this world in the month of November, he left to the convent, £1 13s 4d; and he left as much for the building of the new gate.

John Martin, the executor of John Pekvyle, bestowed for building the chancel in the infirmary, 10 marks. And the same John Pekvyle, Simon and Alice and their wives were received into the fraternity of this church on the day of the Conversion of St Paul; and they bestowed 10 marks for the work of the church.

Henry Porter, 'fowcher', bestowed for the benefit of the new fabric in the infirmary, 10 marks; and to each monk in the convent, 8d, for the souls of his parents, whose names have been received in the fraternity of this monastery.

## 39. A prohibited saint cult at Frithelstock Priory, 1351–52

Monasteries of all kinds possessed miraculous images or relics, venerated by their lay neighbours. The canons of the small Augustinian priory of Frith-elstock in Devon were also active in promoting popular veneration in the mid-fourteenth century, although in this instance they incurred the wrath of their diocesan, Bishop John Grandisson of Exeter. Following his first letter, Grandisson was informed by his commissioners that the prior and canons had caused the altar and image to be removed, leaving the chapel deserted but not destroyed; and this partial compliance prompted his second missive. Neverthe-less, despite the bishop's fulminations, the chapel in question was still standing in the mid-eighteenth century.

Translated from *The Register of John de Grandisson, Bishop of Exeter, 1327–1369*, ed. F. Hingeston-Randolph, 3 vols (London and Exeter, 1894–99), II, 1110–12 (Latin).

### The first letter of Bishop Grandisson

John, etc. to the beloved sons in Christ, the dean of Hartland, and the vicars of the churches of Monkleigh and Buckland Brewer, of our diocese, greeting, grace and blessing. Although, according to the constitutions and precepts of the Holy Fathers, and other canonical sanctions, no-one ought to build a church or perpetual chapel without the foundation stone having been blessed and laid, and without a cross having been first set up in the place, by the diocesan, nor even to erect an altar by their own audacity there; however, it has reached our hearing that the religious men, the prior and convent of Frithelstock, of the order of St Augustine and our diocese, whose simplicity or ignorance of the law should not excuse them, on their own initiative and risking sacrilege, have caused to be built and raised a certain building under the name of a chapel near the wood called Wadeclyve, close to their monastery, in our diocese, not only without our licence but against our expressed will; and to have erected an altar in the same building, and also an image, or rather a counterfeit of one.

And although this building – which we treat with contempt and condemn, and, as much as it pertains to us, we consider and also proclaim profane and condemned, having been built not for the devotion of faith but from the quest of greed, as the profits of the exploits clearly proclaim – is not to be thought a chapel but rather a house of idolatry; nevertheless, some of our parishioners (which is more painful to report), whom the same prior and convent had caused to deviate from the true faith through their empty, heinous and condemned assertions, having forsaken their parish churches and other sacred places properly consecrated to God by bishops, and instead flocking to this profane place by reason of pilgrimage, are not afraid to engage in sacrifice to idols or rather more truly in sorcery.

Since, therefore, out of the pastoral concern enjoined to us, we are bound to confound devious errors (the more frequent they are, the more they lead astray from the divine law and the more serious the danger for souls they carry for our subjects), we have commanded … that the plantation of such idolatry – as depraved superstition and heretical wisdom – should be uprooted; and so should the opportunity to wander[26] and for lewdness for the claustral monks of the same monastery, to the offence of Him to whom they have vowed by their own will to give service in their monastery, abandoning the pleasures and delights of the world.

Therefore, we enjoin and command to you, jointly and separately, ordering strictly that, going to the said profane place in person, you should warn and effectually persuade the prior and convent, enjoining them, just as we enjoin and command by the tenor of the present letters, that they should destroy the aforesaid building, erroneously named a chapel, erected and constructed against our prohibition, before the present solemn festival of Christmas, for the term finally appointed to them by you; and that they should destroy or cause to be destroyed and pulled down the altar at their own expense, under pain of greater excommunication to the said prior, and suspension to the said convent with due threats, if they have not obeyed our warnings with effect.

Prohibiting to all Christ's faithful that henceforth they should by no means approach the aforesaid place by reason of pilgrimage, or make any kind of offerings there, under pain of the greater excommunication written above. What you have done in the aforesaid matter, and how you have executed this mandate of ours, you should certify us, before the present festival of the Epiphany of the Lord [6th January], by your letters patent, having this tenor. Given at Chudleigh, on the 17th day of the month of November, AD 1351 …

## The second letter of Bishop Grandisson

John, etc. to the beloved sons in Christ, the dean of Hartland and the vicars of the churches of Monkleigh and Buckland Brewer, of our diocese, greeting, grace and blessing … A little while ago, we understood surely that against the sacred canons – out of the irreligious and

26 I.e. to leave the monastic enclosure.

profane acquisitiveness of a certain regular, canon in name but not in deed – a certain chapel has been built, in commemoration rather of the proud and disobedient Eve, or the lewd Diana, than of the most humble and obedient Blessed Virgin Mary, in a wood outside the precinct of the monastery of Frithelstock, of the order of St Augustine, of our diocese, leading more to dissoluteness than devotion and to worldly utility than the salvation of souls. This chapel, proceeding according to the sacred canons, we ordered not unjustly to be pulled down. This holy and canonical mandate of ours, the prior and the others of the convent are not attending to, but rather, depending on their own discretion and disobedience, they permit the chapel to remain intact.

Since, therefore, urged on by our conscience, we are unable to ignore such damnable presumption without remedy, we command you, firmly enjoining you by virtue of obedience that you should warn the said prior and convent a first, second and a third and final time, enjoining them, just as we enjoin and command by the tenor of the present letters, that, within twenty days from the time of this your warning made to the prior and convent … they should cause the said house, erroneously named chapel, to be broken up right up to the churchyard, and its foundations pulled down. And when it has been dismantled as above, they should transfer and take, or at least cause to be taken, the timber and the greater stones into the priory's precinct, to be turned to its advantage and convenience; and this is under pain of greater excommunication for the prior and suspension for the convent, if they do not obey your warnings, or rather more truly ours, with effect … And you should likewise exhort the prior and convent that they should reverently engage, as is fitting, in that devotion to the Glorious Virgin Mary which the Holy Spirit will inspire in them in the chapel of the Blessed Virgin Mary built within the precinct of the priory, completely abandoning and moving away from all kinds of irregular lewdness and the opportunity for wandering.

To these things, you should peremptorily cite the prior, or cause him to be cited, so that he may appear before us or our commissary, on the Monday before the present feast of the cathedra of St Peter [20 February], to answer in person concerning such great disobedience, wantonness and contempt … Given at Chudleigh, on the 28th day of the month of January, A. D. 1352 …

# XI: THE SOCIAL SERVICES OF LATE MEDIEVAL MONASTERIES

Religious houses were expected to serve not only the spiritual but also the practical needs of their neighbours and patrons. These social services took three main forms: hospitality, education and charity. It is clear that monasteries took these responsibilities seriously, although it should be remembered that they were only one of several institutions providing for social welfare in late medieval England, and that this was always a secondary role of canons, nuns and monks. The nature, extent and changing face of monastic hospitality, education and charity are illustrated below, and also in several other documents in this collection (see the cross-references in the introductions to individual sources).

## 40. Monastic hospitality: Henry VI's visit to Bury St Edmunds Abbey, 1433–34

The Benedictine Rule states that monasteries are to treat all visitors as if they were Christ, while the social customs of the day required all major landowners to be generous hosts. Monasteries also owed hospitality to their patron, who was in many cases the king. Few royal visits were as extended as that of the young Henry VI to the wealthy Benedictine abbey of Bury St Edmunds in 1433–34, however, which lasted four months. This account of the visit, entered by Abbot William Curteys of Bury into his register, outlines both the advantages and the disadvantages of this responsibility. For other perspectives on monastic hospitality, see **22, 52**.

Translated (with minor corrections of transcription from British Library, Add. MS 14848) from W. Dugdale, *Monasticon Anglicanum*, ed. J. Caley, H. Ellis and B. Bandinel (London, 1846), III, 113n (Latin).

## Concerning the coming of King Henry VI to the monastery of [Bury] St Edmunds

When the most serene prince and lord, the lord Henry VI, by the grace of God king of England and France and lord of Ireland, was ruling and presiding in his Parliament at Westminster, in the twelfth year of his reign and age, on the feast of All Saints [1st November], as is the custom of the royal house, the king with his council finally determined that he would carry through and complete the solemnities of the next Christmas then following at the monastery of Bury

St Edmunds, and reside there continually until the feast of St George [23rd April]. When the truth of this proposed expense was disclosed to William Curteys, then abbot of the said monastery, being personally in his manor of Elmswell with his household, the abbot, although struck by such a novelty – since in no chronicles he was able to have found did the king of England, at least at that time, decree his stay there by royal edict – all the same gladly and cheerfully allowed such new things. And starting on the journey to the monastery within a few days with his retinue and household, he fittingly adorned his palace (which at that time severe degradation and ruin was threatening) with various structures and lavish buildings, having summoned and hired eighty craftsmen and labourers for the space of one month for the completion of this work; accordingly he was able to shore up every part of the palace with the necessary strengthening. He had with him besides one hundred officials of every rank at that time, entertaining the advance-party of the royal visit.

And so that the coming of such a prince – doubly crowned, presiding by hereditary right over the rule of two kingdoms[27] – should be received with worthy honour, the abbot called to him the alderman and the more powerful men of the town [of Bury St Edmunds], and discussed with them what kind and colour of clothing they should wear at the meeting of the prince. Although many of the commons of the town were of different opinions, nevertheless at last they agreed unanimously, allured as one by the abbot's advice, that the alderman and burgesses should be content with scarlet, and the lesser folk with red cloth with hoods the colour of blood.

With the day of the royal arrival dawning, on Christmas Eve, the alderman, burgesses and commons of the town, to the number of five hundred horsemen, in the aforesaid dress, attended on the pleasing Newmarket Plain to meet the king. These attendants, coming before the great din of the royal party and stretching for the length of one mile, led the king up to the precinct of the monastery, to the middle way between the gate and the south door of the monastery (the procession did not dare to receive him on the other side because of the deformity of the ruined [western] bell-tower and the falling of unsound stones). Here, grasped by the arms of the earl of Warwick, the king descended from his palfrey and, turning himself towards the procession at a place covered all around with silk cloth, he knelt there to worship the image of

27  Henry VI was crowned king of England in 1429 and king of France 1431, the latter coronation in accordance with the treaty of Troyes (1420).

the cross. When the king had been received with all processional solemnity, with all the brethren of the monastery standing by in precious copes, the venerable fathers the bishop of Norwich and the aforesaid abbot, both dressed in pontificalia,[28] solemnly censed him. And when he had been sprinkled with holy water by the hand of the abbot, and the cross had been brought by the same abbot to the royal mouth to be kissed first, the procession led on to the high altar, going forth with the antiphon *Ave rex gentis Anglorum*, the notes of the harmony sweetly poured out by playing organs.

When the solemnities of the procession were finished, and the prayers offered at the shrine to God and to St Edmund, the king gave sincere and special thanks to the abbot for the good deeds and expenses he had most courteously made for his household. This settled, he took himself together with the nobles to the abbot's palace, and the splendour of this celebrated palace, its model furnishing being superior to others, much pleased everyone. There on the feast of Christmas, after High Mass was celebrated in the monastery, following a solemn procession in which he walked crowned, the king occupied the great hall among the guests at dinner and completed the solemnities of the feast there up to Epiphany [6th January]. Meanwhile the abbot bestowed many precious gifts on the king. Indeed, he visited also the nobles and their servants with notable sums of gold, to be divided among them each according to his rank ...

Thus therefore with the passing of the season of Christmas, the king asked for the prior's chamber, where he stayed with his nobles until the 23rd day of January, on account of the sweet breeze from the waters close by there, the healthy air and the delightful fragrance of the vineyard. Through the open gates of this vineyard he frequently went with the earls and barons, for the sake of walking and hunting, to the open fields and the flourishing woods, where by the attack of the hunting dogs the deceit of the fox was avenged and the speed of the hares was made lame.

And at last (as the human condition is accustomed to turn aside to various things and always to desire new things) the king, having heard that the abbot's manor of Elmswell was situated in a delightful place, had been very suitably repaired and was endowed with fish-ponds and also surrounded by ditches and woods, decided in his mind to make a stay there for a time. He took himself to the said manor on the 23rd day

28 The robes and insignia of a bishop, also permitted to mitred abbots (see above, p. 119 n. 65).

of January with the earls, barons and other notables in great number, where he rejoiced as much as possible in the catching of fish and birds, whose aerial power, submitting to the blows, was completely overthrown by the attack of birds of prey. The abbot on repeated occasions appeased the king with various lavish presents, at one time of swans, pheasants, partridges and other game, and at another time of pickerel, pikes, eels and other fish in no small number. And his generosity in these and other things was received by the king and his men with worthy praise.

And at length, with the vigil of the Purification of the Blessed Virgin [1st February] dawning, he returned to the palace of the monastery. When the solemnity of this feast had been completed, he returned again to the aforesaid manor, continuing there approvingly with his accustomed recreation until the beginning of Lent. Returning at that time for the whole of Lent, he remained in the prior's chamber until the feast of Easter came, whose solemnities he kept in the palace.

At length, when the time of his removal to London had arrived, the duke of Gloucester and the other nobles, together with the more powerful knights, esquires and servants of the royal court, on account of the singular and special affection which they held towards the king and martyr, St Edmund; and considering besides the purity and moral cleanliness of the religion, the intercession of prayers, the masses and the other divine offices celebrated most devoutly in the monastery; having first made anxious request in this regard before the abbot to be made partakers of all the above, they were admitted into the fraternity of the monastery in perpetuity.

Therefore, the king on his return, lying prostrate before St Edmund, discharged devout and humble prayers to God and the blessed martyr. And at length rising, following the duke of Gloucester and the other nobles, he passed over to the chapter house, where having sent immediately for the abbot, even though he was the patron and founder there, he nevertheless willed (as he asserted) to be received in the fraternal number of the monastery, just like the other nobles. In the view of the nobles standing around, according to the royal petition, the abbot immediately received the king piously and devoutly, and having given him a kiss as a sign of the fraternal bond, he added him to the said number, to be made a partaker in all the prayers, masses and other good works to be carried out there in perpetuity.

And then soon after, with the nobles standing by, the duke of Gloucester, lying prostrate before the king, sincerely implored him that his royal highness would deign to return thanks to the abbot on account of the tireless kindness which he had rendered towards him and his men in gifts and expenses. The king without a pause cheerfully received the abbot by hand, and thanked him many times. And saying farewell to everyone, he earnestly commended himself and his men to God and to St Edmund and to the prayers of the abbot and his brethren.

## 41. The education of Bridget Plantagenet at St Mary's Abbey, Winchester

Many nunneries were involved in the education of children in the later middle ages, providing schooling for girls and also for young boys. The nunnery of St Mary's Winchester, a relatively wealthy house, is recorded to have had twenty-six aristocratic girls studying there in 1536, including Bridget Plantagenet, the daughter of Viscount Lisle (the illegitimate son of Edward IV). For nunnery schools, see also **6, 18**.

Translated from *The Lisle Letters*, ed. M. St Clair Byrne, 6 vols (Chicago, 1981), III, nos 537, 539, V, no. 1226 (English).

### Elizabeth Shelley, abbess of St Mary's Winchester, to Lady Lisle, 2nd October 1534

My singular and special good lady, I heartily recommend myself to your good ladyship, informing you that I have received from your servant this summer a side of venison and two and a half dozen peewits. And whereas your ladyship writes that you sent me an ermine cap for your daughter, surely I have seen none; but the tawny velvet gown that you write of, I have received. I have sent to you, by the bringer of your letter, your daughter's black velvet gown. Also I have caused kirtles[29] to be made of her old gowns, according to your writing. And the 10s you sent is laid out for her, and more, as it shall appear by a bill of reckoning which I have made of the same. And I trust she lacks nothing that is necessary for her. And I pray that Jesus may always preserve my good lord and you to His pleasure, the 2nd day of October …, Elizabeth Shelley, abbess.

### Elizabeth Shelley, abbess of St Mary's Winchester, to Lady Lisle, 26th February 1535

After due recommendation, may it please your good ladyship to know that I have received your letter, dated the 4th day of February last past, by which I do perceive your pleasure is to know how mistress Bridget

29 I.e. tunics.

your daughter does, and what things she lacks. Madam, thanks be to God, she is in good health, but I assure your ladyship that she lacks convenient clothing, for she has neither a whole gown nor kirtle, except the gown and kirtle that you sent her last. And also she has not one good partlet[30] to put over her neck, and only one good coif[31] to put upon her head. Therefore, I beseech your ladyship to send to her such clothing as she lacks, as quickly as you may conveniently.

Also the bringer of your letter showed to me that your pleasure is to know how much money I have received for mistress Bridget's board, and how long she has been with me. Madam, she has been with me a whole year ending the 8th day of July last past, and as many weeks as is between that day and the day of making this bill, which is thirty-three weeks; and so she has been with me a whole year and thirty-three weeks, which is in all four score and five weeks. And I have received from mistress Katherine Motton, 10s, and from Stephen Bedham, 20s; and I received the day of making this bill from John Harrison, your servant, £2; and so I have received in all, since she came to me, towards the payment for her board, £3 10s. Also, madam, I have laid out for her, for mending her gowns and for two Matins books, four pairs of hose and four pairs of shoes, and other small things, 3s 5d. And, good madam, any pleasure that I may do your ladyship and also my prayer you shall be assured of, with the grace of Jesus, who may preserve you and all yours in honour and health. Amen. Written at Winchester, the 26th day of February, by she who is at your commandment, Elizabeth Shelley.

### Elizabeth Shelley, abbess of St Mary's Winchester, to Lady Lisle, 21st September 1538

Madam, in my most lowly manner, my duty remembered, this is to advertise your ladyship, that on the 14th or 15th day before Michaelmas, mistress Waynam and mistress Fawkenor came to Winchester to see mistress Bridget Lisle, with whom came two of my lord's servants; and they desired to take mistress Bridget to Sir Anthony Windsor's to amuse her for a week. And because she was out of clothing, so that master Windsor might see her, I was the better content to let her go; and since that time she has come no more to Winchester. In this, I beseech your ladyship to think no unkindness of me for my lightly sending her away: for if I had not thought that she would come back, she should not have gone there at that time. And I thus refer myself to your ladyship, and I

30 A female garment worn over the neck or the upper part of the chest.
31 A cap.

beseech Jesus long to preserve you and all yours. Written at Winchester the 21st day of September by your poor bedewoman, Dame Elizabeth Shelley.

### 42. The appointment of a schoolmaster at Llanthony Secunda Priory, 1502

Male monasteries also provided education for local children, but their clientele was rather different from that of nunneries. This indenture provides details about how the grammar school of the wealthy Augustinian canons of Llanthony Secunda in Gloucester was to operate, and for whom. See also **34, 44** for further materials about the schools of monks and canons.

Translated from *A Calendar of the Registers of the Priory of Llanthony by Gloucester 1457–66, 1501–25*, ed. J. Rhodes, Gloucestershire Record Series, 15 (2002), 60–1 (Latin).

This indenture was made on the 12th day of September, the 18th year of the reign of King Henry VII [1502] between the lord Edmund, prior of the house and church of the Blessed Mary of Llanthony by Gloucester and the convent of the same place on the one part; and Thomas Browning, a literate man, on the other part. It witnesses that between the aforesaid parties the following agreement has been made: namely that Thomas in his own person shall hold and supply a grammar school within the priory of Llanthony in a certain appropriate place assigned to him by the prior and convent, from the day of St Michael the Archangel next following after the grant of the present letters for the duration of his natural life, while he is able-bodied; and if he should become impotent of body, then by his deputy, sufficiently trained in Latin grammar. And, at appropriate times each day, he shall faithfully instruct, educate and teach every canon and boy being in this priory coming to this school freely and diligently in Latin grammar, to the best of his ability.

Taking and holding from the prior and convent annually during the aforesaid term, for his learning and diligent labour thus employed in the said science, one tenement with the adjacent garden for his house in a certain street of Gloucester called Severn Street now appointed and assigned to him, built and repaired, and moreover to be repaired, at the cost and expense of the prior and convent themselves.

And beyond this, Thomas shall have every day within the priory honest and sufficient food and drink suitable for him, and towards night-time every day for his livery one loaf with an appropriate portion of ale. And he shall have annually one gown of the livery of the prior of Llanthony's gentlemen at that time, just as that prior shall happen to give and distribute to other gentlemen for their livery. And he shall have four marks of legal English money at the usual four terms of the year, namely at the feasts of Christmas, the Annunciation of the Blessed Mary, the Nativity of St John the Baptist and St Michael the Archangel, by equal portions to be paid to him faithfully during the aforesaid term.

And it will be well permitted to Thomas to receive and teach within the priory in the place assigned to him as many other scholars as shall happen to come to him, for his own need and necessity; receiving from them school fees as agreed between them, without any opposition from the prior and convent and their successors during the aforesaid term: on condition that those secular scholars should not make or cause to be made any loss, prejudice or detriment to the priory in any way while they are residing there and living soberly and honestly.

And for observing well and faithfully every one of these agreements on the part of this Thomas, he has sworn a corporal oath concerning them before the prior and convent. In witness of which, we the aforesaid prior and convent have affixed our common seal to one part of this indenture, remaining in the possession of Thomas; and I, Thomas, have affixed my seal to the other part of this indenture remaining in the possession of the prior and convent and their successors. Given in our chapter house of Llanthony, the day and year written above.

## 43. The reconfiguration of monastic charity at Gloucester Abbey, 1516

Monasteries provided charity in a number of ways. Leftover food was distributed to the poor; gifts of money were made by the superior and obedientiaries; and more institutionalised charity was offered through the management of hospitals, almshouses and almonry schools. The following document, from the large Benedictine abbey of Gloucester, reflects the growing movement away from indiscriminate charity in late medieval England. Further insight into monastic almsgiving, and attitudes to it, can be found in **7, 10, 22, 28, 48, 50**.

Translated from *Historia et Cartularium Monasterii Sancti Petri Gloucestriae*, ed. W. Hart, 3 vols, Rolls Series, 33 (1863–67), III, lxxxiii–lxxxix (English and Latin).

... ⌈In times past⌉ it has pleased the honourable fathers and governors,

abbots of this holy monastery, with the consent of their brethren ... to
order ... that the alms of the whole house be distributed by the almoner,
from the proceeds of the manor of Standish, in corn, which in common
years amounts to the sum of £16; and also with other petty alms, such
as thirteen frieze gowns[32] distributed by the town monk,[33] and 2s in
money to each of thirteen poor men yearly, to be paid by the cellarer,
besides the abbot's alms dish, which amounts to the sum of 8d per week.
In times past the alms of Standish, to the aforesaid sum, have been
distributed first in money and then afterwards in bread and now finally
in corn within the monastery, the customary gathering for which has
caused much inconvenience and disorderly behaviour (such as brawling,
swearing, blaspheming and fighting, with the infectious gathering of
sick and unthrifty persons) to the great disquiet of the monastery and
troublesome disturbance to its officers and inhabitants ... And since it
is left and stands at and in the disposition and pleasure of the abbot for
the time being, with the consent of his brethren, to make alteration and
reformation as aforesaid, it has therefore pleased William [Malvern],
by God's permission abbot of the monastery, by the whole assent and
consent of the convent there, the year of Our Lord God 1516 ... – the
grace of the Holy Ghost first invoked and desired, to the praise of God
and for the redemption of the founders' souls, with other benefactors,
brothers and sisters, both quick and dead – to ordain, assign and establish a certain fraternity in the honour of the Holy Cross, of thirteen
poor men commonly to be called Peter's Men. These men are to pray
devoutly each day for the founders and benefactors, brothers and sisters
of the monastery, and to be found and maintained from the said ill-used
proceeds, altered from corn to money, with further aid and help added
by the provision of the abbot and convent ... forever to be observed in
the form and manner that follows hereafter.

In the name of God, Amen. Seeing that anything without distinct
order may not long continue or endure, we order, decree and authorise
by this present ordinance and statute that thirteen poor, honest men
are to be assigned and elected by the abbot of the time. Fathers and
brothers of his convent are first and principally to be preferred to the
same position; secondly, servants who over a long period have spent
their youth well in true service of this monastery; thirdly, tenants of
the monastery, impoverished and impaired and not able to continue
and maintain their tenures (and namely from the lordship of Standish),

32 Gowns made with a coarse woollen cloth.
33 The Gloucester obedientiary responsible for the house's property in the town.

and not without reasonable cause; and after them generally men of the town and country near about, in default of the others aforesaid. Of these poor men, one of the most discreet and honest shall be assigned by the abbot to be prior over them, and to take precedence over them in all places. To be distinguished from them, he shall continually wear a black scapular,[34] and he shall receive on Saturday afternoons each week 9d (the other twelve receiving 8d apiece in good money from the subprior). We, the abbot and convent, commit to him the charge, oversight, governance and correction of the others, as well as the receipt and payment of money ... and, as part of his reward for his charitable labours, he shall enjoy and receive each year half of all kinds of forfeitures, fines and penalties paid [by the poor men], on making a true account to the abbot of the monastery for the time being, on the feast of Michaelmas. The other half of the said forfeitures is to be delivered to the precentor[35] by the abbot, to be used for the repair of the books in the choir.

Furthermore we ordain and assign the town monk to prepare and ordain for the said brethren, before the feast of St John the Baptist each year, thirteen honest gowns and one scapular of black cloth, not under the price of 20d per broad yard. Every man should receive at least three broad yards for his gown and hood, or more if their stature so requires; and the scapular and the said gowns are to be made with tight sleeves and tight at the front. They are to wear continually a large hood about their necks and a great pair of beads likewise at all times, when they are not actually praying, with the arms of the monastery embroidered and affixed on their right shoulders to the value of sixpence each, and a cross of red and blue prominent on their breasts ... providing always that their outermost clothing and hood is always black and honest, and will be left (if they depart) for those who succeed them in the monastery. It is provided also that the hood and beads of every one of them at their first entry will be consecrated at the rood altar by the subprior (or one in his place saying the Mass of the Holy Cross there), the poor man kneeling there in his gown during the Mass.

And after Mass, clothed with hood and his beads, he is to be brought down immediately to his place by the subprior, and to swear there to observe the confidential matters of the monastery. At his first entry he is to sit in the lowest place of all his company, and so to continue at all times until another enters. And at his first beginning, he is to enter with

---

34 A short cloak worn about the shoulders, particularly associated with the religious orders.

35 See above, p. 131 n. 87.

his company at the long peal of Prime, standing outside their stalls with their faces to the prior, attending to the names of the founders read by him, which are contained in a table there, and to pray specially for them. After that, they are to enter into their stalls, and kneel there in their order with their beads in their hands, devoutly praying all the time of Prime. When this is done, they shall follow their prior in twos up to the high altar and kneel there on the lower step, the prior also in their midst, praying devoutly during the Mass said there for the founders; and then come down again to their stalls, and say there a Pater Noster, Ave and Credo.[36] They are then to depart and go at their liberty – although not to the common plays – until the High Mass, commonly the last Mass.

And furthermore they are to be at the beginning of all requiem masses for the founders contained and noted in their table, and at those for all abbots of the monastery, and at the High Mass of that day. And they are to continue in their stalls as aforesaid until these masses are ended, except at the time of the elevation of the Blessed Sacrament at the high altar and the altars in the body of the church. The precentor or his deputy should always ensure that at the beginning of every solemn Mass of requiem and *Dirige*[37] ... he comes down to their stalls, expressing to their prior the name or names of those for whom the said *Dirige* or Mass is to be sung. And when these masses are ended, they should so depart until the first peal of Evensong, and then come into the refectory and sit there on the bench at the lowest end in their order, and drink there twice every day in the summer until Michaelmas from the first Sunday in Lent, and only once in the other seasons of the year, receiving every day one loaf from the panter.[38] And after they have drunk quickly they are to depart and prepare themselves in their stalls at the beginning of Evensong or *Dirige*, standing up at the time of the Magnificat, and when Evensong has ended to depart for the day, from the feast of Michaelmas to the first Sunday in Lent; and on other days in the year they are to be at Compline. Providing always that they enter their stalls before the beginning of Prime, masses, Evensong, *Dirige* and Compline, as aforesaid.

Furthermore, in all processions about the church, cloister or elsewhere, we will that they go two by two in order behind all other men, with the prior going before them, and so return to their stalls. And at all times

---

36 See above, p. 145 n. 101.

37 See above, p. 105 n. 42.

38 The officer in a household responsible for the supply of bread and for the pantry.

when they walk in the church, cloister, refectory and dormitory, and in other ordinary places, they are to proceed quietly in discreet silence, soberly and without laughing or chattering at any time. Provided always that there is no service or further obligation required from the poor men by any of our brethren, or anyone else, apart from what is assigned and enacted by this present document, other than the abbot … shall deem necessary.

Furthermore, on our seven principal feasts they are to be served first, and grace is to be said by the abbot in his hall, if he is present; and there every one of them shall receive one penny from the abbot. And if it happens that any of the poor men by reason of actual sickness are absent any week or days, they are to receive only half their wages. And evermore, so that they do not depart or go out of the town without having asked and obtained express licence from the abbot … during the time of their absence they are neither to receive nor to be paid wages. And furthermore, for every Prime, Mass, *Dirige*, Evensong, Compline and procession, as aforesaid, where they are wholly absent, they are to lose a halfpenny every time. And for their absence from part of the said Hours apart from those already specified, notwithstanding urgent necessity such as passing water or other such necessary causes, they are every time to lose ¼d. And for not wearing the said habit, hood or beads as before assigned, on every occasion they are seen so transgressing they are to lose a halfpenny. And their prior should make due report and account on the Saturday to their paymaster concerning all their transgressions and forfeitures, on pain of losing 4d …

# XII: RELATIONS WITH LAY NEIGHBOURS

Religious houses did not just interact with their secular neighbours as providers of religious and social services. Collectively they also possessed large estates and manifold rights and privileges, according them considerable power over many layfolk. Monasteries were important employers, and did much to enhance the economies of their localities. But their wealth and privileges might also bring the religious into conflict with their neighbours over specific grievances. This section illustrates the sometimes troubled relations between monasteries and neighbouring tenants, townsmen and parishioners; although it should be read alongside Chapters IX–XI, which show more positive facets of monastic contact with lay society. For additional material concerning religious houses' legal disputes, see **52**, **54**.

## 44. The monastery as employer: the household list of Butley Priory, 1538

Every monastery was a major employer, of both permanent staff and temporary labour. The well-known Butley household list is one of the fullest and most revealing sources for this wider monastic community. Made at the suppression of this medium-sized priory of Augustinian canons in Suffolk, it reflects the Tudor government's concern (manifested in the 1536 Act for the Suppression of the Lesser Monasteries) that widespread unemployment should not result from the closure of religious houses. For other material on monastic employment, see for example **6**, **7**, **42**, **52**.

Translated from *The Register or Chronicle of Butley Priory, Suffolk, 1510–1535*, in A. G. Dickens, *Late Monasticism and the Reformation* (London, 1994), 71–3 (English).

|  |  |
|---|---|
|  | John Norwiche |
|  | James Denyngton |
|  | Roger Chipnam |
|  | Reynold Westerfeld |
|  | John Harwiche |
| The names of the canons – | Nicholas Oxborowe |
|  | John Bawdesey |
|  | Thomas Ryvers |
|  | Thomas Woodebrege |

Henry Denyngton
Robert Yngham
John Colcestr'

Number: 12

| | |
|---|---|
| Chaplains – | Edward Mar, reader of the lecture<br>William Sutton, chaplain |
| Under-steward of the lands – | William Royston, under-steward and keeper of the register |
| Surveyor of the lands – | William Cookeson, surveyor and outrider |
| | Edmund Burwell, keeper of the granaries for corn<br>Richard Stoker, keeper of the infirmary<br>Henry Crampton, an old and enfeebled man |
| Yeoman waiters and those executing other offices – | Thomas Bekett, carver<br>William Pawling, lame and enfeebled<br>John Crewe, at the appointment of the duke of Suffolk<br>John Mallyng, usher of the hall<br>John Maners, keeper of the swans and poultry |
| In the pantry and buttery – | Richard Denny<br>Richard Lyon<br>William Bastyan |
| Barber – | Thomas Mannyng |
| Master of the children – | Robert Fale |
| Children kept from alms for learning – | Denys Cookeson<br>Thomas Brooke<br>John Ide<br>William Fale<br>Richard Hoode<br>Austin Brooke<br>William Burwell |
| In the kitchen – | John Knott, chief cook<br>Bartholomew Fereby, under-cook<br>Robert Bestowe, a boy in the kitchen |

| | |
|---|---|
| Slaughterman – | Alexander Dawson |
| Sheep-reeves and attending to the cattle and pasture – | John Jaye<br>Robert Haughfen |
| Clerk in the church – | Walter Lavas |
| Horsekeepers – | Thomas Bene<br>Robert Pyke |
| Cooper of the brewing vessels and other necessaries – | William Cooke |
| Keepers of the scaleboat, heaving boat,[39] the ferry and weirs – | Simon Pullen<br>Thomas Pullen<br>John Studham<br>William Nevell<br>Robert Reve |
| The smith – | Thomas Clerke |
| Warreners – | Thomas Punt<br>Thomas Furton |
| Bakers and brewers – | William Sampson<br>Robert Byngley<br>John Alen |
| Maltsters – | Thomas Munday<br>William Hill |
| Porter – | William Sympson, an impotent man |
| Keeper of the gardens and ponds – | William Drue |
| Laundresses and in the dairy – | Joan Haughfen<br>Margaret Heyward<br>Joan Mathewe<br>Katherine Woodcrofte<br>Joan Cooke<br>Joan Barfoote |
| Servants in husbandry – | John Chaundeler, bailiff of husbandry<br>Austin Chaundeler<br>William Parker<br>William Stookes<br>William Cokett |

39 Apparently boats used at the landing-place and for transporting goods respectively.

|                                                 | Robert Mersshe |
|                                                 | Thomas Derker |
|                                                 | Robert Eve |
|                                                 | Robert Mannyng |
|                                                 | John Haughfen |
|                                                 | Austin Kempster |
|                                                 | William Wheteley |
|                                                 | Henry Chaundler |
|                                                 | Henry Kyng |
| Carters –                                       | John Leche |
|                                                 | Robert Smyth |
|                                                 | Robert Hethe |
|                                                 | Robert Halowtree |
| Shepherds –                                     | Robert Vynterer |
|                                                 | Thomas Jay |
| Woodmakers –                                    | Thomas Legge |
|                                                 | John Fox |
| Keeper of the swine –                           | William Shelle |
| Wrights for making and mending ploughs and carts – | John Bryghtwell John Gawge |
| For making candles and keeping the fish house – | John Ingram Henry Punte |
| Bedemen, who are impotent –                     | John Kempster Augustine Adams |
|                                                 | Number: 84 |

## 45. Crowland Abbey and its neighbours

The late medieval Crowland chronicle (a continuation of an earlier chronicle of this large Benedictine abbey in fenland Lincolnshire) is a rare source of its kind from the second half of the fifteenth century. As well as assessing each abbot's rule, the chronicler provides an account of disputes of various kinds involving the monastery. The following extract, taken from the sections on Abbot Richard Crowland (1476–84) and Abbot Edmund Thorp (1485–97) relates the problems each faced with their neighbours.

Translation taken from *The Crowland Chronicle Continuations, 1459–1486*, ed. N. Pronay and J. Cox (London, 1986), 166–9, 184–9 (Latin).

Powerful neighbours, let me not say enemies, therefore, observing the simple innocence and the innocent simplicity of the man [Abbot Crowland], rose up on all sides against the most pious person, at the same moment. Some, the men of Deeping in fact, gathering together to the number of 300 men, forced their way into the marsh of Cogge-sland, which undoubtedly belongs to the demesne[40] of the monastery, and carried off the reeds which had been collected by the men and by the tenants of the monastery, throwing into the water or beating whomever they came across. Finally they made an assault on the village of Crowland and so frightened the most pious father that he was compelled to leave his chamber and go down into the nave of the church to answer their insolence in his calm and priestly gentleness. Moreover although it was necessary, to avoid the flooding of the Holland, to cut the bank of Coggesland marsh, especially in winter, if any dangerous flood occurred (indeed this had been done once this season already with the most beneficial results for the district of Holland), those officials of Deeping, putting their sickle, as it were, in another's harvest, unjustly as well as presumptuously imposed intolerable amercements on the abbot. They levied distraints[41] and took grain coming from Langtoft and Boston along the water-way which runs from Deeping; and (which showed their great inhumanity) they cruelly transfixed with arrows the cellarer's guard-dog.

In other places also there was no lack of ungrateful factions amongst laymen (although they too were nearby tenants of this place) which in many ways disturbed the peace of the excellent father. Thus the tenants and parishioners of Whaplode, having exerted themselves in opposition to the power and rights of this monastery, attacked brother Lambert Fossdyke, seneschal of the place, with unheard-of violence while he was forbidding them to uproot trees growing in the cemetery and if he had not shut himself up securely in the church, in the sacristy no less, behind locked doors, he would have been in no small fear for his life.

But all this kind of disturbance is slight in comparison ... [manuscript illegible] which William Ramsey, abbot of Peterborough, then our over-close (would that I could say good!) neighbour created concerning the marsh of Alderland and other lands and rights which belonged, without doubt, to this monastery. In these affairs, which were long in dispute, you might have seen the lamb arguing with the wolf, the mouse with the cat. However, since all this litigation was finally brought to an

40 See above, p. 89 n. 14.
41 See above, p. 91 n. 18.

end by the arbitration and award of lord Thomas Rotherham, recently
bishop of Lincoln, ordinary of this place and subsequently archbishop
of York, (as is fully recorded in certain letters of attestation then drawn
up, where it is quite plain which side's interest and honour more fully
concerned him), we have decided to conclude the whole tragic story at
the time of the death of this father, Abbot Richard ...

At the start of his [Abbot Thorp's] tenure of office he prudently turned
his attention to the interference which his predecessors had endured
from their ungrateful, proud and almost wild neighbours and those
closest to them and missed no opportunity of seeing that everything
was settled and restored in every respect. Three principal problems
were outstanding: the first concerned the precinct of Crowland which
was strongly disputed by the men of Moulton and Weston; the second
concerned the boundaries, the lordship and the system of common
pasture in Coggesland involving the tenants of the monastery and
those of Deeping; the third problem concerned the marsh of Alderland
which seemed to have been brought to a very expensive though imperfect end, straightway, by the aforesaid arbitration.

The burden of the first problem was thrown utterly and completely
upon the shoulders of Abbot Lambert [Fossdyke, 1484–85] although,
as we have already stated, he had held office only for a short time.
The malice of the populace in those parts, indeed, produced such
hostility that in fact they harassed everything belonging to the monks
sometimes with dire threats, sometimes by fierce deeds; and when at
last they realised that with such behaviour they would not be able to
escape unharmed the snares for breaking the peace of the kingdom, as
if they were quite confident in their cause, they very presumptuously
brought a complaint against this monastery before the king's council
... The justices, however, prudently observed that it was necessary to
proceed with caution and moderation in the presence of a noisy mob;
having found that the allegation of these men was without substance,
because they had never had such possession of the pretended rights of
common [in the abbey precinct], they dismissed the principal issue and
gave decisions on those problems which seemed urgent concerning the
excessive flow of water from the height of the precinct into Holland
below ...

Edmund who succeeded him, to his praise, made an end to these happen-
ings in Abbot Lambert's time, when, through many outstanding acts
of devotion, he drew to his side in favour and assistance those very
powerful men, the chief inhabitants of Moulton, a family called Welby,

of very honourable standing, whom the local people were not accustomed to oppose.

The second problem, which concerned the inhabitants of Deeping has been so handled hitherto – through the patience of Abbot Edmund and his monks and the prudent counsel of the most illustrious mother of the lord king, to whom the lordship of Deeping is known to belong – that, with God's protection, the monastery seems unlikely to lose its rights or to incur the displeasure of powerful men with whom it cannot be on equal terms, however much those people, naturally ferocious, may strive always to preserve their boundaries.

The third problem, however, which was always found to be the greatest and most knotty of all, remained to come into the hands of Abbot Edmund as though he were the first to have been found worthy to settle this whole business and without whom nothing could have been achieved ...

[The arbitration award of Archbishop Rotherham is here summarised, which gave Crowland the option of either delivering lands worth £10 per year to Peterborough Abbey or financing the appropriation of the parish church of Bringhurst on behalf of Peterborough.]

Edmund, by the advice and consent of the chapter, decided to make every effort and to tackle the second course, namely to bring about the appropriation of Bringhurst church to the perpetual use of the monastery of Peterborough. This could not be accomplished, there being a statute of the realm in the way, without first having and obtaining the royal licence. He applied whatever zeal, hard work and expense seemed necessary for this task so carefully and diligently through friends that at last they deservedly achieved the fulfilment of their purpose, for he obtained royal letters patent for a licence of this sort addressed to the abbot and convent of Peterborough. Someone else will perhaps write more fully about them and about the whole process which ensued, at its proper place below.

## 46. An agreement between Reading Abbey and town, 1507

One of the main flashpoints between monasteries and their neighbours concerned the so-called monastic boroughs: towns such as Reading which were subject to the rule of the monastery, rather than self-governing like royal boroughs. After several generations of intermittent conflict between townsmen and Benedictine abbey, the following agreement was brokered in 1507, allowing the guild merchant (the association of merchants, with exclusive rights of trading in the borough) a greater say in town affairs.

Translated from *Records of the Borough of Reading: Diary of the Corporation*, ed. J. Guilding, 4 vols (London, 1892–96), I, 105–8 (English).

It is to be had in mind and known that in the year of Our Lord God 1507 ... in the time of Christian Nicolas, then mayor of the guild merchant of the borough of Reading, certain variances and grievances of long standing were in dispute between Abbot John Thorne, the lord of Reading, and the mayor and burgesses of the town, over the past nineteen years, concerning the approving of the corporation of the guild merchant, and the ordering of the constables and wardens, along with other articles. The mayor, with Richard Cleche and Thomas Carpenter, burgesses and former mayors of the guild, with the assent and consent of all burgesses of the town, by way of complaint, showed these variances and grievances to Dr [Richard] Fox, lord privy seal and bishop of Winchester, and to Lord [Giles] Daubeney, chamberlain to our sovereign lord [Henry VII]. On seeing the evidences of both parties, the same lords willed and desired the mayor and Richard and Thomas, burgesses, to abide by the direction of Robert Rede, knight, chief justice of the Common Bench at Westminster, and John Kyngesm-ylle, justice of the same Bench. At this, the said justices, having seen the evidences, first gave sentence and affirmed that the mayor and burgesses of the guild merchant were corporate;[42] and concerning all the other premises, to bring about forever a full conclusion and a continual peace between the parties, the lord chamberlain and justices determined and concluded in the manner and form following ...

First, concerning the making of the warden of the guild merchant, it is advised by the said lord and justices that the burgesses of the guild shall name and present three good and able burgesses of the guild to the abbot yearly on the feast of St Michael the Archangel, if the same abbot is in Reading within eight days following the same feast; and if he is absent from Reading during this time, then to name and present the three people to the prior, chamberlain or sub-chamberlain of the monas-tery ... And in the monastery, they are to desire and ask the abbot, if he is present (or in his absence the prior, chamberlain or sub-chamberlain) to choose and admit one of the same three people to be warden of the guild; and that the abbot ... admit one of the three people at his pleasure

---

42 I.e. the guild merchant was legally authorised to act as a single body in the courts, with its own privileges distinct from those of its members.

to be warden of the guild merchant for a year next ensuing. And the person so chosen warden in the presence of the abbot, if he is present, is to be sworn to him ... according to the effect and words contained in an old final agreement made in the time of King Henry III.[43] And all other things and articles comprised in the same agreement shall be firmly observed between the abbot and the warden of the guild and its burgesses ...

And concerning the election of the two constables and the ten wardmen of the five wards in the town of Reading to be made hereafter as often as necessary, it is moved by the lord and justices that the abbot shall allow the warden of the guild and the commonalty, householders of the town, and the majority of them, to choose one able and discreet person from the burgesses of the guild to be one constable, and five honest burgesses to be five of the wardmen of the said five wards. And also the warden, burgesses and commonalty, householders of the town, are to choose another able person of the commonalty at large, who is not a burgess of the guild, to be the other constable of the town, and another five able people of the commonalty at large besides the five burgesses of the guild, who are not burgesses of it, to be the other five wardmen of the town. And all these elections are to be made in the abbot's leet and lawday[44] of his town; and also both the constables and ten wardmen are to be admitted and solemnly sworn only in the same leet and lawday, before the abbot's steward, or his deputy, truly to do and exercise all things pertaining to their offices in the town.

And as to the making of burgesses of the guild, it is directed by the lord and justices that whenever any person shall be enabled and named by the warden and burgesses of the guild to be a burgess of the same, then the warden of the guild ... shall inform the abbot of this a fortnight before this person is to be made a burgess, and require the abbot ... to assign a monk of the monastery to survey and be present at the assessing of the fine of this person. And the abbot shall henceforth, on every such reasonable request, assign or cause to be assigned one of his co-monks to do the same, with one half of every such fine given over to the use of the abbot and his successors, and the other half to the use of the warden and burgesses of the guild, to be applied to the common profit of the guild. And that the fine of a legitimate son of every burgess

43 An agreement of the 1250s, by which the monastery recognised the guild merchant in return for the power to choose its warden and receive fines from its members and chepyngavell, a payment made in return for licence to trade in the town.

44 I.e. the court of the town (held by its lord) and the day of its meeting.

of the guild should be only four shillings when he is made burgess; and if the fine of any foreigner hereafter to be made a burgess is testified in any of the said courts by six burgesses of the guild, in the form that has been used in times past, to be reasonable ... then the said co-monks of the abbot are not to refuse that fine, but that person is to be admitted as a burgess for the same fine so testified.

And concerning chepyngavell, which is a yearly fine only of every burgess of the guild, which time out of mind has been paid yearly to the abbot's predecessors by every burgess of the guild; that is to say, every burgess of the guild has paid 5d yearly, and the widow of every burgess of the guild 2½d yearly, at the feast of St Peter ad Vincula, for their occupation of trading in the town. For this fine of chepyngavell, it is thought by the lord and justices ... that every burgess of the guild and widow ... shall and may freely buy and sell all kinds of merchandise in their houses and shops in the town, and also buy and sell all kinds of merchandise and things saleable in fairs and markets of the town out of their houses and shops. And it is advised by the lord and justices that from henceforth the abbot shall allow the warden of the guild and its burgesses to set up stalls in the empty grounds of the town, without paying anything other than the yearly fine of chepyngavell, always providing that the same stalls are not to the prejudice or nuisance of any inhabitant of the town, or any obstruction of passage in any highway or street of the town. And if these stalls are to the nuisance of any of the inhabitants or an obstruction of the highway, then this is to be reformed only by the abbot's bailiffs. And from all other inhabitants of the town, who are not burgesses, the abbot shall take and have such fines and customs for their trading in the town as he and his predecessors have had there time out of mind.

And as to the determination of the right of the flesh shambles or butchery in the town, which the warden of the guild and its burgesses claimed, it is advised by the lord and justices that the warden of the guild and its burgesses hereafter shall show their evidences for them before my lord bishop of Winchester and the lord chamberlain, and that then both parties should be ordered further by the said lords on seeing this.

## 47. The dispute over Wymondham Church, 1409–10

Another group whose interests could potentially be compromised by a neigh-bouring monastery were parishioners. A significant proportion of monas-teries (both male and female) shared churches with parochial congregations, and occasionally – as at Wymondham (Norfolk), the site of a small Benedic-tine priory, in the early fifteenth century – this led to conflict. Following the royal investigation ordered below, the dispute was finally taken to Archbishop Arundel of Canterbury who permitted the parishioners to have their own bell-tower. The church at Wymondham is still today dominated by its two large and competing towers.

Translated from National Archives, C66/382, m.1d (Latin).

The king to his beloved and faithful men, Thomas de Morleye, knight, Thomas Erpyngham, knight, Simon Felbrygg, knight, Edmund Oldehall, Robert Marcham, John Wyntur and Thomas Derham, and to our sheriff of Norfolk, greeting. The prior, beloved to us in Christ, of the priory of Wymondham, which is a cell of the church of St Albans of the foundation of our ancestors and is of our patronage, has shown to us that although he and his predecessors as priors of the same place have held in peaceful possession the nave[45] of the aforesaid priory church with all its profits from time out of mind; and also the parishioners of the priory have been governed in their coming to the church by the sounds of the priory bells over the same period, and they have never had their own bells, so that the prior and his other monks should be not at all disturbed in their divine service, as is the usage in various abbeys and other priories; – however, a certain William Groute, Thomas Boteler and Robert Kempe, confederated out of their malice, thus associated with very many other wrongdoers, parishioners of the priory, broke a certain tower of the priory church by force and arms, and hung three bells there to the disturbance of divine worship and to the disquiet of the prior himself, and also contrary to possession and custom. They also broke other strong walls of the priory, ejected the prior from his parlour, and kept him out of it for three days; and they walled up and fortified the doors between the chancel of the choir and the nave of the church, so that the prior was not able to leave or enter the church, in procession or otherwise (as he has been accustomed to throughout the aforesaid time); and they impeded the prior so that he could not receive his victuals or the other profits of the church; and they threatened the prior concerning his life and the maiming of his limbs; and they made

45 The part of the church used by the parishioners of Wymondham.

assaults against his men and servants from day to day, besides making and perpetrating many other grievances, transgressions and extortions there to the manifest annihilation of the priory.

As a result of which, the prior has entreated for a remedy to be graciously provided by us in this matter. We, not wishing the prior to be injured in this matter, assign you jointly and singly by the ways and means which you think best to inform yourselves concerning the above; and if the bells thus hung should exist, then to remove and get rid of them, and to guard them safely until there will be alternative provision; and to reform the broken walls and other transgressions thus perpetrated in the manner you think or esteem best according to your sensible discretion; and also to open or cause to be opened the door and entry thus walled up and fortified in the same manner, just as it was of old before the said transgressions were committed; and moreover to enjoin the wrongdoers on our behalf that they should in future desist from such injuries, gatherings, extortions and other transgressions against the prior, under the danger which is due; and to arrest and commit to our prison all those whom you find as opponents or rebels in this matter, guarding them there safely and securely until they may provide surety before you, or any of you, that they will completely desist and cease henceforth in future from these injuries, extortions and transgressions against the prior. We therefore command to you that you should diligently attend to the above matters and perform and execute them in the aforesaid form. We firmly command each and every sheriff, mayor, bailiff, minister and our other faithful men and subjects, both within and without liberties by the tenor of the present letters that they should attend to, advise and aid you in the execution of the above as is fitting. Witnessed by the king at Westminster, the 8th day of February [1410].

# XIII: CRITICISM OF THE MONASTIC LIFE

Numerous observers made comment on the monastic life in late medieval and early Tudor England, and much of this comment was critical. This is partly because the genres of writing that discussed the Church tended to focus on faults thought to be in need of reform. Chaucer's famous depictions of monks and nuns in *The Canterbury Tales*, although hardly flattering, were arguably no more than conventional literary portrayals of these types. The following selection includes not only literature, but also the political and financial manifesto of the Lollards, and an unusual but suggestive episode from fourteenth-century Exeter. The Lollard, Erasmian and evangelical critiques of pre-Reformation monasticism are all represented here, although it should be remembered that none of these sets of opinions seems to have been widely held among the population at large.

## 48. William Langland, *The Vision of Piers Plowman*

This extract, from one of the most famous poems of late medieval England (here taken from the so-called B-text version, completed *c.* 1379), presents Langland's diagnosis of monastic failings and his prescription for reform. A harsher critic than Chaucer, and more concerned with rectifying abuses, Langland's attitude towards monasticism was nevertheless ambivalent. In the first passage given below, the personification of Wrath discusses his experiences in convents; whereas the second passage is taken from the character Clergy's denunciation to Piers of the faults of churchmen.

Translated from *The Vision of Piers Plowman: a Critical Edition of the B-Text based on Trinity College Cambridge MS B.15.17*, ed. A. Schmidt (London, 1987), 47–8, 110–12 (English).

> I, Wrath, never rest
> But I must follow this wicked folk, for such is my lot
> I have an aunt, a nun and an abbess
> She would rather swoon or die than suffer any pain.
> I have been cook in her kitchen, and the convent served
> Many months with them, and with monks too.
> I was the prioress's pottager and for other poor ladies,
> And made them stews of squabbling – that Dame Joan was a bastard,
> And Dame Clarice, a knight's daughter – and her father was a cuckold,

And Dame Pernel, a priest's wench – to be prioress never
For she had a child in cherry-time,[46] all our chapter knows it!
From wicked words I, Wrath, made her worts,[47]
Till 'You lie!' and 'You lie' leapt out at once
And one hit the other across the mouth;
Had they had knives, by Christ! each would have killed the other.
St Gregory was a good pope, and had a good foresight
That no prioress should be priest – for he perceived
They would have been disgraced the first day, they can so badly keep
secrets.
         Among monks I might be, but many times avoid,
For there are many fierce folks my friends to espy
Both prior and subprior and our father abbot;
And if I tell any tales, they take themselves together,
And make me fast Fridays on bread and on water;
And I'm charged in the chapter house as if I were a child,
And beaten on the bare arse – and no breeches between!
And so have I no liking with those folks to dwell;
I eat there unwholesome fish and weak ale drink.
But other times when wine comes, when I drink wine in the eve
I have a flux of a foul mouth for five days after.
All the wickedness I know about any of our brethren,
I cough up in our cloister, that all our convent knows it.
         . . .
Amongst righteous religious this rule should be held.
Gregory, the great clerk and the good pope,
Rehearses in his *Moralia* the rule of religion
And says this as an example that they should follow after:
'When fish lack either the sea or fresh water,
They die for drought, when they lie dry;
So religion flops about and dies
In those who out of convent and cloister crave to live.'
For if heaven is on this earth, and peace to any soul,
It is in the cloister or schools, by many reasons I find,
For in cloister no man comes to quarrel or fight,
But all is obedience there and books, to read and to learn.
         In the schools there is scorn unless a clerk will learn,
And great love and liking, for all of them teach each other.

46 I.e. the cherry season.
47 Vegetable dishes.

But now Religion is a rider, a roamer through streets,
A lord of love-days[48] and a land buyer,
A rider on a palfrey from manor to manor,
A pack of hounds at his arse as if he were a lord;
And unless his servant kneel, who his cup brings,
He scowls at him and asks him who taught him courtesy?
Little business have lords to give land from their heirs
To religious who regret not if it rains on their altars.
      In many places there they are parsons,[49] by themselves at ease,
Of the poor they have no pity – and that is their pure charity,
But they think themselves as lords, their land lies so broad.
      But there shall come a king and confess you religious,
And beat you, as the Bible tells, for the breaking of your rule,
And amend nuns, monks and canons,
And put them to their penance – to return to their pristine state,
And barons with earls beat them, by 'Blessed the man'[50] teaching,
Will take what their children claim, and tell you straight:
'Some [trust] in chariots and some in horses. They are bound, etc.'[51]
And then friars in their refectory shall find a key
Of Constantine's coffers, in which is the cash
That Gregory's godchildren [i.e. the monks] have wickedly spent.
      And then shall the abbot of Abingdon and all his successors forever
Have a blow from a king, and incurable the wound.
That this will be true, seek you who look often at the Bible:
"How have oppressors come to nought?
How has the tribute ceased to be paid?
The Lord has broken the staff of the wicked,
The rulers' rod that punished the people;
He has given them an incurable wound."[52]

48 A day appointed for the arbitration of a dispute.
49 I.e. the rector, who had appropriated the bulk of the parish church's income.
50 The opening line of Psalm 1: 'Blessed is the man that walks not in the counsel of the ungodly, nor stands in the way of sinners, nor sits in the seat of the scornful.'
51 Psalms xx. 7–8: 'Some trust in chariots, and some in horses: but we will call upon the name of the Lord our God. They are bound and have fallen: but we are risen, and are set upright.'
52 From Isaiah xiv. 4–6.

## 49. The Order of Brothelyngham, 1348

The following document, from the register of Bishop Grandisson of Exeter [cf. **39**], describes an unusual but intriguing outbreak of anticlericalism in that city. Whether this episode was meant in jest or more seriously is open to interpretation, but the particular actions of this group certainly appear to be a comment on the monastic life of the day.

Translated from *The Register of John de Grandisson, Bishop of Exeter, 1327–1369*, ed. F. Hingeston-Randolph, 3 vols (London and Exeter, 1894–99), II, 1055–6 (Latin).

John, etc., to our beloved sons in Christ, the official to the archdeacon of Exeter and the dean of Christianity of Exeter, and also Sir Robert de Eglosayl, rector of the church of St Paul, Exeter, greeting, grace and blessing. Since holy religion should be planted in the field of the Lord for this reason, that it may produce in it the flowers of honour and the plentiful fruits of honesty, by virtue of our office, we are rightly provoked to cut off thorns and thistles, by which so holy a plantation may be disgraced or disturbed. It has reached our hearing, indeed, not without grave concern, that in our city of Exeter a certain abominable sect of certain malicious men, under the name of the Order, indeed rather the Error, of Brothelyngham, has newly risen up, at the instigation of the sower of evil works. This 'Order', evidently making not a convent but an unlawful and suspect conventicle, put a certain lunatic and madman in charge (at any rate one most aptly suited to their works) going by the name of abbot. And dressing him in the monastic habit, they set him up in the theatre, as if worshipping their idol; and at the blowing of a horn (which they had set up for a bell), they accompanied him through the streets and spaces of the same city, on some days now elapsed, with a very great crowd on horseback and on foot. They took clerics and laymen then standing by in their way, and pulled out others from their houses, and they held them against their will for a very long time by reckless and sometimes sacrilegious daring, until they had extorted from them certain sums of money for the place of sacrifice, or rather more truly of sacrilege. And, although these things may seem to have been ventured under the colour and clothing of a play and indeed in jest, however this is, without any doubt, robbery and pillage inasmuch as it was taken from the unwilling.

Wishing therefore that the aforesaid disgraceful and detestable sect, damnably mocking holy religion and bringing concerns in many different ways to the devotion of religious men (besides threatening similarly the disturbance of the peace of the kingdom and the Church) should not be propagated any further, with the loss of souls and danger to bodies and property; we firmly enjoin you, jointly and singly, and command that, on this present Sunday, in our cathedral church, and in every church and chapel of the city and its suburb, you should prohibit, or cause to be prohibited, publicly and distinctly (just as we also, by the tenor of the present letters, more strictly prohibit) that from now no-one in the city or suburb – under the pretext of this not Order, as we have said, but Horror – should presume to make such conventicles, nor take part in them, nor in any way to enter, defend or maintain this most dangerous and suspect sect, under penalty of greater excommunication, to be threatened against those acting to the contrary and any of them. Denouncing also generally to all whom this matter touches, that if they do not obey these your warnings (or rather more truly ours) with effect, we will not only proceed according to canonical sanctions against them and each one of them, as their guilt demands; but we will also describe the matter, so perilous and pernicious, as an example to his royal majesty, so that worldly severity may by swift remedy restrain and punish those whom ecclesiastical discipline does not coerce ... Given in our manor of Chudleigh, the 11th day of July, AD 1348 and the twenty-first year of our consecration.

## 50. The Lollard Disendowment Bill, 1410

The disendowment of the Church was widely discussed in the late fourteenth and early fifteenth centuries, including on more than one occasion in Parliament. This is the context for the following bill, presented to Parliament in 1410, by Lollard sympathisers who opposed the wealth of the Church on ideological grounds. Although the valuations of particular monasteries (mainly male houses of the Benedictine, Cluniac, Cistercian and Augustinian Orders) given here were only estimates, this document shows some familiarity with the monastic scene.

Translated from *Selections from English Wycliffite Writings*, ed. A. Hudson (Cambridge, 1978), 135–7 (English).

To the most excellent redoubtable lord the king, and to all the noble lords of this present Parliament, all the true commons show meekly, saying this truly: our liege lord the king may have from the temporalities[53] of bishops, abbots and priors occupied and wasted proudly,

---

53 Income drawn from manors, granges, urban property, trade or the profits of justice, rather than from parish churches and offerings.

within the realm fifteen earls and 1,500 knights, 6,200 esquires and one hundred almshouses more than he has now at this time, well maintained and truly sustained by lands and tenements. And evermore when all this is performed, our lord the king may have every year a clear gain to his treasury for the defence of his realm £20,000 and more, as it may be truly proved. And reckon that every earl may spend each year 3,000 marks of lands and rents; and every knight 100 marks of rent and four plough-lands in his own demesnes;[54] and every esquire 40 marks with two plough-lands in his demesnes; and every almshouse 100 marks, under the supervision of good and true seculars, because of priests and clerks who have now very nearly destroyed all the almshouses within the realm. And also to ordain that every town throughout the realm should keep all the poor men and beggars who may not work for their sustenance, according to the statute made at Cambridge; and, in case the aforesaid commons might not continue to sustain them, then the aforesaid almshouses might help them.

And as for how all this might be done, will you know that the temporalities of bishops, abbots and priors extend to the sum of 322,000 marks per year. That is to say the temporalities of the archbishop of Canterbury with the two abbeys there, Shrewsbury, Coggeshall and St Osyth's are worth per year 20,000 marks. Those of the bishop of Durham and the abbey there, 20,000 marks. The archbishop of York and the two abbeys there, 20,000 marks. The bishop of Winchester and the two abbeys there, 20,000 marks. St Mary's Clerkenwell with the estates, 20,000 marks. And so amounts the first 100,000 marks.

The bishop of Lincoln with the abbeys of Ramsey and Peterborough, 20,000 marks. The abbeys of Bury and of Gloucester, 20,000 marks. Of the bishop of Ely with the two abbeys there, and Spalding and Lenton, 20,000 marks. Of the bishop of Bath and the abbeys of Westminster, St Albans and Ogbourne, 20,000 marks. Of the bishop of Worcester with the abbeys there and Gloucester, Eynsham, Abingdon, Evesham and Reading, 20,000 marks. And so amounts the second sum, 100,000 marks.

Of the bishop of Chester with the abbey there and 'Bannastre',[55] and of the bishop of London, St David's, Salisbury and Exeter, 20,000 marks. Of the abbeys of Rievaulx, Fountains, Jervaulx, the abbey of Grace Dieu, Wardon, Vale Royal, Whalley and Salley, 20,000 marks.

54 See above, p. 89 n. 14.

55 It is not clear which religious house this refers to.

Of the abbeys of Leicester, Waltham, Guisborough, Merton, Oseney and Cirencester, 20,000 marks. Of Dover, Battle and Lewes, Coventry, Daventry and Thorney, 20,000 marks. Of Bristol, Northampton, Thornton, Kenilworth, Hailes, Winchcombe, Pershore, St Frideswide's [Oxford], Notley and Wellow, 20,000 marks. Of Carlisle, Chichester, Hereford, Rochester, St Mary Overy [Southwark], St Bartholomew's [Smithfield], Sawtry, Huntingdon and Swineshead, 20,000 marks. And so amounts the third sum, 100,000 marks.

Of the bishop of Norwich with the abbey there and Crowland, 10,000 marks. Of Malmesbury, Bruton, Tewkesbury, Dunstable, Sherborne, Taunton, Byland and Burton, 12,000 marks. And so amounts the fourth sum, 22,000 marks.

And perhaps any bishopric or abbey or priory may be wholly kept to help reach that aforesaid sum of 322,000 marks, so that every person above-said may clearly be served as is written above. And then there shall remain clearly £20,000 and more every year for the king's treasury.

And yet furthermore there may be got £100,000 of further temporalities, wasted and occupied among worldly clerks, and found from there 10,500 priests and clerks. And every clerk paid £2 per year. And 6,200 squires in the manner before-said.

And thus in all the realm men may have fifteen earls, 1,500 knights and esquires more than are now sufficiently endowed, and still from there fifteen universities and 15,000 priests and clerks sufficiently founded by temporal alms, if it pleases the king and lords to spend them to that use, and the king for his treasury £20,000 per year. And still one hundred almshouses, every house having 100 marks with land to feed all the needy poor men with no cost to the town, but only of the temporalities alienated in mortmain and wasted among proud worldly clerks. These proud clerks, for all that is taken away of their temporalities, may still spend per year in their spiritualities as it is assessed in the exchequer clearly £143,734 10s 4½d.

And still we have not touched on colleges, chantries, the white canons [the Premonstratensians], cathedral churches with their temporalities, and churches with their temporalities, and churches appropriated by monks, of charterhouses, and nor of French monks, glebes, Bonhommes, hospitals, hermitages or the crutched friars.

And therefore all the true commons desire for the worship of God and the profit of the realm that these worldly clerks, bishops, abbots and priors who are such worldly lords, be put to live by their spiritualities;

for they do not live now nor carry out the office of true curates as prelates should, and they do not help the poor commons with their lordships as true secular lords should; nor do they live in penance or in bodily labour, as true religious should by their profession. But from every estate they take pleasure and ease and put away from themselves labour, and take profits that should come to true men. Their life and evil example have been vicious so long that all the common people, both lords and the simple commons, are now so vicious and infected through the arrogance of their sin that scarcely any man fears God or the devil.

To which bill at that time no answer was given.

## 51. Desiderius Erasmus, the letter to Abbot Paul Volz

Desiderius Erasmus (c. 1467–1536) was the most celebrated writer of his day, winning a wide audience among the educated elites across Europe. This letter, to a Benedictine abbot of Erasmus's acquaintance, was used as the preface to the 1518 edition and subsequent editions of his popular work, the *Enchiridion Militis Christiani* ('The Handbook of the Christian Knight'). The *Enchiridion*, first published in 1503 and translated into English in 1533, develops some of Erasmus's ideas about religious reform, including that of the monastic life, which Erasmus had himself experienced unhappily as a young man.

Translation taken from *The Correspondence of Erasmus: Letters 842 to 992, 1519 to 1519*, ed. R. Mynors, D. Thomson and P. Bietenholz, *Collected Works of Erasmus*, VI (Toronto, 1982), 87–90 (Latin).

Not but what these men will find it more desirable that recruits to the religious life should be honourable and genuine rather than numerous. And would that it had been provided by law that no one under the age of thirty should put his head into that kind of noose, before he has learnt to know himself and has discovered the force of true religion! In any case those who take the Pharisees as the model in their business, and course over land and sea that they may make one proselyte, will never be short of inexperienced young men whom they can get into their net and try to persuade. Everywhere the number of fools and simple people is enormous.

I at least would hope, and so I doubt not do all truly religious men, that the religion of the Gospel might be so deeply loved by all that they would be content with this, and no one go off in search of a Benedictine or Franciscan rule; and Benedict himself and Francis would, I am sure, hope the same thing. Moses rejoices to find himself obscured by the glory of Christ; and they would rejoice likewise, if our love for the law of the Gospel made us despise all human codes. How I wish all Christians lived in such a way that those who are now called religious might seem hardly religious at all! Even today this is true in not a few cases; for why need I conceal what is well known? And yet in ancient days the first origin of the monastic life was a retreat from the cruelty of those who worshipped idols. The codes of the monks who soon followed them were nothing but a summons back to Christ. The courts of princes were in old days more Christian in name than in their manner of life. Bishops were soon attacked by the diseases of ambition and greed. The primitive fervour of the common people cooled. Hence the retreat aimed at by Benedict and Bernard [of Clairvaux] after him, and then by many more. It was the banding together of a few men aimed at nothing but a pure and simple Christianity.

If anyone were to study with attention the life and rules of Benedict or Francis or Augustine, he will find that they had no other ambition than to live with friends who joined them willingly a life according to the teaching of the Gospel in liberty of spirit; and that they were compelled to lay down some rules for dress and food and other external things, for they were afraid that, as often happens, more importance might be ascribed to the constitutions of human origin than to the Gospel. They had a horror of riches; they avoided honours, even in the church. They laboured with their hands, in order not only to be a burden to no man, but to have to give to others in need; they occupied mountain-tops, they made their nests in marshy places, they lived in sandy wastes and deserts. And then they ruled this great concourse of men without violent language and whipping and prisons, but solely by teaching and exhorting, by mutual service and by examples of godly life.

Such were the monks so loved and praised by Basil and defended by Chrysostom; to them was appropriate, in any case, what St Jerome writes to Marcella – that choirs of monks and virgins are a blossom and most precious stone among the adornments of the church. On this tribute monks of all kinds pride themselves astonishingly today; they shall be welcome to claim the praise if at the same time they follow the example ...

Such were the first beginnings of monasticism, and such its patriarchs. Then gradually, with the passing of time, wealth grew, and with wealth ceremonies; and the genuine piety and simplicity grew cool. And though we see monasteries everywhere whose ways have sunk

lower than the laity, even so the world is burdened with fresh foundations, as though they likewise were not likely to fall in the same way.
Once, as I said, the monastic life was a refuge from the world. Now men
are called monks who spend all their time in the very heart of worldly
business and exercise a kind of despotism in human affairs. And yet
because of their dress, or because of some name they bear, they claim so
much sanctity for themselves that compared with them they think other
people hardly Christians. Why do we so closely confine the professed
service of Christ, which he wished to be as wide open as possible?

If we are moved by splendid names, what else, I ask you, is a city
than a great monastery? Monks obey their abbot or those who are
set over them; citizens are obedient to their bishop and their pastors,
whom Christ himself, not human authority, set over them. Monks live
in leisure and are fed by the liberality of other people, possessing in
common what has come to them without effort on their part (of wicked
monks I say nothing for the present); citizens, each according to his
means, share what they have won by their own industry with those in
need. Then as concerns the vow of chastity, I would not dare to unfold
how little difference there is between celibacy of the ordinary kind and
chastity in wedlock. Last but not least, we shall not greatly feel the lack
of those three vows[56] which are man's invention in someone who has
kept in sincerity and purity that one great vow, which we took in our
baptism not to man but to Christ.

Then if you compare the wicked men in both classes, there is no question
that laymen are preferable. Compare the good, and there is very little
difference, if there is any at all, except perhaps that they who live a
religious life under less compulsion seem more truly religious. The
result is therefore that no one should be foolishly self-satisfied because
his way of life is not that of other people, nor should he despise or
condemn the way of life of others. But in every walk of life let this be the
common aim of us all, that to the best of our power we should struggle
towards the goal that is set before us all, even Christ, exhorting and
even helping one another, with no envy of those who are ahead of us in
the race and no scorn for the weak who cannot yet keep up with us …

56 Chastity, poverty and obedience, the three vows which all monks, canons and nuns
   swore to uphold on their profession.

## 52. An evangelical attack on monasteries: *Rede Me and Be Nott Wrothe*

This evangelical satire is ascribed to Jerome Barlowe and William Roye, two former Observant friars who had fled 1520s England because of their reformist leanings. It was printed in Strasbourg in 1528 to be smuggled into England, although many of the copies were intercepted by the authorities. Its targets include Cardinal Wolsey and the friars, but considerable space is given to a critique of monasticism which reflects the general contours of evangelical opinion on the subject.

Translated from J. Barlowe and W. Roye, *Rede Me and Be Nott Wrothe*, ed. D. Parker (Toronto, 1992), 101–3, 129–31 (English).

Jeffrey:    O Lord God, what good days
These monks have in abbeys
And do neither sweat nor swink [work].
They live in wealthiness and ease,
Having whatsoever they please,
With delicate meat and drink.
Wherewith they force their bellies so full
That to all goodness they are dull,
Making merry with Gill and Joan.
They sit sleeping in a corner,
Or mumbling their Paternoster,
Their mind nothing thereupon.
Be they ever so strong or stark [stout],
They will exercise no kind of work
Nor labour bodily.

Watkin:    Are you here, Jeffrey mate?

Jeffrey:    Yes, why do you come so late?
I am eager for you to stay.

Watkin:    I was troubled with the estates,
I curse all their foolish pates [heads]
For coming here this day.

Jeffrey:    So may I prosper, I thought the same,
Howbeit the steward was to blame,
That he did no better purvey?

Watkin:    By your faith, had you better fare,
In the cloister, where as you were,
Under the rule of the monastery?

Jeffrey:        Fare indeed? They eat their bellies full,
                Every man as much as he will,
                And none says black is his eye.

Watkin:         What do they for it, anything?

Jeffrey:        Truly nothing but read and sing,
                Passing the time with sport and play.

Watkin:         That is a life indeed for the nones [while],
                You were a fool by these ten bones,
                When you came from them away.

Jeffrey:        Oh, I think myself most fortunate,
                That from their life I am separate,
                Seeing it is so abominable.

Watkin:         What abomination is therein?

Jeffrey:        Alas, mate, all together is sin,
                And wretchedness most miserable.

Watkin:         What a man of religion,
                Is reputed a dead person
                To worldly conversation?

Jeffrey:        It is of a truth they are dead,
                For they are of no use or stead [profit],
                To Christian men's consolation.
                And as a dead, stinking carcass,
                Unprofitably blocks a space,
                If it be kept above ground:
                So in their life superstitious,
                Of wicked crimes enormous,
                No kind of profitableness is found.

Watkin:         Yet their order is very strait [strict]?

Jeffrey:        Yes, but these use such a conceit,
                That they make it easy enough.
                More easy by the twenty part,
                Than to labour in some art,
                Or to go with the cart or plough.

Watkin:         They have each man the world forsaken,
                And a spiritual life taken,
                Consisting in ghostly [spiritual] business.

Jeffrey:        What call you the world, I pray?

Watkin:     Wealthy riches and pleasures gay,
            And occasions of sinfulness.

Jeffrey:    Then they are in the world still,
            For they have all that they will,
            With riches and possessions.
            And as touching the realm of vice,
            Pride, wrath, envy and avarice,
            With other sinful transgressions.
            In this world that we do name,
            There is none so far out of frame [fit],
            And who live in such outrageousness.

[A lengthy section on the friars follows, before the conversation turns again
to the possessioners]

Watkin:     I see then he were a very child,
            Who would any more abbeys build,
            If the goods should be so ill-spent.

Jeffrey:    It were far better, I suppose,
            To pluck down a great many of those,
            Which are already of costly building.

Watkin:     Our lord forbid, that were a pity,
            For they keep hospitality,
            Wayfaring people harbouring.
            Husbandmen and labourers,
            With all common artificers,
            They cause to have great earning.
            Their towns and villages,
            Without exactions or pillages,
            Under them have much winning.
            They keep also many servants,
            Retaining farmers and tenants,
            Who by them have their living.

Jeffrey:    Hospital abbeys you find but few,
            As though some of them for a show
            To blindfold the people's sight.
            Perhaps they will not deny,
            If a gentleman come that way,
            To give him lodging for a night.
            But if poor men to there resort,
            They shall have full little comfort,

Neither meat, drink, nor lodging.
Saving otherwise perhaps,
They get a few broken scraps,
Of these cormorants'[57] leaving.

Watkin:    Well, yet their fare considering,
It is I know no small thing,
What they leave daily at their board.

Jeffrey:    Yes, but through false lurkers,
And unthrifty abbey lubbers,[58]
To poor folk little they afford.
For the best meat away they carve,
Which for their harlots must serve,
With other friends of their kin.
Then pilfer the serving officers,
With the yeomen who are waiters,
So that their crumbs are but thin.
And whereas you make relation,
That men of sundry occupation,
By them are set unto labour.
It is about such foolishness,
Concerning no profitableness,
To their neighbours' succour.
In building of chambers curious,
Churches, and houses, superfluous,
To no purpose expedient.
So that they may satisfy,
Their inordinate fantasy,
They care for no detriment.
Set dice and card players aside,
And throughout the world so wide,
They waste their goods most in vain.
Their pride makes many a beggar,
Few, or none faring the better,
Except an idle rascal or twain [two].
Their towns sometime of renown,
Lewdly they cause to fall down,
The honour of the land to mar.
They sue their subjects at the law,

57 Cormorants were associated with insatiable greed in the middle ages.

58 A popular Reformation term to refer to idle and superfluous monastic servants.

Whom they make not worth a straw,
Arraigning them guiltless at the bar.
And that I may now report,
To their lordships a great sort,
With whom they had controversies.
Namely, St Edmund's Bury,
With various others a great many,
Under the hold of monasteries.
Furthermore, there as I did moan,
All husbandmen they have undone,
Destroying the land miserably.

Watkin: To prove that, it were very hard.

Jeffrey: Take heed how farmers go backward,
And you shall see it with your eye.
For the land's wealth principally,
Stands in exercise of husbandry,
By increase of cattle and tilling.
Which as long as it does prosper,
The realm goes backwards never,
In stable felicity persevering.
The abbeys then full of covetousness
Whom possessions could not suffice,
Ever more and more encroaching.
After they had despoiled gentlemen,
They undermined husbandmen,
In this manner them robbing.
Where a farm for £20 was set,
Under thirty they would not it let,
Raising it up to so high a sum.
That many a good householder,
Constrained to give his farm over,
To extreme beggary did come ...

# XIV: MONASTERIES AND THE CROWN

As major landholding institutions with much local power and influence, the larger monasteries were always in close contact with the Crown. Abbots and priors served on royal commissions, collected taxes and sometimes acted as royal councillors, diplomats and chaplains. Occasionally heavy financial demands on religious houses were also made by the king, especially at times of war. However, in the decades leading up to the Dissolution, the involvement of the Crown in monastic affairs became increasingly pressing. One manifestation of this was the greater public role now required from many superiors, such as the abbot of Tavistock. But these years also saw greater Crown intervention in monastic affairs, including interference in elections, heavier taxation and the growing conviction that the reform of religious houses should be undertaken by the government – although there was no hint of what this 'reform' would ultimately involve.

## 53. The new privileges of the abbots of Tavistock

The public role and status of the abbot was changing in the later middle ages, as the following two documents relating to the wealthy Benedictine abbey of Tavistock (Devon) indicate. The privileges obtained by the abbots of Tavistock were already held by many other large monasteries, but their wider extension in this period is of interest.

Translated (with minor corrections of transcription from National Archives, C66/485 and C66/621) from W. Dugdale, *Monasticon Anglicanum*, ed. J. Caley, H. Ellis and B. Bandinel (London, 1846), II, 502–3.

The king to all those to whom, etc., greeting. You should know that we of our special grace have granted and given licence on behalf of us and our heirs, as much as is in us, to John Dynyngton, abbot of the house and church of the Blessed Mary and St Rumon of Tavistock; that he himself may be able to prosecute before the lord supreme pontiff, the present pope, and have licence to use the mitre, amice, sandals and other pontifical emblems,[59] and to give blessings in solemn services of masses and to give remission by the same authority and the means that any bishop may use; and that the same abbot may be able to prosecute

---

59 See above, p. 191 n. 28.

likewise any other provisions concerning that matter before the afore-said pontiff, and to enjoy them for himself and his successors in perpe-tuity. And besides we have granted from our more abundant grace, and have given licence to the abbot, that he may receive apostolic letters and bulls concerning the aforesaid provisions, and to execute, exercise, read and cause to be read everything contained in the same provisions, and to use and enjoy them and each one of them freely and wholly, quietly, peacefully and safely according to the power, form and effect of the same letters and bulls and each of them. Not wishing that the same abbot or his proctors, supporters, advisors, helpers and those adhering to him in this matter, or any other solicitors, readers or publishers of the aforesaid letters and bulls, or any of them, be impeached, disturbed, perturbed, molested in anything or oppressed by us or our heirs, notwithstanding the Statutes of Provisors[60] and any other statutes, ordinances, provi-sions or acts whatsoever made to the contrary ... Witnessed by the king at Westminster, the 3rd of February [1458].

The king to all those to whom, etc., greeting. You should know that we, specially moved by certain considerations and from the special devotion which we bear and hold to the Blessed Virgin Mary, mother of Christ, and to St Rumon, in whose honour the abbey of Tavistock (which is of the foundation of our noble ancestors, formerly kings of England, and of our patronage) is dedicated; hence it is that of our special grace, and out of our certain knowledge and pure motive, we will our same abbey or monastery to rejoice in the honour, privilege and liberties of the spiritual lords of our Parliament, and that of our heirs and successors. Therefore we have granted, and by the present letters we grant, on behalf of us, our heirs and successors, as much as is in us, to our beloved in Christ Richard Banham, abbot of Tavistock, and his successors and each one of them who will be abbot there at that time, that he should be and will be one of the spiritual and religious lords of our Parliament, and that of our heirs and successors, rejoicing in the honour, privi-leges and liberties of the same. And moreover from our more abundant grace, desiring the advantage of our said monastery, with its distance to be considered, so that if any abbot of the time should happen to be absent on account of the advantage of the monastery in not coming to our Parliament, or that of our heirs and successors, this absence we have pardoned to the abbot by the present writings. On the condition however that he then shall pay for any such absence from each whole

60 Statutes issued in 1351 and 1390 limiting the pope's ability to provide (i.e. present) candidates to Church livings in England.

Parliament in our exchequer, by himself or by an attorney, five marks
to us or our heirs and successors, whenever this shall happen in the
future ... Witnessed by the king at Westminster, the 23rd of January
[1514].

## 54. Lay interference in monastic affairs: the abbot of Faversham's reply to Thomas Cromwell, 1536

From the late 1520s, government interference in monastic elections became
increasingly common, with both Wolsey and Cromwell seeking to install their
own candidates as superiors. Attempts were also made to force vacancies,
although this was harder to bring about. This letter from the Cluniac abbot
of Faversham (Kent) indicates the new pressures being applied on religious
houses on the eve of the Dissolution.

Translated from *Three Chapters of Letters, Relating to the Suppression of the
Monasteries*, ed. T. Wright, Camden Society, original series, 26 (1943), 103–7
(English).

May this letter be delivered to the right honourable, his especial good
Master Secretary [i.e. Thomas Cromwell].

Right worshipful sir, after humble recommendations according to
my most bound duty, with similar thanks for your benevolent mind
always showed towards me and my poor house, to your goodness had
and accustomed; it may please you to be informed that I lately received
your loving letters dated the 8th day of this present month, concerning
a resignation to be had of the poor house which I, under God and the
king's highness my sovereign lord, of long time (though unworthy of
such a cure) have had the administration and rule of, because of the
age and debility that are reported to be in me. So it is, right worshipful
sir, I trust I am not yet now so enfeebled or infirm, either in body or
memory, or by any extremity of age (which, for the most part, debility
always readily accompanies), or by any immoderate affliction of any
great continual infirmity; but rather I may (high thanks be to God for
this!) accommodate myself to the good order, rule and governance of
my poor house and monastery as well as ever I could since my first
promotion to the same office, although I may not so well perhaps ride
and journey abroad as I might have done in times past.

But admit the particular office of an abbot to consist (as I must refute,
for we profess a rule very different from that) in journeying forth
and surveying the possessions of his house, in which case agility and

patience of labour in journeying were much required indeed. Although
I myself am not so well able to take pains in this as I have been in my
younger years (at which time I trust I took such pains that I have less
need to survey the same at this present time), yet I have such faithful
approved servants whom I have brought up in my poor house from
their tender years – and those of such wit and good discretion, joined
with the long experience of the trade of such worldly things – that
they are able to furnish and supply those parts, I know very well, in all
points much better than I ever could myself, or than it would have been
expedient or decent for me to have done. Again, on the other hand, if
the chief office and profession of an abbot is (as I have always taken it)
to live in chastity and solitude, to be separate from the intermeddling
of worldly things, to serve God quietly, to distribute his resources in
the refreshing of poor needy persons, to have a vigilant eye to the good
order and rule of his house and the flock committed to him in God,
I trust, your favour and benevolence obtained (which I very humbly
request of you), I myself may and am as well able still now to supply
and continue those parts as ever I was in all my life, as concerning the
sufficiency of my own person.

Yet doubtless it might be much more ease and quiet to me, as you have
persuasively argued in a very friendly and vehement manner in your
letters, to resign my office on the provision of such a reasonable pension
as your good mastership should think suitable and convenient; in which
surely I would not at all doubt your worship and conscience, but have
much trust in the same, not only because of the great goodness and
good impartiality which I hear everywhere commonly reported of you,
but also for the great favour and benevolence which I have always found
in you. And perhaps in my own mind I could very well be content and
fully persuaded in my own part to do so, for the satisfaction and fulfilment of your loving proposal, for I am nothing less than ambitious.
But I do esteem more in this matter the miserable state and condition
that our poor house should stand in, if such a thing should come to
pass, than I do my own private office and dignity – the administration
of which, though it is somewhat more painful to me than it has been
accustomed in the past, yet God forbid that it should seem irksome or
tedious to me.

Moreover, I pray your good mastership, to whom I wish all these things
were as openly and manifestly known as they are to me, our poor house
and monastery because of various and many insupportable costs and
charges which we have sustained, as much from the king's highness

as otherwise partly by reason of various great sums of money which it was left indebted in, in the time of my last predecessor there (who, as it is well known in the country, was only a very slender husband to the house); and partly because of various and many great repairs, both of the buildings of our church and of other housing, which were allowed to fall into great ruin and decay, insomuch that some of them were likely to fall clean down to the ground; and in the reclaiming of various marshes belonging to our monastery which the violent rages and surges of the implacable sea had won and occupied, being now since my time well and sufficiently repaired and fully mended, as the place itself may sufficiently declare, to the inestimable costs and charges of our poor house; and partly again because of the great costs, charges and expenses which we have had and sustained by and through the occasion of various and many lawsuits and actions which we have been compelled to use and pursue against various of our tenants for the recovery of various rights of our monastery, for a long time unjustly detained and obstinately denied by the same tenants; and partly also because of various and many great sums of money which we have paid and lent to the king's highness, both in tenths and subsidies and otherwise, amounting in all to the sum of £2,000 and above, to our great impoverishment – and the house is still now at this present time indebted to various of our friends and creditors by more than the sum of £400, as you shall be further instructed in detail whenever it pleases you to demand a further and more exact declaration of this.

If it might please Almighty God that I live and with your good favour continue in my office for the space of six or seven years at the furthest, I do not doubt that I should see these sums well repaid and satisfied again. But if I should now at this present time resign my said office (the case standing as it does) undoubtedly our poor house, being now so far indebted already by means of the occasions remembered above – the burdensome charges of the First Fruits and Tenth[61] which would be due to the king's highness now immediately upon this resignation added and accumulated to this – should be entirely impoverished and utterly decayed and undone forever in my mind, which I am very well assured your goodness would not covet to bring to pass. And therefore Christ forbid that I should ever so heinously offend and commit against Almighty God and the king's highness my sovereign lord, that by my instigation or consent, so fine and ancient a foundation – built and

61 A tax payable to the Crown by all churchmen, introduced in 1534, consisting of the first year's net income of their benefice and an annual tenth thereafter.

dedicated in the honour of St Saviour by so noble and victorious a prince and one of the king's most noble ancestors, whose very body together with the bodies of his dear and well-beloved queen and also the prince, his son, lies buried in honourable burial there,[62] and are all three kept in perpetual memory with continual intercession and commendations of prayers – should be utterly and irrecoverably decayed and undone, as it must surely be if any such resignation should now be had.

Therefore, when you have tenderly considered and deliberately pondered the whole matter of the above, right worshipful sir, I do not doubt that you will continue the accustomed favour and benevolence which you have always borne towards our poor monastery, and so doing you shall not only please and content Almighty God our Saviour, but also bind us to be your continual bedemen and to pray to God during our lives for the prosperous state of your good mastership, long to endure with much increase of honour. Dated at our poor monastery, the 16th day of this present month of March, AD 1536.

By your bedeman and daily orator, John, abbot of Faversham.

### 55. Plans for monastic reform, 1529

In the months before his fall from power, Cardinal Wolsey sought to acquire a number of papal bulls for the rationalisation of English monasteries. This document, a draft produced during discussions among Wolsey's circle over what powers should be sought from the pope, reflects an increasing interest in monastic reform in early Tudor England. Although the papal curia granted bulls meeting all Wolsey's requests, albeit with some modifications, these bulls were never acted upon. However, this reforming programme may have influenced the early stages of the Dissolution process in the following decade.

Translated from National Archives, SP 1/54, fos 37–40v (Latin).

### Three instructions for bulls to be obtained concerning the state of religion

1.) Instructions for a commission to be obtained for erecting abbacies into bishoprics.

Let a commission be directed to the legates, and let it be entreated on behalf of his royal majesty.

---

62 King Stephen, Queen Matilda and their son, Eustace earl of Boulogne, who were buried in the church, which was of Stephen's foundation.

Let a faculty be granted for the erection of abbacies into bishoprics in monasteries of any order; for dividing and partitioning their possessions and portions; for assigning and appointing new dioceses and territories, and also establishing archdeaconries and uniting parish churches to them; and for consecrating the abbots who subsequently obtain these offices as bishops, and providing them with such things as the hat, rochet[63] and the other clothing to the likeness of bishops, notwithstanding their profession as a regular.

2.) Instructions for a faculty to be obtained to suppress monasteries of any order, up to the [collective] yearly value of 6,000 ducats.

Let a commission be directed to the most reverend cardinal of York [i.e. Wolsey]. Let it be entreated on behalf of his royal majesty.

The substance of the appeal is: since two colleges have been built, one by Edward [III] king of England, the king's ancestor, in the castle of Windsor, the other by Henry VI in the university of Cambridge, he [i.e. the king] has decided to complete them in accordance with their ancient institutes, and to leave in them a pious and perpetual memory of himself; and since the church in England is so well endowed, it is expedient that the endowment which belongs to small monasteries should to some degree be diverted to better uses, rather than it continue to grow and be increased by new offerings; and since there are in this country such monasteries whose wealth it would be both sensible and beneficial to divert to such good causes; let therefore a faculty be granted to suppress any monasteries of any order, to the [collective] annual rent of 6,000 ducats, with their fruits, possessions and rents to be applied to the colleges of Windsor and also of the blessed Mary and St Nicholas, Cambridge, commonly called King's College, and to other pious places ...

3.) Instructions concerning monasteries to be converted and the state of religion to be settled.

Let a commission be directed to the most reverend cardinal of York and Cardinal Campeggio, legate *de latere*.

Let it be entreated on behalf of his royal majesty. Let the true cause be the conservation of religion which cannot be observed unless by religious communities dwelling together in any adequate number and sufficient congregation; but the religious dispersed in these very small

---

63 A linen vestment, worn by a bishop.

and imperfect monasteries do nothing other than bring religion into disrepute and confirm a bad opinion of religion.

Accordingly let it be committed to these cardinals that those monasteries of any order, both of men and of women, where the full number of religious – that is, twelve – cannot be nourished out of those fruits of the monastery in which they live, by their judgement should be united and annexed to other monasteries, and one perfect thing constituted out of many imperfect; and the number of religious and how many paupers are to be given alms should be prescribed certainly; they should enclose nuns and religious women with walls, according to the canonical sanctions published in this regard; and finally they should do all things generally which seem necessary for the state of religion to be settled and for right order to be confirmed, etc., also under ecclesiastical penalties and censures.

# REFERENCES FOR PRINTED WORKS CITED

Adams, R., ed. (1989), *Desiderius Erasmus, The Praise of Folly and Other Writings* (New York)

Andrews, F. (2006), *The Other Friars: The Carmelite, Augustinian, Sack and Pied Friars in the Middle Ages* (Woodbridge)

Aston, M. (1984), '"Caim's Castles": poverty, politics and disendowment', in *The Church, Politics and Patronage in the Fifteenth Century*, ed. R. B. Dobson (Gloucester), 45–81

Baskerville, G. (1937), *English Monks and the Suppression of the Monasteries* (London)

Bell, D. (1995), *What Nuns Read: Books and Libraries in Medieval English Nunneries* (Kalamazoo)

—— (1999), 'Monastic libraries: 1400–1557', in *The Cambridge History of the Book in Britain*, vol. III: *1400–1557*, ed. L. Hellinga and J. Trapp (Cambridge), 229–54

Bernard, G. (2005), *The King's Reformation: Henry VIII and the Remaking of the English Church* (New Haven)

Bond, C. J. (2001), 'Monastic water management in Great Britain: a review', in *Monastic Archaeology: Papers on the Study of Medieval Monasteries*, ed. G. Keevill, M. Aston and T. Hall (Oxford), 88–136

Bonney, M. (1990), *Lordship and the Urban Community: Durham and its Overlords 1250–1540* (Cambridge)

Bowers, R. (1994), 'The musicians of the lady chapel of Winchester Cathedral Priory, 1402–1539', *Journal of Ecclesiastical History*, 45, 210–37

—— (1999), 'The almonry schools of the English monasteries, c. 1265–1540', in *Monasteries and Society in Medieval Britain*, ed. B. Thompson (Stamford), 177–222

Bowker, M. (1981), *The Henrician Reformation: The Diocese of Lincoln under John Longland 1521–1547* (Cambridge)

Brooke, C. (2003), *The Age of the Cloister: The Story of Monastic Life in the Middle Ages* (Stroud)

Brown, A. (1995), *Popular Piety in Late Medieval England: The Diocese of Salisbury 1250–1550* (Oxford)

Burgess, C. (1988), '"A fond thing vainly invented": an essay on Purgatory and pious motive in later medieval England', in *Parish, Church and People*, ed. S. Wright (London), 56–84

—— (1990), 'Late-medieval wills and pious convention: testamentary evidence reconsidered', in *Profit, Piety and the Professions in Later Medieval England*, ed. M. Hicks (Gloucester), 14–33

—— (2005), 'St George's College, Windsor: context and consequence', in *St George's Chapel Windsor in the Fourteenth Century*, ed. N. Saul (Woodbridge), 63–96

Cassidy-Welch, M. (2001), *Monastic Spaces and their Meanings: Thirteenth-Century Cistercian Monasteries* (Turnhout)

Catto, J. (1985), 'Religion and the English nobility in the later fourteenth century', in *History and Imagination: Essays in Honour of H. R. Trevor-Roper*, ed. H. Lloyd Jones, V. Pearl and B. Worden (London), 43–55

Clark, J. (2000a), 'Reformation and reaction at St Albans Abbey, 1530–58', *English Historical Review*, 115, 297–328

—— (2000b), 'Selling the holy places: monastic efforts to win back the people in fifteenth-century England', in *Social Attitudes and Political Structures in the Fifteenth Century*, ed. T. Thornton (Stroud), 13–32

—— (2002) 'The religious orders in pre-Reformation England', in *The Religious Orders in Pre-Reformation England*, ed. J. Clark (Woodbridge), 3–33

—— (2004), *A Monastic Renaissance at St Albans: Thomas Walsingham and his Circle, c. 1350–1440* (Oxford)

Clay, R. M. (1914), *The Hermits and Anchorites of England* (London)

Cobbett, W. (1827), *A History of the Protestant Reformation* (London)

Coldstream, N. (1986), 'Cistercian architecture from Beaulieu to the Dissolution', in *Cistercian Art and Architecture in the British Isles*, ed. C. Norton and D. Park (Cambridge), 139–59

Colvin, H. (1951), *The White Canons in England* (Oxford)

Coppack, G. (2002), 'The planning of Cistercian monasteries in the later middle ages: the evidence from Fountains, Rievaulx, Sawley and Rushen', in *The Religious Orders in Pre-Reformation England*, ed. J. Clark (Woodbridge), 197–209

Coppack, G. and M. Aston (2003), *Christ's Poor Men: The Carthusians in England* (Stroud)

Coulton, G. G. (1923–50) *Five Centuries of Religion*, 4 vols (London)

Cross, C. (1988), 'Monasticism and society in the diocese of York, 1520–1540', *Transactions of the Royal Historical Society*, 5th series, 38, 131–45

—— (2002), 'Yorkshire nunneries', in *The Religious Orders in Pre-Reformation England*, ed. J. Clark (Woodbridge), 145–54

Davis, V. (1993), *William Waynflete, Bishop and Educationalist* (Woodbridge)

Dickens, A. G. (1987), 'The shape of anti-clericalism and the English Reformation', in *Politics and Society in Reformation Europe*, ed. E. Kouri and T. Scott (Basingstoke), 379–410

Dickinson, J. C. (1950), *The Origins of the Austin Canons and their Introduction into England* (London)

Dobson, R. B. (1973), *Durham Priory 1400–1450* (Cambridge)

—— (1992), 'The religious orders 1370–1540', in *The History of the University of Oxford*, vol. II: *Late Medieval Oxford*, ed. J. Catto and R. Evans (Oxford), 539–80

—— (1995), 'The monks of Canterbury in the later middle ages, 1220– 1540', in *A History of Canterbury Cathedral*, ed. P. Collinson, N. Ramsay and M. Sparks (Oxford), 69–153

—— (1999a), 'The monastic orders in late medieval Cambridge', in *The Medieval Church: Universities, Heresy and the Religious Life*, ed. P. Biller and R. B. Dobson, Studies in Church History, Subsidia 11 (Woodbridge), 239–69

—— (1999b), 'English and Welsh monastic bishops: the final century, 1433– 1533', in *Monasteries and Society in Medieval Britain*, ed. B. Thompson (Stamford), 348–67

—— (2003), '"The clergy are well lodged": the transformation of the cathedral precinct at late medieval Durham', in *The Medieval English Cathedral*, ed. J. Backhouse (Donington), 23–40

Dodds, B. (2004), 'Estimating arable output using Durham Priory tithe receipts, 1351–1450', *Economic History Review*, 57, 245–85

Doyle, A. I. (1988), 'The printed books of the last monks of Durham', *The Library*, 6th series, 10, 203–19

—— (1990), 'Book production by the monastic orders in England (*c.*1375– 1530): assessing the evidence', in *Medieval Book Production: Assessing the Evidence*, ed. L. Brownrigg (Los Altos Hills), 1–19

Duffy, E. (1992), *The Stripping of the Altars: Traditional Religion in England, 1400– 1580* (New Haven)

Dutton, M. (1999), 'Chaucer's two nuns', in *Monasteries and Society in Medieval Britain*, ed. B. Thompson (Stamford), 296–311

Dyer, C. (2005), *An Age of Transition? Economy and Society in England in the Later Middle Ages* (Oxford)

Ellis, R. (1997), 'Further thoughts on the spirituality of Syon Abbey', in *Mysticism and Spirituality in Medieval England*, ed. W. Pollard and R. Boenig (Woodbridge), 219–43

Emery, A. (1996–2006), *Greater Medieval Houses of England and Wales, 1300–1500*, 3 vols (Cambridge)

Erler, M. (2002), *Women, Reading and Piety in Late Medieval England* (Cambridge)

Evennett, H. (1958), 'The new orders', in *The New Cambridge Modern History*, vol. II: *The Reformation 1520–1559*, ed. G. Elton (Cambridge), 275–300

Farnhill, K. (2006), 'The guild of the Annunciation of the Blessed Virgin Mary and the priory of St Mary in Walsingham', in *The Parish in Late Medieval England*, ed. C. Burgess and E. Duffy (Donington), 129–45

Field, S. (2002), 'Devotion, discontent and the Henrician Reformation: the evidence of Robin Hood stories', *Journal of British Studies*, 41, 6–22

Fleming, P. (1984), 'Charity, faith, and the gentry of Kent 1422–1529', in *Property and Politics: Essays in Later Medieval English History*, ed. A. Pollard (Gloucester), 36–58

—— (2000), 'Conflict and urban government in later medieval England: St Augustine's Abbey and Bristol', *Urban History*, 27, 325–43

Froude, J. A. (1867–83), *Short Studies on Great Subjects: Series I-IV* (London)

Gasquet, F. A. (1893), *Henry VIII and the English Monasteries*, 5th edn (London)

Gilchrist, R. (1994), *Gender and Material Culture: The Archaeology of Religious Women* (London)

—— (2005), *Norwich Cathedral Close: The Evolution of the English Cathedral Landscape* (Woodbridge)

Gilchrist, R. and B. Sloane (2005), *Requiem: The Medieval Monastic Cemetery in Britain* (London)

Gillespie, V. (1989), '*Cura pastoralis in deserto*', in *De Cella in Saeculum: Religious and Secular Life and Devotion in Late Medieval England*, ed. M. Sargent (Cambridge), 161–81

—— (1999), 'Dial M for mystic: mystical texts in the library of Syon Abbey and the spirituality of the Syon brethren', in *The Medieval Mystical Tradition in England, Ireland and Wales: Exeter Symposium VI*, ed. M. Glasscoe (Cambridge), 241–68

—— (2000) 'The book and the brotherhood: reflections on the lost library of Syon Abbey', in *The English Medieval Book*, ed. A. Edwards, V. Gillespie and R. Hanna (London), 195–208

—— (2002), 'Syon and the New Learning', in *The Religious Orders in Pre-Reformation England*, ed. J. Clark (Woodbridge), 75–95

Golding, B. (1995), *Gilbert of Sempringham and the Gilbertine Order c. 1130–c. 1300* (Oxford)

Graham, R. (1929), *English Ecclesiastical Studies* (London)

Gransden, A. (1975), 'A democratic movement in the abbey of Bury St Edmunds in the late twelfth and early thirteenth centuries', *Journal of Ecclesiastical History*, 26, 25–39

Greatrex, J. (1994), 'The English cathedral priories and the pursuit of learning in the later middle ages', *Journal of Ecclesiastical History*, 45, 396–411

—— (2002), 'After Knowles: recent perspectives in monastic history', in *The Religious Orders in Pre-Reformation England*, ed. J. Clark (Woodbridge), 35–47

Greene, J. (1989), *Norton Priory* (Cambridge)

Grenville, J. (1997), *Medieval Housing* (London)

Gribbin, J. (2001), *The Premonstratensian Order in Late Medieval England* (Woodbridge)

Haigh, C. (1975), *Reformation and Resistance in Tudor Lancashire* (Cambridge)

—— (1987) 'Anticlericalism and the English Reformation', in *The English Reformation Revised*, ed. C. Haigh (Cambridge), 56–74

—— (1993), *English Reformations: Religion, Politics and Society under the Tudors* (Oxford)

Haines, R. (2003), 'Regular clergy and the episcopate in the provinces of Canterbury and York during the later middle ages', *Revue Bénédictine*, 113, 407–47

Hanna, R. (2000), 'Augustinian canons and Middle English literature', in *The English Medieval Book*, ed. A. Edwards, V. Gillespie and R. Hanna (London), 27–42

Harper-Bill, C. (1985), 'The labourer is worthy of his hire? Complaints about diet in late medieval English monasteries', in *The Church in Pre-Reformation Society*, ed. C. Barron and C. Harper-Bill (Woodbridge), 95–107

—— (1988), 'Dean Colet's Convocation sermon and the pre-Reformation Church in England', *History*, 73, 191–210

Harper-Bill, C. and C. Rawcliffe (2004), 'The religious houses', in *Medieval Norwich*, ed. C. Rawcliffe and R. Wilson (London), 73–119

Harrison, F. Ll. (1963), *Music in Medieval Britain*, 2nd edn (London)

Harvey, B. (1977), *Westminster Abbey and its Estates in the Middle Ages* (Oxford)

—— (1993), *Living and Dying in England 1100–1540: The Monastic Experience* (Oxford)

—— (2002), 'A novice's life at Westminster Abbey in the century before the Dissolution', in *The Religious Orders in Pre-Reformation England*, ed. J. Clark (Woodbridge), 51–73

Hatcher, J. (1986), 'Mortality in the fifteenth century: some new evidence', *Economic History Review*, 2nd series, 39, 19–38

—— (1996), 'The great slump of the mid-fifteenth century', in *Progress and Problems in Medieval England*, ed. R. Britnell and J. Hatcher (Cambridge), 237–72

Heal, F. (1990), *Hospitality in Early Modern England* (Oxford)

Heale, M. (2004a), *The Dependent Priories of Medieval English Monasteries* (Woodbridge)

—— (2004b), 'Dependent priories and the closure of monasteries in late medieval England, 1400–1535', *English Historical Review*, 119, 1–26

—— (2006) 'Monastic-parochial churches in late medieval England', in *The Parish in Late Medieval England*, ed. C. Burgess and E. Duffy (Donington), 54–77

—— (2007), 'Training in superstition? Monasteries and popular religion in late medieval and Reformation England', *Journal of Ecclesiastical History*, 58, 417–37

—— (2008a), '"Not a thing for a stranger to enter upon": the selection of monastic superiors in late medieval and early Tudor England', in *Monasteries and Society in the British Isles in the Later Middle Ages*, ed. J. Burton and K. Stöber (Woodbridge), 51–68

—— (2008b), 'Colleges and monasteries in late medieval England', in *The Late Medieval English College and its Context*, ed. C. Burgess and M. Heale (York), 67–86

Heath, P. (1984), 'Urban piety in the later middle ages: the evidence of Hull wills', in *The Church, Politics and Patronage in the Fifteenth Century*, ed. R. B. Dobson (Gloucester), 209–34

Hoyle, R. (1995), 'The origins of the Dissolution of the monasteries', *The Historical Journal*, 38, 275–305

Hudson, A. (1988), *The Premature Reformation: Wycliffite Texts and Lollard History* (Oxford)

Huizinga, J. (1924), *The Waning of the Middle Ages* (London)

Hume, D. (1780), *The History of England from the Invasion of Julius Caesar to the Revolution in 1688*, 8 vols (Dublin)

Jones, M. and M. Underwood (1992), *The King's Mother. Lady Margaret Beaufort, Countess of Richmond and Derby* (Cambridge)

Kaartinen, M. (2002), *Religious Life and English Culture in the Reformation* (Basingstoke)

Kermode, J. (1998), *Medieval Merchants: York, Beverley and Hull in the Later Middle Ages* (Cambridge)

Kershaw, I. (1973), *Bolton Priory: The Economy of a Northern Monastery 1286–1325* (Oxford)

Knowles, D. (1948–59), *The Religious Orders in England*, 3 vols (Cambridge)

—— (1963), *The Monastic Order in England: A History of its Development from the Times of St Dunstan to the Fourth Lateran Council, 940–1216*, 2nd edn (Cambridge)

—— (1969), *Christian Monasticism* (London)

Knowles, D. and R. N. Hadcock (1971), *Medieval Religious Houses: England and Wales*, 2nd edn (London)

Lawrence, C. H. (2000), *Medieval Monasticism: Forms of Religious Life in Western Europe in the Middle Ages*, 3rd edn (London)

Lee, P. (2001), *Nunneries, Learning and Spirituality in Late Medieval English Society: The Dominican Priory of Dartford* (Woodbridge)

Lovatt, R. (1992), 'The library of John Blacman and contemporary Carthusian spirituality', *Journal of Ecclesiastical History*, 43, 195–230

Luxford, J. (2005), *The Art and Architecture of English Benedictine Monasteries, 1300–1540: A Patronage History* (Woodbridge)

MacCulloch, D. (1996), *Thomas Cranmer: A Life* (New Haven)

Makowski, E. (1999), *Canon Law and Cloistered Women: Periculoso and its Commentators, 1298–1545* (Washington DC)

Mann, J. (1973), *Chaucer and Medieval Estates Satire: The Literature of Social Classes and the General Prologue to the Canterbury Tales* (Cambridge)

Marshall, P. (2003), *Reformation England 1480–1642* (London)

—— (2006), 'Anticlericalism revested? Expressions of discontent in early Tudor England', in *The Parish in Late Medieval England*, ed. C. Burgess and E. Duffy (Donington), 365–80

Martin, J. (1998), 'Leadership and priorities in Reading during the Reformation', in *The Reformation in English Towns, 1500–1640*, ed. P. Collinson and J. Craig (Basingstoke), 113–29

Matthew, D. (1962), *The Norman Monasteries and their English Possessions* (Oxford)

Mayer, T., ed. (1989), *Thomas Starkey: A Dialogue between Pole and Lupset*, Camden Society, 4th series, 37

Morris, R. (1979), *Cathedrals and Abbeys of England and Wales: The Building Church, 600–1540* (London)

Myers, A., ed. (1969), *English Historical Documents, IV, 1327–1485* (London)

Newman, C. (2000), 'Employment on the estates of the priory of Durham, 1494– 1519: the priory as an employer', *Northern History*, 36, 43–58

Oakley, F. (1979), *The Western Church in the Later Middle Ages* (Ithaca, NY)

Olin, J. (1969), *The Catholic Reformation: Savonarola to Ignatius Loyola* (New York)

Oliva, M. (1998), *The Convent and the Community in Late Medieval England: Female Monasteries in the Diocese of Norwich, 1350–1540* (Woodbridge)

Orme, N. (2006), *Medieval Schools from Roman Britain to Renaissance England* (New Haven)

—— (2008), *The Victoria History of the County of Cornwall, II: Religious History to 1559* (London)

Pantin, W. A. (1944), 'The monk-solitary of Farne: a fourteenth-century English mystic', *English Historical Review*, 59, 162–86

Parish, H. (2005), *Monks, Miracles and Magic: Reformation Representations of the Medieval Church* (London)

Pearsall, D. (2001), '"If heaven be on this earth, it is in cloister or in school": the monastic ideal in later medieval English literature', in *Pragmatic Utopias: Ideals and Communities, 1200–1630*, ed. R. Horrox and S. Rees Jones (Cambridge), 11–25

Platt, C. (1984), *The Abbeys and Priories of Medieval England* (London)

Power, E. (1922), *Medieval English Nunneries c. 1275 to 1535* (Cambridge)

Raban, S. (1982), *Mortmain Legislation and the English Church 1279–1500* (Cambridge)

Renna, T. (1987), 'Wyclif's attacks on the monks', in *From Ockham to Wyclif*, ed. A. Hudson and M. Wilks, Studies in Church History, Subsidia 5 (Oxford), 267–80

Rhodes, J. (1993), 'Syon Abbey and its religious publications in the sixteenth century', *Journal of Ecclesiastical History*, 44, 11–25

Riley, H., ed. (1863–64), *Thomae Walsingham, quondam monachi S. Albani, Historia Anglicana*, Rolls Series, 2 vols, no. 28

Robinson, D. (1980), *The Geography of Augustinian Settlement in Medieval England and Wales*, British Archaeological Reports, British Series, 80

Rollason, L. (1999), 'The *Liber Vitae* of Durham and lay association with Durham Cathedral Priory in the later middle ages', in *Monasteries and Society in Medieval Britain*, ed. B. Thompson (Stamford), 277–95

Roper, S. (1993), *Medieval English Benedictine Liturgy: Studies in the Formation, Structure, and Content of the Monastic Votive Office, c. 950–1540* (New York and London)

Rosenthal, J. (1972), *The Purchase of Paradise* (London)

Rushton, N. (2001), 'Monastic charitable provision in Tudor England: quantifying and qualifying poor relief in the early sixteenth century', *Continuity and Change*, 16, 9–44

Sargent, M. (1976), 'The transmission by the English Carthusians of some late medieval spiritual writings', *Journal of Ecclesiastical History*, 2, 225–40

Savine, A. (1909), *English Monasteries on the Eve of the Dissolution* (Oxford)

Scase, W. (1989), *Piers Plowman and the New Anticlericalism* (Cambridge)

Schmidt, A., ed. (1978), *William Langland, The Vision of Piers Plowman: A Complete Edition of the B-Text* (London)

Schofield, A. (1966), 'The second English delegation to the Council of Basel', *Journal of Ecclesiastical History*, 17, 29–64

Shagan, E. (2003), *Popular Politics and the English Reformation* (Cambridge)

Smith, D. (2006), 'The phantom prior of Mount Grace', *Monastic Research Bulletin*, 12, 46–9

Spear, V. (2005), *Leadership in Medieval English Nunneries* (Woodbridge)

Stöber, K. (2007), *Late Medieval Monasteries and their Patrons: England and Wales, c. 1300–1540* (Woodbridge)

Swanson, R. (1989), *Church and Society in Late Medieval England* (Oxford)

—— (2002), 'Mendicants and confraternity in late medieval England', in *The Pre-Reformation Church in England*, ed. J. Clark (Woodbridge), 121–41

—— (2004), 'Books of brotherhood: registering fraternity and confraternity in late medieval England', in *The Durham Liber Vitae and its Context*, ed. D. Rollason, A. J. Piper, M. Harvey and L. Rollason (Woodbridge), 233–46

Tanner, N. (1984), *The Church in Late Medieval Norwich*, Pontifical Institute of Medieval Studies, Studies and Texts LXVI (Toronto)

Thompson, A. H., ed. (1914–29), *Visitations of Religious Houses in the Diocese of Lincoln, 1420–49*, Lincoln Record Society, 3 vols, nos 7, 14, 21

—— ed. (1940–47), *Visitations in the Diocese of Lincoln, 1517–31*, Lincoln Record Society, 3 vols, nos 33, 35, 37

Thompson, B. (1994a) 'The laity, the alien priories, and the redistribution of ecclesiastical property', in *England in the Fifteenth Century*, ed. N. Rogers (Stamford), 19–41

—— (1994b), 'Monasteries and their patrons at foundation and Dissolution', *Transactions of the Royal Historical Society*, 6th series, 4, 103–26

—— (1999), 'Introduction: monasteries and medieval society', in *Monasteries and Society in Medieval Britain*, ed. B. Thompson (Stamford), 1–33

—— (2002), 'Monasteries, society and reform in late medieval England', in *The Religious Orders in Pre-Reformation England*, ed. J. Clark (Woodbridge), 165–95

Thompson, E. M. (1930), *The Carthusian Order in England* (London)

Thompson, M. (2001), *Cloister, Abbot and Precinct in Medieval Monasteries* (Stroud)

Thomson, J. A. F. (1965), 'Piety and charity in late medieval London', *Journal of Ecclesiastical History*, 16, 178–95

—— (1993), *The Early Tudor Church and Society 1485–1529* (Harlow)

Threlfall-Holmes, M. (2005), *Monks and Markets: Durham Cathedral Priory 1460– 1520* (Oxford)

Tillotson, J. (1989), *Marrick Priory: A Nunnery in Late Medieval Yorkshire*, Borthwick Paper, no. 75

Vauchez, A. (1997), *Sainthood in the Later Middle Ages* (Cambridge)

Watkins, A. (1994), 'Merevale Abbey in the late 1490s', *Warwickshire History*, 9, 87–104

—— (1996), 'Maxstoke Priory in the fifteenth century: the development of an estate economy in the Forest of Arden', *Warwickshire History*, 10, 3–18

Webber, T. (1997), 'Latin devotional texts and the books of the Augustinian canons of Thurgarton Priory and Leicester Abbey in the late middle ages', in *Books and Collectors 1200–1700: Essays Presented to Andrew Watson*, ed. J. Carley and C. Tite (London), 27–41

Youings, J. (1971), *The Dissolution of the Monasteries* (London)

—— (1990), 'The monasteries', in *Rural Society: Landowners, Peasants and Labourers 1500–1750*, ed. C. Clay (Cambridge), 71–120

Zarnecki, G. (1972), *The Monastic Achievement* (London)

# INDEX